Ethnic Media in America:

Images, Audiences and Transforming Forces

Book Three

Guy T. Meiss
Alice A. Tait

KENDALL/HUNT PUBLISHING COMPANY
4050 Westmark Drive   Dubuque, Iowa 52002

Cover image courtesy of Corel.

Copyright © 2004 by Kendall/Hunt Publishing Company

ISBN 0-7575-0816-2

Printed in the United States of America
10 9 8 7 6 5 4 3 2 1

DEDICATION

For Carthage College, where I first experienced community and learned to appreciate diversity.

Guy T. Meiss

For my grandchildren: Leiah B. Smith, Joseph (Tresby) C. Smith, III, Brigham K. Smith, and Robert A. Smith.

Alice A. Tait

"When diversity is used as a mask for stigmatized difference, it presents policymakers and managers with the dilemma of how to treat target populations under diversity programs: If those other populations are truly empowered, the whole social fabric will have to be rewoven, for stigmatization is an aspect of social control, and destigmatization implicates loss of control.

"Fortunately, the term *diversity* has another meaning, that of variety or multiformity. In this sense, diversity means something more like the proliferation of subtypes of one overarching group, maintaining commonalities while recognizing dissimilarities.

"With this [latter] approach to reframing diversity...cultural diversity—can be understood as *the normal human variation in the systems of meaning by which groups understand and enact their everyday lives, which they acquire through experiential apprenticeship.*"

Banks, Stephen P. (1995). *Multicultural Public Relations:*
A Social-Interpretive Approach (pp. 17-18). Thousand Oaks, Calif.: Sage.

CONTENTS

SERIES FOREWORD

For this series, we have adapted an integrated framework suggested by Paul M. Hirsch for research-ing the American mass communication system.[1] It identifies five levels of analysis: (1) institutional, which examines relations between media organizations and the cultural, political, economic and technological environments in which they operate; (2) individual media organizations and their administration; (3) the occupational roles and gate keeping processes of those media organizations; (4) the symbolic content they create; and (5) the characteristics of the audiences for their products.

In this series, our primary focus is on ethnic media—a subsystem of that social institution called the American mass communications system, comprising the various media industries (e.g., print, broad-cast, films, recordings and advertising) that create the symbolic content of news, information and entertainment. We primarily examine the media organizations of four major ethnic groups we call ALANA—African, Latina/o, Asian and Native American.

Historically, research into the role of ethnic groups in American media has generally focused on the negative and exclusionary portrayals of ALANA and other groups (e.g., Arab Americans) in main-stream (i.e., Eurocentric) mass media news, information and entertainment content. Discussions of the results of such studies have emphasized the harmful effects those images have on ALANA indi-viduals, their culture and the broader society.

More recently, scholars have also begun to track the effects of the multiculturalism movement on minority hiring by Eurocentric media organizations and on patterns of minority ownership in the broadcast industry.

A related, but less studied research agenda—the subject of this series—involves the media organiza-tions that ALANA groups control, significantly influence or own. Unfortunately there has been a dearth of information about the structure and operation of such mass media organizations, the orga-nizational roles and careers of their gatekeepers, the nature of the images they produce and distrib-ute, and the effects those images have on their audiences.

Three basic questions underlie the series: (1) Why do ALANA groups seek to control or significantly influence Eurocentric media, or even own their own media systems? (2) Are ALANA groups and society in general better served when they themselves control, significantly influence or own mass media organizations? (3) What challenges do ALANA groups face in seeking these forms of empow-erment? This three volume series, *Ethnic Media in America*, provides as comprehensive an answer to these questions as currently exists in the research.

This volume, *Images, Audiences and Transforming Forces*, is the third and final in the series, *Ethnic Media in America*. It examines communications theory about the interaction of minority groups and mass media, the stereotypical ALANA images of Eurocentric media, ALANA models for improving ethnic portrayals, and the nature of ALANA audiences, including how they use and derive gratifica-tion from the media and the effects of those mediated experiences on them.

Volume one, *Building a System of Their Own*, explores why ethnic groups seek to control, influence and, especially, own mass media organizations and provides examples of Native-American and

African-American experiences in building their own media institutions, emphasizing the cultural, philosophical, economic, legal/regulatory and political environments in which that takes place.

Volume two, *Taking Control*, examines the management, structuring, goals, policies and philosophy of ALANA-owned media organizations, their marketing and advertising strategies, their economic problems, and the effects of new technology (e.g., the internet and video games) on their struggle. It also provides insights into how ALANA organizations and individuals (e.g., trade associations, entrepreneurs, producers, authors, actors and critics) act as gatekeepers, influencing both ALANA and Eurocentric mass media.

Understanding the American mass communications system—including its ALANA subsystem—requires an interdisciplinary approach; therefore, we have drawn on the work of experts in mass communications, speech communication, organizational communication, media studies, women's studies, ethnic studies (including individual ALANA programs), history, sociology, economics, business and law. Contributing scholars represent both quantitative and qualitative research methods, including survey research, content analysis, case studies, critical analysis, ethnographic studies, and historical, legal/regulatory and economic analysis.

We are gratified by the interest this ALANA project has generated in the diverse community of scholars researching minority involvement with the media, and we hope the conceptual framework of the series will stimulate a research agenda to build on the body of knowledge gathered in the three volumes of *Ethnic Media in America*.

Guy T. Meiss
Alice A. Tait

---

[1] Hirsch, P.M. (1977). Occupational, Organizational, and Institutional Models in Mass Media Research: Toward An Integrated Framework, in P.M. Hirsch, P.V. Miller & F.G. Kline (eds.), *Strategies for Communication Research* (pp. 13–42). Beverly Hills, CA: Sage.

ACKNOWLEDGEMENTS

The editors wish to thank Central Michigan University's Faculty Research and Creative Endeavors Committee and contributors to the Dow Jones High School Journalism Workshop for financial support that aided in the preparation of this manuscript.

We want to acknowledge James Hageman, Sue Ann Martin, Maria Marron and Richard Davenport, current and former Central Michigan University administrators, for providing support and encouragement along the way.

We also owe a debt to colleagues Harvey Dorrah and Robert Perry for their thoughtful and timely advice at various stages in the development of this volume.

We gratefully acknowledge the patience, perseverance and hard work of a cadre of student assistants, including Manav Bahl, Farrah McDaniel, Heather Sowinski, Melissa Thomas, Melissa Brown, Fatima Sylvertooth, Danielle Silva and Kevin Keeley, as well as the staff support of Tricia Kierst, the Journalism Department's former administrative secretary.

Finally, we would like to thank the scholars we have met along the way—both those whose work we have included in the series and those who have expressed interest in the ALANA project and shared their ideas about ethnic media in America.

INTRODUCTION

The Oprah Winfrey Show, Stand and Deliver, The Joy Luck Club, Dances With Wolves. Amos and Andy, Chico and the Man, The Adventures of Charlie Chan, Custer's Last Stand. Aunt Jemima, the Frito Bandito, the railroad coolie, the drunken Indian. The good, the bad and the ugly. Impressive images of African, Latino, Asian and Native Americans (ALANA) in mainstream, Eurocentric media. Images that we all experience in varying degrees that affect our view of ourselves and others. Images that help create our attitudes, opinions and beliefs about the way we relate to each other. Positive, but until recently, more often negative, images that permeate our society. And sometimes, as currently with Asian Americans, an absence of image, suggesting to some critics that that group plays no significant role in our society.

What reactions might one expect from ALANA and other ethnic groups to living in such a mediated world? The answer depends largely on two non-media factors: (1) the economic, political and cultural milieu at the time groups encounter unacceptable images and (2) the vision of society that those groups and their individual members choose to try to implement. Milieu circumscribes the possibilities for change—the constraints on and impetus for ethnic mobility. Vision defines a point on the assimilation-separation continuum that ethnic groups choose to move toward vis-à-vis the dominant society.[1]

In mass media, those factors lead ALANA and other ethnic groups either to accept the status quo as the price for evolutionary assimilation or to seek to control, significantly influence or own their own media. This series, *Ethnic Media in America*, explores the latter path. Volumes one and two, *Building a System of Their Own* and *Taking Control*, explored how ALANA developed organizational mechanisms of control and ownership. The contributors to this volume detail the history of unacceptable images in mainstream media and provide insights and actual models for how ALANA control, influence and ownership can alter mainstream media portrayals—or offer society viable alternatives. Whether critics believe those changes in mainstream media are sufficient—or could ever be—depends on their vision of society and how mass media can help achieve it.

This preoccupation with mediated images raises the question: How powerful are they? For decades, mass communications researchers have studied the effects of media on individuals, groups and society. They have teased out a range of theories from minimal to powerful effects, many of which are proffered by our contributors to justify ALANA concerns and efforts toward improving ethnic portrayals. But some of those contributors also caution us that ethnic groups are not homogeneous, and determining the effects of image on them is not easy. So, while we have used the acronym ALANA as shorthand for African, Latino, Asian and Native Americans, each has a distinctiveness and complexity that must not be obscured. For example, many of those we call Latino Americans prefer to view themselves and the world from their unique heritage (e.g., Mexican, Cuban or Puerto Rican). Moreover, ALANA audiences interact with media images as both individuals and members of groups with distinct social, political and cultural experiences, so that an African American and a Latino American, for example, may interpret the same images in quite different ways.

In Part One, "Ethnic Images and Their Impact," two articles present the theory and research underlying minority interaction with mainstream and African-American media. In chapter one, Byron Renz discusses the prosocial nature of the mass media, along with other institutions in society, to bring new individuals and groups—whether from birth or immigration—into the American family, as it were. In chapter two, Tamika Carter and Richard Allen shift our focus to the audiences for images and examine how mainstream and Black mass media influence the interrelationship of group identity and self-concept among African Americans. Their analysis re-enforces Renz's observation that media impact is complex, not easily predictable and often may have unintended consequences.

According to Renz, mass-mediated images, the symbolic products media organizations produce and distribute, potentially facilitate the assimilation and integration of ethnic groups into mainstream society. Media images—especially those presented in a dramatic or narrative form, whether in news or entertainment—can introduce, reinforce or change attitudes, opinions, beliefs and values of members within a group as well as those of one group toward another. He explains that "media create a **cognitive convergence of thought** that allows the mind to accept an association of images" (e.g., members of two different ethnic groups interacting). But whether an interaction is seen as positive or negative depends on the interpretation one gives to the event, recognizing that the formation of attitudes, opinions, beliefs and values is a complex process in which media images are but one variable. Whether assimilation or integration take place, he cautions, depends on a variety of economic and political forces that influence a minority group's interest or lack of interest in assimilating or integrating into the dominant society.

Renz describes three theories that help explain how people learn to fit in by attending to mass media: (1) *social organization*, the way people learn the norms and sanctions of a society and recognize and accept the roles and ranks of society; (2) *modeling*, how people learn, through vicarious identification with characters in drama, models of acceptable and unacceptable behavior; and, (3) *construction of meaning*, how people come to adopt words and concepts that influence their behavior toward themselves and others.

In chapter two, Carter and Allen examine several databases from national surveys to explain the role media play in influencing the interconnected nature of African-Americans' feelings toward themselves (self-esteem) and feelings toward their group (group identity). They conclude that negative images of African Americans emanating from mainstream media (i.e., White) legitimate class, race and gender inequalities for commercial purposes and, thus, perpetuate the dominant White culture. Conversely, Black media are filters of information that advocate social and political change and raise racial consciousness. Specifically, the data suggest, "Mainstream television had a negative influence on Black autonomy, a negative influence on African self-consciousness and a negative influence on self-esteem. Mainstream print media had a negative influence on self-esteem and a positive relationship with African self-consciousness…Black print media on the other hand exhibited a positive influence on self-esteem, a positive influence on closeness to elites, a positive influence on Black autonomy and a positive influence on African self-consciousness. Exposure to Black television and movies was negatively linked to Black autonomy and African self-consciousness."

Parts two and three of this volume provide composite pictures of two ALANA groups—Latino Americans and African Americans. Each set of three articles explores the good, the bad and the ugly images of those groups in mainstream and ethnic media. But, the authors also offer suggestions and/or models for transforming the bad and the ugly into more positive ALANA image-making, based on their orientation toward the assimilation, integration (pluralism/multiculturalism) or separation of ethnic groups. First, part two.

Interested in the influence of ethnic media images (i.e., narrative visuals) on Latinas' self-esteem, Melissa Johnson, Prabu David and Dawn Huey Ohlsson analyzed the non-advertising, women's photographs in 13 Latina magazines to understand whether they provide an alternative to mainstream media stereotypes. The content analysis revealed that Latina magazines' female images "fulfill pluralistic media functions like empowerment and promoting ethnic pride [e.g., negating mainstream stereotypes of fat and lazy Latinas]. They help cement a standard of U.S. Latino identity and beauty that has the potential to unite subgroup ideals of beauty. But in perpetuating the thin ideal, Latina magazines also are assimilationist in that they replicate a standard for Anglo-American women that has been promoted in U.S. general market media."

Motivated by concerns uncovered in her earlier field research with Chicano-Latino audiences that described "how women and men experience ease of consumption as well as struggle to find cultural fulfillment in both mainstream and Spanish-language media," Diana Rios examines the roles of one of Hollywood's few successful Latinas, Rosie Perez. Rios uses a new feminist approach, the *mesitza-womanist perspective*, to describe, critique and evaluate Perez's on-screen characters and their traits. Here in chapter four, this multicultural perspective is used as an analytical device, but it also offers readers a model for constructing more complex and diverse representations of Latinas and other women of color.

In chapter five, a team of scholars complete our case study of Latino experiences with media images. Gloria Ruiz, Beatriz Robinson, Susan Angulo, Gary Feinberg, Judy Bachay and Edward Blackwell have developed a unique, multidisciplinary approach to assessing and encouraging *cultural competence* in film and television. They use the term "to suggest that valuable representations of diverse groups reflect realistic, thoughtful, and nuanced (as opposed to stereotypical) portrayals." First, the authors detail the extent to which film and television have created stereotypical Hispanic[2] images that discount differences of national origins, socioeconomic status, geography, physical characteristics and linguistics. Second, they explain why such *cultural incompetence* alienates and negatively affects Hispanic and other ethnic minorities. Finally, rather than a list of instructions, they advance a set of global questions (i.e., questions appropriate to pose when depicting any ethnic group). The approach is meant to encourage film and television professionals and critics (and, presumably, thoughtful consumers) to reflect "on the possible existence of stereotypical portrayals and patterns in media productions," in order to promote culturally competent films and programs that appeal to a broad audience for both mainstream and ethnic media products.

The authors of Part Three focus on the powerful, dramatic narratives of film and television to analyze the images of African Americans in mainstream media and to suggest how they can be improved. Like Rios earlier, Brenda Cooper and Rebecca Brasfield employ a feminist analysis of the work of women and men of color—actors, authors and directors—in both mainstream and ethnic media, concluding that even ALANA control, significant influence or ownership does not necessarily produce culturally competent images.

In chapter six, Cooper painstakingly details how three White male directors—Bille August, Steven Spielberg and Brian Gibson—translated the literary texts of three women authors of color—Latina Isabel Allende's *The House of Spirits*, African-American Alice Walker's *The Color Purple*, and African-American Tina Turner's *I, Tina*. She concludes that, although they did not consciously intend to, each director co-opted the authors' narrative themes—women's empowerment over sexism and racism, spiritualism, male violence and discrimination—by employing various hegemonic devices[3] (e.g., marginalization and omission) that reinforce patriarchy and its inherent White privilege—the very things those women were challenging—while appearing to honor diversity. Cooper's critique highlights by negative examples how these films could have portrayed the complicated social, moral and political world the authors intended. But her analysis also raises disturbing questions about how effective ALANA can be in introducing multicultural/pluralistic worldviews into mainstream media.

Chapter seven also takes up the literary texts of two African-American women, Alice Walker and Terry McMillan, and the translation of their novels into the Hollywood film productions of *The Color*

Purple and *Waiting to Exhale*. Rebecca Brasfield brings a revolutionary feminist perspective to her analysis. She maintains that the only way to break the assimilative nature of mass media, whether Eurocentric or ethnic, is to create narratives in which characters go beyond *personal* empowerment to acquire political consciousness or engage in social activism toward the destruction of racism, sexism and other sources of oppression in the dominant society. Thus, Brasfield raises provocative questions about whether ALANA groups and society as a whole are *necessarily* better served when they control, significantly influence or own mass media.

Alice Tait's chapter eight concludes Part Three's examination of African Americans and media images by summarizing the relevant media effects theory and research as it relates to society in general, children in particular, and then African Americans exclusively. But her unique contribution comes in the form of a model for evaluating and transforming inadequate and inappropriate African-American media portrayals. Unlike Ruiz et al.'s universal approach, Tait's model, based on her previous research into Black public affairs television programming, glorifies African-American distinctiveness by using elements of traditional Afrocentric philosophy.

Part Four, "The Ethnic Audiences," returns to Carter and Allen's focus on media audiences, their complexity, their distinctive characteristics and the level of their involvement with particular forms of media.

Fernando Delgado's essay in chapter nine seeks to "provoke conversation and further exploration into what the evolving presence of Latina/os in the mainstream media actually means to producers and consumers of mass media." While acknowledging the deficiencies and distortions in Latino media images, he argues that the meaning found in films is not fixed in the text but is subject to the perceptions and interpretations of the audiences, in effect, in the *communicative moment* between the media text and multicultural audience members. Citing research that suggests Latino audiences decode media messages differently from other audiences (particularly when the content represents, or is perceived to represent, them).[4] Delgado stresses that scholars and media professionals should see audience members as active participants with divergent cultural experiences and ethnic identities that affect their responses to ALANA portrayals.

Brenda Cooper, Lisa Duke and Michelle Sisson, authors of the final two chapters, embrace the active audience concept that Delgado champions. Cooper compares how Black and White university students interpret Spike Lee's *Do The Right Thing*; Duke and Sisson compare how Black and White girls interpret teen magazines. Each approaches the investigation from a different research tradition (reception research and reader response theory), but both aim to understand how their respective audience members create meaning that is culturally and personally relevant as they interact with either film or magazine texts. Cooper analyzed students' open-ended, self-report essays; Duke and Sisson, in-depth interviews with the teens. Their findings, however, were similar. Cooper found, "…contradictory interpretations of *Do The Right Thing* between the non-African Americans [i.e., White and Hispanic, men and women] and the African Americans, based on their cultural subjectivities and corresponding discourses." Duke and Sisson found that Black and White girls, experiencing the same Eurocentric ideal of beauty, read or decoded the message differently. For example, "White girls, who are more culturally aligned with the material in the major teen magazines, consistently invest more authority in the magazine's counsel and images of beauty, regardless of age." And, "Instead of translating their relative exclusion from the major teen magazines into negative self-assessments, Black girls generally viewed the magazines as biased and largely irrelevant to their ideas about beauty, though enjoyable for other reasons." Both case studies provide richly nuanced findings and conclusions.

The contributors to this volume have provided an array of perspectives on the ethnic *Images, Audiences and Transforming Forces* at work in modern American mass media. Collectively, they complete the series' answer to the questions we posed at the outset: (1) Why do ALANA groups seek to control or significantly influence Eurocentric media, or even own their own media systems? (2) Are ALANA groups and society in general better served when they themselves control, significantly influence or own mass media organizations? (3) What challenges do ALANA groups face in seeking these forms of empowerment?

But, in doing so, they have raised other interesting and important questions about how successful ALANA strategies for controlling, significantly influencing and owning their own media can be in creating alternative images in economically viable ways for pluralistic audiences.

Guy T. Meiss

---

[1]There is no definitive array of terms to describe relative points on the continuum. Nor do scholars always agree on the definition of the terms generally used. However, the authors in this series adhere to the following paradigm: **assimilation....integration (sometimes called pluralistic or multiculturalism)...separation**. Working definitions include: **assimilation**—absorption of minority groups into the dominant culture with the possibility of influencing the majority, but more often with the loss of minority distinctiveness; **integration**—bringing minority groups into equal membership with the majority, where all groups operate out of a similar set of values; **Pluralistic and multiculturalism**—similar to integration, but emphasizing mutual respect among the groups, where distinctive identities are preserved and sometimes emphasized or glorified; **separation**—rejection of the dominant culture and glorification of ethnic differences.

[2]The terms Latino and Hispanic are used interchangeably in these chapters, although scholars sometimes define them differently. For example, Melissa Johnson et al. say: "Latino refers to U.S. residents who self-identify with the indigenous or Spanish-speaking cultures of Mexico, Puerto Rico, Cuba, Central America and South America. Hispanics are also of European Spanish origin...."

[3]According to Cooper: "Hegemonic devices...represent the specific narrative strategies used in media to contain and suppress challenges to the dominant ideological ideals of a culture."

[4]Similarly, Carter and Allen discuss how individual self-esteem is an inseparable part of being a member of a social group for African, Asian and Latino Americans.

Ethnic Images and Their Impact

Theoretical Foundation Underlying Minority Group and Media Interaction

Byron Renz

The basic premise underlying this chapter is that the mass media help shape a psychological climate conducive to creating new types of relationships between people of one type of group and people from other types of groups. The specific concern here is with the climate created when ethnic groups or non-English-language linguistic groups interact with the mainstream society. This chapter sets forth the theoretical foundation that helps explain the nature of the role played by the media in the integration of minority groups into the dominant society.

Overview

This chapter first examines the process which allows images on a screen—or mediated images generated on the "screen" of the mind through the written word or sound—to become juxtaposed in a way that will allow one image to influence another, a process referred to here as the *cognitive convergence of thought*.

The second section examines the power of the dramatic form in media content construction and suggests that the form of the drama serves as a type of multiplier, which has the potential to modify attitudes, opinions and behaviors of members of one group in relation to members of another group.

The third section of this chapter examines the paths of group influence that exist between the media and the groups that use the media. Media influence can exist within groups, where it serves to introduce, reinforce, or change atti-

tudes, opinions, beliefs and values of group members. Media influence is also significant when it functions between groups, where it introduces, reinforces or changes the attitude-belief structure of one group toward the other.

The fourth section examines the significance of the image of people in the mass media in general and suggests that image is an important dimension in creating or modifying attitudes, opinions, values and beliefs of one individual toward another and of one group toward another.

The fifth section shifts the focus from image concerns in relation to minority groups and media use to economic and political forces that have an influence on minority groups' interest in (or lack of interest in) assimilating or integrating into the majority society. Such forces affect minority media concerns because ideas and impressions gained from the media are inextricably intertwined with minority interest in adapting to a society for personal gain, as well as for personal comfort and stability. To omit a discussion of assimilation and integration in a chapter on minority media concerns would be like trying to understand the elephant by examining only its trunk. In other words, one variable alone would be examined in an effort to understand a multivariate structure.

The sixth section explores mass communication theory to suggest the way in which it supports the impact of media messages on people's attitudes, opinions, beliefs and value structures. Three branches of existing mass communication theory directly address the premise that the mass media play a role in creating a psychological climate that allows individuals of various groups to behave differently with one another as a result of certain types of exposure to the images of other group members in mediated form.

The first of the three relevant theories is *social organization*. Social organization theory explores the way that people learn the norms and sanctions of a society and recognize and accept the roles and ranks of a society. The mass media become one of the societal instruments through which such learning and recognition occurs. The second theory is *modeling*. Modeling theory suggests a related path of behavior acquisition through vicarious identification with characters in drama, which then function as behavior models for the media user. The third theory is *construction of meaning*. Construction of meaning theory stresses the importance of the development of words to define elements in our surroundings.

The seventh section of this chapter explores the way that the theories play themselves out in illustrative television and radio series, both in the United States and abroad.

The eighth, and final, section of this chapter explores several topical ideas and issues of concern to minority groups and their individual members. The questions associated with these issues range from the use of the media as a linguistic reinforcement mechanism to the extent to which minority group members may become integrated into the dominant society. But, why can the picture generated as part of a media message influence behavior?

Cognitive Convergence of Thought

The media create a **cognitive convergence of thought** that allows the mind to accept an association of images. When we see an image of two people interacting—members of two different ethnic groups, for example—the mind, first, notices the association and, second, provides an interpretation of it. If the two people are interacting harmoniously and seem to be working cooperatively toward some common goal, the chances are fairly great that the mind's interpretation will be positive. Therefore, seeing images of persons of different ethnic groups or alternative lifestyles interacting in the pursuit of common social endeavors has two results. First, it creates the idea that juxtapositions (physical proximity) between the two types of people are possible. People of different ethnic groups, for example, can interact without conscious awareness of the ethnic difference or without feeling uncomfortable about the difference. Second, as the mind interprets the nature of the relationship between the two types of people, the interpretation will tend to be positive if the nature of the depicted interrelationship is positive. For example, if an African American and a Caucasian are seen working together in a common cause, a viewer's interpretation of the relationship will suggest that the interaction is natural and comfortable. This is what is meant by a positive interpretation of relationships.

Therefore, the idea that two different types of people can interact harmoniously has to be created initially by showing the two people together. By seeing the two people together, the mind learns to accept that reality. The two images seen together allow for a convergence of thought. We learn to accept the association as natural when we see the two persons cooperating to accomplish some meaningful end. This results in an acceptance of an association of images.

The image relationship between two people first creates an awareness of the possibility of such an association; then, it sets the stage for a **mental interpretation of the event**, including the emergence of some attitude toward the situation. If no attitude exists regarding the nature of the relationship, an opportunity arises for the development of an attitude. There is a prosocial (as well as an antisocial) potential in the depiction of two people interacting with one another. That is, showing people of different ethnic groups interacting with one another may not always be interpreted positively. However, absent some stimulus that may trigger a negative reaction to a scene that is intended to be positive, most viewers will tend to start thinking positively about the nature of the relationship.

A basic premise underlying this chapter is that the mass media create a psychological climate that allows individuals of various groups to behave differently with one another as a result of certain types of exposure to the images of other group members in mediated form. But, what does it mean to say that the mass media create a "climate"? In physical terms, a climate describes the atmospheric conditions that we react to on a daily basis. If we live in a cold climate, we anticipate the air temperature, the humidity level, and the wind velocity that we will encounter when we leave our homes and dress accordingly and adapt ourselves psychologically to the impact that those weather conditions will have on our bodies and minds.

When we talk about a psychological climate, we are concerned with a world of virtual reality. Sensory impressions in a virtually real environment stimulate our minds in essentially the same way as sensory impressions stimulate our minds in the real world. The sensory impressions then ready our bodies to respond to the anticipated conditions of the physical world in which we will find ourselves a few moments later.

Therefore, receiving stimuli in a virtual world can lead to learning, to conditioning, and to a sense of possible and appropriate associations in our environment. Stimuli from the media create a virtual reality for us. We can learn from those stimuli. We develop associational patterns from those stimuli. We are exposed to the words that are used to describe objects and events in our virtual environments. The main difference is that our bodies don't subsequently move through the actual environment. Nevertheless, our minds become conditioned to direct our bodies to respond in one way rather than another when our bodies eventually move through the actual environment. That is the reason why the effect of media messages on the mind is extremely important in anticipating behavioral patterns.

In other words, as we move through the world, sights, sounds and physical sensations create the data that our brains analyze and interpret. This is our reality of existence. The sights and sounds that we receive from a television screen or that we conjure up when lost in the description of a novel also constitute sensory data that are fed to the brain for analysis and interpretation. This is virtual reality. Both types of reality allow us to construct our composite meaning of the world around us.

In effect, the reality of life is drama, or, perhaps, it is more accurate to say that the dramatic form of media formatting approximates the experiences of real life more closely than any other form, such as news, interviews, lectures, or music. For that reason, dramas on television, at the movies or in novels create an experience that we analyze and interpret much as we do life experiences themselves.

This is significant for minority concerns with the media, because images that we interpret as positive tend to reinforce our beliefs about the world around us. Intragroup positive images—that is, favorable images of our own ethnic, religious or social group—may reinforce the image of the self as a respectable member of one's own group. Intergroup images—that is, images that we see of other ethnic, religious, or social groups—may serve to sensitize members of one group to the values, perspectives and expectations of the other groups. Both activities have the potential of fostering harmony within the society as a whole.

The unintended positive interpretation by some people of the character of Archie Bunker in Norman Lear's television series *All in the Family* is an example of how tricky interpretations of scenes with prosocial intentions can be and how unintended consequences may result from the construction of prosocial media messages.

All in the Family, which originally aired in 1971, was a sitcom that blended comedy and social commentary in about equal parts. The series constituted one of the first efforts on television to explore topics that were present in everyday life but were considered taboo at the time—open discussion of racial prejudice, male impotence and female breast cancer, for example.

All in the Family was the prototype of a show based on a dysfunctional family, a practice that became fashionable in sitcoms of the 1990s and continues today. In the 1970s, as the war in Vietnam dominated newscasts, the parents, Archie and Edith, and the grown children, Mike and

Gloria, could be seen seated at the piano, singing about the good old days. From there, the dialogue evolved into ethnic slurs by Archie and caustic criticism of President Richard Nixon by "Meathead" Mike.

The program's avowed intent was to poke fun at the prejudices of the time and, by making fun of them, to show how absurd the beliefs were. Archie was depicted as a closed-minded bigot. His character was intended to serve as a negative reference point for the prosocial beliefs of the younger and more socially liberal son-in-law, Mike. However, many people interpreted Archie as the hero who embraced a stronger and more stable belief system than Mike did.

Nevertheless, in a prosocial sense, if two people are seen interacting harmoniously in the pursuit of common goals, at least the possibility of a harmonious relationship between the two people is suggested. Of course, attitude formation is sufficiently complex that a positive one-to-one relationship cannot be guaranteed. That is the reason for the caution suggested in terms such as "possible" and "potential." In essence, then, cognitive convergence (bringing the images into a physical relationship in the mind) brings the images into the realm of cognitive acceptability (creating the potential for the development of positive attitudes).

The Power of the Dramatic Form in Media Content Organization

The media format that seems to provide the most power for attitude modification is the drama. Dramatic forms create the opportunity for vicarious identification to occur, and attitude formation studies indicate that vicarious identification facilitates the attitude modification process. When we feel ourselves at one with a character on the screen—or in the mental images that we conjure up from the pages of a novel—we tend to suspend our disbelief and reduce the barriers that defend our attitudes against formation or change. This principle applies to all mass media—print, audio, and audio-visual media. With print and audio media, however, it is still *image* that allows for identification—the motion picture that arises in the mind. Therefore, when considering image in relation to attitude formation, it is important to realize that it is the form in which the image is cast—more than the image itself—that creates the potential for attitude modification.

As mentioned previously, the dramatic form in media approximates our daily existence. Even though the dramatic form is a contrived and structured entity—with beginning, middle, end, plot points and climax—the viewer who submerges himself into the unfolding events on a screen (a television screen or the screen of our imagination) senses that he is experiencing life itself. Therefore, the attitudes, opinions, beliefs, and values that the viewer is subjected to in screen "life" have the potential to influence the viewer's attitude and belief system.

This potential effect of the media on beliefs obviously affects all types of persons and all social groups, but minority groups are also subject to the force field of values interwoven into dramatic screen constructions. The writer and producer interpose these values in the screenplay either consciously or unconsciously. Therefore, where minorities are concerned, it is possible to introduce values into a drama that—intentionally or unintentionally—will create certain impressions about the minority group. For example, in the early 1970s, some Hispanic groups criticized Sam Peckinpah for depicting Mexicans in his films of that time as shiftless, lazy, and irresponsible. Peckinpah's response to such criticism was to say that it was an attack on artistic license. In other words, the story needs to be told by the screenwriter in his own way, and let the values fall where they may. Regardless of the merit of Peckinpah's argument, many media producers consciously construct dramas to reflect a certain value system, as Lear did with *All in the Family*. The point is that values (and attitudes, opinions and beliefs) are present in virtually every drama and become part of the force field of influence that we encounter every day.

The Dynamics of Minority/ Majority Group Influence

It is important to understand where the influence of values is particularly relevant in a discussion of minority groups and the media affecting them—in what types of societal groups. Values function as an influential fabric within groups and between groups. Value systems affect minorities in two basic ways. First, values can affect how a minority person feels about himself in relation to other members of his own group—*intragroup* influence of media values. For example, if a minority person sees other members of his own group holding positions of social respect and authority—such as professional, managerial or governmental positions with decision-making power—he will come to accept that image as reality and, therefore, as a societal role that is possible. If a minority person sees screen heroes who represent members of his own ethnic or social group interacting and communicating effectively, maintaining a family and providing positive support for their communities, the values associated with these activities will be seen as possible for the minority group members themselves. In other words, the viewer will come to accept the images as reality.

However, having those values depicted on-screen not only makes them seem possible, but they also become instructive. It shows the minority viewer what values are associated with the various roles of society. If a person wants to become a doctor, that person will need to adopt the basic value system of the medical profession. The screen depiction shows the viewer what the value system is and intimates how it can be adopted by showing models of the behavior that is associated with acceptance into a particular social structure.

The second way in which value systems affect minority groups is by showing them the values of the majority group—*intergroup* influence of media values. Most minority group members feel the need (or want) to communicate effectively with majority group members with whom they interact. This is often necessary to function effectively in a job or to interact successfully socially. One of the ways in which a minority group member can learn the value system of the majority is by seeing those values depicted in media drama. Whether the minority group member decides to adopt those values or not, he at least acquires an understanding of them. Such an understanding facilitates effective communication.

Correspondingly, intergroup influence also occurs when majority group viewers see minority group members engaged in some activity on a screen. Therefore, intergroup influence cuts both ways. Minority group members perceive the values of the majority group, and majority group members perceive the characteristics and values of the minority group. This is the concept of intergroup influence of the media.

In sum, where minorities are concerned—regardless of whether these are ethnic, linguistic, cultural or gender minorities—attitudes about themselves may be formed, changed or reinforced in relation to their own group (**intragroup influence**). In addition, attitudes of the minority group member may be formed, changed or reinforced in relation to the majority group (the first way that influence cuts in **intergroup communication**). Likewise, majority group attitudes may be formed, changed or reinforced in relation to a particular minority group (the second way that influence cuts in **intergroup communication**). "Interaction" with those groups on the screen becomes a part of our composite experience with those groups. Therefore, seeing the image of a minority person onscreen introduces that type of person into the field of our perceptions, and thus it becomes part of our field of experience. Recognition is the first step in understanding and acceptance. Immersion in the value system is the second step. Finally, recall that the opportunity to "understand that person" is maximized if the character is shown in a dramatic context—playing a particular role in life, following the norms (standards of conduct) that are associated with that role, interacting with others on the basis of one's rank in society and behaving within the context of the sanctions (both pro and con) associated with that role.

When a minority person is experienced in a dramatic setting (or when a minority person experiences a majority person in the same type of setting), the viewer has an opportunity to come to understand not only what the person looks like and how he behaves, but also the full social character of that person. Attitudes arising from that type of understanding have the potential of being deeper and more fully formed than an attitude arising from the experience of a moving image alone. That is the reason that issues revolving around societal integration and minority rights and privileges may be dealt with in a composite manner in the media if dramatic forms are employed to create an experience in which one person is involved with another.

The Significance of Image in Media Content

Image and value transfer are related concepts. Image, in relation to attitude formation, is significant both from the standpoint of the influence of that image internally in groups of like characteristics (a particular minority group, for example) and the influence that cuts across groups of unlike characteristics (a minority group and the majority group or one minority group, such as African Americans, and another minority group, such as Hispanics). We must have an image of a person engaged in some life activity before an influence can occur that affects our attitudes, opinions, values and beliefs. The significance of image in relation to minorities cuts three ways. In its most obvious form, a minority person, seeking acceptance in a dominant majority society, is concerned about the image of his group in the larger society (intergroup influence). Full political, economic and social acceptance of that person will ultimately depend upon the image held of the minority group by the dominant group.

However, the sword cuts in two other directions as well. First, minority groups will develop attitudes toward the majority based on the minority's image experience with the majority (the second way in which intergroup influence may work). That image experience may come partially (or largely) from experiences with the majority in dramatic forms in the media.

Although the concern so far has been with minorities and majorities within a given society (the United States, in this case), minority and majority image generation can occur on a worldwide scale, as well as on a national, regional and local scale. For example, in the early twenty-first century, America is considered something of a "majority" entity in world politics and economics. Yet, many people in the world experience America and Americans almost entirely through the media. Therefore, the image of the social role played by Americans is shaped for most people by the images of Americans conveyed through television and film.

The third way in which the sword cuts concerns the image developed by the minority of itself (intragroup influence). Self-image and self-concept, ultimately, play a role in the way in which a minority will function in society. Within the dominant society in the United States, media images generated specifically for the minority group (primarily through minority media) have enhanced a positive minority self-image. This is a major reason that minority groups often go to considerable lengths to develop their own broadcasting stations (or programs) and their own newspapers and magazines.

With Portuguese-language programming in the United States, a Portuguese-speaking viewer can experience the life and thought processes of a successful Portuguese professional, for example. This tends to reinforce the Portuguese person's sense of the acceptability of his own ethnic and linguistic group. To the extent that the image of the Portuguese professional is incorporated in the mainstream media, the general viewer achieves an awareness of the Portuguese character as someone identifiable with his ethnic group and playing a role that is comparable to that of any other professional of that type. This heightens the awareness of that ethnic group in the society at large. Such awareness tends to reinforce the legitimacy of this linguistic group in and of itself—as well as in American society as a whole.

This constitutes a microscopic perspective on the relationship of the media to ethnic and linguistic groups. But, there is also a macroscopic view of the relationship of the media to ethnic groups and linguistic minorities. That view concerns the ability of the media—along with other societal institutions—to facilitate integration and assimilation in the larger society. Although the focus is different in the macroscopic view, the function of the media in the process of sensitizing groups to the mutual acceptability of one another remains the same. The question arises as to whether the media, in general, can be effective at bringing about a change in attitudes toward groups different from their own through program content. Probably our best guide, at this point, is media theory, which addresses the issue of influence macroscopically, rather than through the microscopic approach of empirical studies.

However, it is important to remember that an examination of minority group integration or assimilation into a larger society must consider several powerful forces—societal institutions—other than the media. One important part of this greater whole is derived from economic theory, which expands the focus from media influence on behavior per se to media influence as but one component of a larger composite body of influence affecting the minority person in his effort to adapt his behavior to a pattern acceptable by the majority society. Political theory, too, becomes a part of the composite body of influence affecting a minority person's mobility within a society dominated by a majority. Culture is the third major building block—aside from the mass media—that shapes the behavior that facilitates or restricts the mobility of minority group members within a dominant society. Economic considerations provide the motivation to change (the impetus); political theory describes the sanctions (the opportunities and limitations) on mobility within a majority society; cultural components provide the lubrication that allows a minority person to move smoothly within the mechanism of the majority society; and media presentations provide a handbook of how change can occur.

Economic, Political and Cultural Forces Affecting Societal Integration

A theoretical foundation for discussing the role of the media in societal integration involves an examination of the power of an economy in relation to the motivation of individuals to em-brace the principles embodied by the dominant economic group in society. Such a motivation may facilitate media use, as well as raise interest in achieving assimilation or integration in the larger society.

The role of the media in societal integration is also dependent upon economic forces and the linguistic and cultural expectations embodied in the engine that drives the economy. A powerful engine, with essentially unidimensional linguistic and cultural expectations, exerts a great force on the process of assimilation; a less powerful engine lacks the unifying power of the strong engine and allows for greater autonomy among the various linguistic and cultural groups comprising the polity.

In other words, a strong economy creates wealth and jobs to a greater extent than a weak economy. On the one hand, if the wealth created by that economy and the jobs generated by that economy use a particular language as an instrument of communication (English, let's say, in the United States, Britain and Australia), a powerful motivation is provided for minority group members to master the language and social customs necessary to get mainstream jobs and to share in the wealth of the society. This is a force that encourages integration or assimilation.

A weak economy, on the other hand, generates less wealth and lower-paying jobs. Correspondingly, there is less motivation for minority group members to master the majority language or adopt majority social patterns. Societies with weak economies, therefore, provide less impetus for minority groups to integrate or assimilate. In societies with weak economies, it is easier for minority groups to remain autonomous.

But, politics also influences the mobility of minority group members within the dominant society. Political theory describes the limits of possibility within the legal constraints of a political system. The underlying political philosophy of a nation's executive, legislative and judicial interests shapes the status of immigrant groups (and their descendants). The ultimate impact that media messages can have on a society is governed by a country's political structure. Those structures that allow full political participation within a democratic society expand the circle of entry into a society to its maximum (permitting assimilation); those structures with a paternalistic bent categorize immigrant groups (and their descendants) as distinct from the indigenous population and as groups to be dealt with differently (even if benignly).

A societal group's culture is a third element in the composite body of influences that govern the behavior that smoothes the path for a minority group member's mobility within the dominant society. The strength and dynamism of a nation's culture dominates, at varying levels, the sensoriums of a country's inhabitants. Powerful cultures intrude vigorously into people's perceptions and thought processes; weaker cultures intrude less. Therefore, specific media impact in societal integration is an organic entity influenced by the economic, political and cultural housing of which the media are a part.

The movement toward assimilation or integration—and the impetus to do so—is dependent upon the linguistic and cultural expectations of the dominant economic group. For example, if English is the language used in business, that fact constitutes a powerful motivator for non-English-speaking people to want to learn English well enough that they can be gainfully employed. Correspondingly, some internalization of the employer group's values allows the minority employee to become stably integrated into the employment structure. Both majority language acquisition and value acquisition, therefore, facilitate job acquisition and retention. Job availability and a relatively high wage scale motivate language learning and value acquisition, and that, in turn, eases the way toward integration or assimilation. Therefore, the power of the economic engine drives both integration and assimilation. Because the majority media use the dominant group's language and tend to reflect the dominant group's values, the minority person may find himself encouraged to interact more or less fully with both the language patterns and value systems reflected in the media—both majority media and his own group's minority media.

Whether minority groups can become integrated into a dominant society—and the extent to which that can happen—depends upon a composite group of factors—economic, politi-

cal and cultural, as well as the image and idea components available from the mass media. However, the significance of image in minority group mobility should not be underestimated. Considerations of minority media come back eventually to the postulates of the three theories of mass communication whose constructs embrace minority media specifically—*social organization* theory, *modeling* theory and *construction of meaning* theory.

The uses of media by minority groups suggest the potential impact of minority media on their own groups. How minority media are used indicates the potential power of those media to generate images, with associated values, for the group itself. Potential impact is the ultimate outcome; the extent and nature of the use of those media suggest the potential of the media to have an impact on attitudes, opinions, beliefs and values.

Mass Communication Theory Relevant to Minority Media Use

Powerful effects media theories—generally accepted at the turn of the twenty-first century—suggest that media impact is cumulative, with its strength being exerted over time. The influence of the media over time—that is, longitudinal effect—seems to operate in the case of media influence in societal integration. For example, over time—when media users are exposed to prosocial interactions among different social groups—there is a cumulative positive effect on the perceptions of one group toward another. (Of course, other image constructions could generate antisocial effects also.)

SOCIAL ORGANIZATION THEORY

One conceptual construction that supports such a positive effect is *social organization* theory, which suggests that the social organization subdivisions of norms, roles, ranking, and sanctions are learned through communication in a social setting. One of those settings is dramatized program matter. When we submerge ourselves in the programming—whether television, film or the novel—we learn (usually subconsciously) what the expectations of the social organization subdivisions are.

For example, social norms, the general rules that all members of a group understand and follow, range widely in significance, from covering one's mouth during a yawn to proscriptions against murder. Learning about the roles people play in life is a central organizing principle that allows people to act in a collective, coordinated manner to accomplish goals that could not be realized if each person acted independently.

One also learns the principle of differential power in society—the creation of ranks—that allows a command structure to be created. It is necessary that everyone recognize social rank and that behavior toward others recognizes rank. Additionally, we need to learn what social sanctions exist and the character of the sanctions. On the one hand, negative sanctions punish persons who deviate from the rules of society. Positive sanctions, on the other hand, reward persons who conform to social rules. Conformity assists the group in goal achievement.

The mass media, particularly through dramatized material, are a major source of patterns of social expectations. Through vicarious identification with characters in a drama, we experience the punishments that accompany social deviance and the rewards associated with social conformity.

Social organization theory suggests that patterns of social organization are learned through contact with others in a social setting—primarily through direct contact with others in social groups, but also through psychologically interactive contacts with others in the media. We see the form of norms, roles, ranking and sanctions. Audience members then assimilate the definitions, and those definitions become the audience members' learned sets of social expectations about appropriate social behavior. Prior understanding of what constitutes desirable behavior facilitates appropriate behavior for participants of groups to which one belongs or will belong. A person learns what to expect from others in response to certain behavior patterns. In addition, one learns how to behave toward others who are playing out their roles in specific groups, and one learns how others can be expected to behave toward us. These steps lead to our knowledge of the social order. Therefore, social organization theory explains long-range and indirect influences of the media. (See, for example, DeFleur and Dennis, 1998; Littlejohn, 2001.)

MODELING THEORY

Modeling theory also supports the argument that media can function positively in societal integration. As we identify vicariously (*vicarious identification*) with characters in a drama, we associate our thinking with the behavior of the characters. The character becomes a model for our behavior. The sequence of events begins with an experience, an encounter with some type of action in a story. If identification with the model occurs, the audience member will want to be like the character. The audience member remembers the behavior patterns of the character and reproduces the actions at some later time. If a positive outcome accompanies the assumed behavior, the new behavior is reinforced. Additional reinforcement makes it likely that the newly modeled behavior will be adopted as a permanent characteristic. (See DeFleur and Dennis, 1998: 471.)

Not only do we learn behaviors from the models with whom we identify (and these models may be media models, as well as real-life models), but we also discover solutions to problems through vicarious identification with models. Behavior modeling, including problem solution through identification with media characters, is advantageous because it is often physically less painful than experimentation with modeled behavior in real life.

According to Albert Bandura, who developed modeling theory, social learning through identification with characters on screen occurs in any of three ways. The first way is what Bandura refers to as *observational* learning. Viewers discover what a particular behavioral pattern is—by seeing it on the screen—and then copy the behavior. Success or failure of the outcome of experimentation with that behavioral pattern will determine whether it is retained and integrated into one's behavioral system or whether the pattern will be abandoned.

Modeling theory also suggests that certain effects are associated with the observation of characters on a screen. Effects may be *inhibitory* or *disinhibitory*. Seeing a screen character being punished for exhibiting certain behavior decreases the likelihood that the viewer will experiment with the behavioral pattern seen on the screen. Various studies have shown that seeing characters being punished for certain behaviors discourages behaviors such as aggression, exploration and antisocial interaction with one's peers.

Conversely, disinhibitory effects occur when a screen character is being seen rewarded for exhibiting threatening or prohibited behavior. Under these circumstances, the viewer is more likely to adopt the behavioral pattern for experimentation. Although vicarious identification is critical in the transfer of behavioral patterns (including their associated value and belief systems), the actual adoption of the behavior is dependent upon the reinforcement contingencies. That is to say, as we watch the characters on the screen, we sense their pleasure or pain as they exhibit certain behavior in relation to the events of their lives.

Some sophistication is called for in the behavioral development of "good guys" and "bad guys" on the screen, however. If the "good guy" defeats the "bad guy" by being more aggressive and wielding more blatant power, the behavioral principle of aggression and direct application of power are conveyed as favorable behavioral patterns (disinhibitory) even though they may simultaneously convey some prosocial principle. (See Bandura, 1965.)

CONSTRUCTION OF MEANING THEORY

Construction of meaning theory also contributes to our understanding of the role of the media in societal integration. Socrates discussed the importance of definitions in our understanding of the world around us. To know something, Socrates said, we have to be able to name it and define it in precise terms and then to be consistent in our use of that meaning. When we begin with a clear and concise definition, and when we follow the rules that standardize connections between words for aspects of our environment,

we are then able to reason logically from premises to conclusions to reach truth. The knowledge that we have about some aspect of our environment governs our behavior toward it. Plato said that our knowledge of the world not only depends on what we perceive with our senses, but also on what we agree upon with other people are the meanings of events in the world around us. (See DeFleur and Ball-Rokeach, 1989.)

According to construction of meaning theory, human memory makes the development of knowledge possible. Knowledge exists as concepts, which are structures of meaning that are named or labeled and remembered by people. Meanings for concepts are developed either through direct experience of the senses or through symbolic interaction in a language community. Language consists of symbols that allow us to label things and thus create meanings on which we all agree. Communication is made possible through the conventions that standardize the links between symbols and meaning. The symbols and conventions of language that are agreed upon and used shape our perceptions of the physical and social world, our interpretation of that world and our consequent conduct toward that world. Therefore, in a world of media, the question that arises concerns the extent to which program content results in our constructing shared meanings for the world of reality that we cannot experience directly.

Therefore, as we see an image associated for us in televised narrative settings (and news could be considered a "narrative setting" in this context), that image association becomes our reality, and we develop a vocabulary to describe it. We see the images of characters of various ethnic backgrounds juxtaposed and interacting in pursuit of societal goals. That image is a psychological experience and becomes a segment of our reality. As we develop a vocabulary for that reality and define it, the reality assumes meaning. The creation of meaning includes devising rules that govern the choice of words that are used to discuss ethnic association. At that point, we are able to reason logically from our premises about ethnic association to our conclusions that constitute an acceptance of the premises. We then have knowledge not only about ethnic group existence, but also about the nature of our relationship to it. That knowledge governs our behavior toward it.

When a concept becomes clear through the invention of a word and when we standardize rules that allow us to connect words in meaningful expressions about our environment, then we can reason logically from a premise to a conclusion in an effort to discover truth. That focus on language symbols that create meanings has a direct bearing on media and their role in societal integration.

The Application of Theoretical Principles of Minority Images in the Media

What do these theories suggest, collectively, about the role of the media in societal integration? It seems likely that the media can start sensitizing people to the possibility of coexistence and co-involvement in societal functions. As characters representing different ethnic or linguistic groups interact in their efforts to achieve common goals, the audience members come to associate the juxtaposition and interaction of the characters in their thought processes. The pattern of association is remembered. This association of images, over time, suggests that juxtaposition is possible, and then that it is normal.

For example, in the serial drama *ER*, men and women from different ethnic groups play roles within the social stratification of a hospital. Created by Michael Crichton, *ER* concerns the work and lives of a group of emergency room medical personnel in a Chicago hospital. Each episode tells the story of another day in the emergency room, from the frenetic to the banal, and from the joyous to the heartbreaking. The stressful life in the emergency room is intensified by rapid pacing and interwoven plot lines, and the dramatic emotional swings of the characters. The scripting puts the viewer at the doctor's shoulder, viewing the other players in that world from the doctor's perspective.

Doctors are represented by African Americans, Asians and women, as well as by Caucasian males. A similar diversity of ethnic groups and genders is represented at the level of the nurse and the hospital support staff. Repeated exposure of viewers to the interrelationships among the characters at each social level sensitizes the person, who has become vicariously immersed in the program, to the normality of a situation where doctors may be, for example, Pakistani, African-American or Caucasian, and male as well as female. A similar expectation would be created at the other levels as well; that is, the role of the nurse, for example, may also be represented normally by different types of people, particularly men as well as women. This sensitization is most effective through dramatic constructions, particularly those that provide an opportunity for vicarious identification with the characters and for repeated periodic exposure to the media-constructed reality. Therefore, the most powerful program types in this category are the soap opera and the serial drama.

This principle is already part of programming practice in various areas of the world. The United States incorporated the principle of image juxtaposition of characters in pursuit of common goals some time ago in its mainstream media. Not only do multi-ethnic characters interact, but they also pursue goals related to current issues of social concern. Serial dramas, such as *ER, L.A. Law* and *St. Elsewhere*, depict multi-ethnic characters pursuing significant social goals which, simultaneously, explore controversial social issues in the stratified narrative structure of the soap opera and serial drama.

As with *ER, St. Elsewhere* is set in a hospital, in this case a public hospital in Boston. The series, which ran from 1982 to 1988, tried to present a realistic view of an institution that reflects the seamy side of life. St. Elsewhere was the nickname for Boston's St. Eligius hospital. The doctors were not cast as heroes, and medical miracles were not part of the script. The show's dialogue was filled with coarse, hospital humor and depicted the daily life-and-death struggles of patients rejected by Boston's more prestigious hospitals.

Characters at the several levels of the hospital staff hierarchy are representative of various ethnic groups and consist of both men and women at all levels. The patients, too, represent a rich ethnic mix; therefore, the viewer is exposed not only to the professional employees interacting with one another in accordance with their professional duties, but also to the professionals interacting with interest, sympathy and love toward the patients that they treat. Employees and patients, regardless of race or gender, are seen working together toward the common goal of medical recovery.

L.A. Law is set in the offices of a major Los Angeles law firm. Aired from 1986 to 1994, the series was created by Steven Bochco (the creator of *Hill Street Blues*) and Louise Fisher (the producer of *Cagney and Lacy* and a former deputy district attorney). The high-powered law firm of McKenzie, Brackman, Chaney, and Kuzak took both criminal and civil cases.

Intertwined plot lines often focused on cases that explored social problems of the time and incorporated office politics and sexual adventures. For example, Stuart and Ann connived to find ways to become partners in the firm. Michael Kuzak was sexually interested in Grace Van Owen, and Becker was sexually interested in many of the women.

The plot lines resembled soap operas. Abby left the firm to set up her own practice, but then decided to return to McKenzie, Brackman. Grace Van Owen was named a judge, but she resigned to join the prestigious law firm. Arnie finally married Corrine, after years of seducing rich and beautiful women, but had an extra-marital affair with his rather plain secretary, Roxanne.

As is true of the hospital dramas, the attorneys are represented by Hispanics, African Americans, and women, as well as by Caucasian males. Characteristic of the dramatic form of literature, the characters in the firm interact collectively to solve the problem represented in the particular episode. However, *L.A. Law* expanded the character roles to include not only various ethnic groups and women, but also other groups striving for full social recognition, such as full-figured women and gays.

In all cases, these groups were integrated into the story line and played out their character roles so as to assist in the mutual effort to solve the central problem presented in the drama. The stratified structure of soap opera and serial drama allows four or five story lines to be played

out during the course of a single program by intercutting among the story lines as they progress within the program time block. This program compression heightens the dramatic impact of the screen presentation and, thus, heightens the impact of the nature of the character interaction on the screen, a positive effect when prosocial character interrelationship is desired.

However, the United States is not the only country in which the principle of sensitization is being incorporated in dramatic programming. In radio, the BBC World Service runs a daily soap opera, *Westway*, which incorporates characters from major immigrant groups in Britain. For example, a series of episodes in 1999 included an Indian living in an English household, who played an integral part in the dramatized activities. *Westway* also explores controversial social issues, such as the status of homosexuals in society (personal experience of the author, 1998-2000).

In developing Eastern Europe, now more than a decade after the end of Soviet occupation, countries are struggling not only to develop economically and politically, but also to reconcile social differences that have often divided residents of the countries into tenuously coexistent groups, separated by differing value and belief systems and by their self-perception.

These are grounded in their sense of world position. For example, a member of a superpower (or former superpower) often exhibits a self-confident, expansionist view of the world. A member of a small country that has experienced occupation by another country and whose people have been subjected to the power, values and beliefs of the occupying political, economic and social system often have to contend with a sense of inferiority. Media images may be marshaled (intentionally or unintentionally) in an effort to adjust to the inferiority complex.

In the Baltic country of Latvia today, Latvian and resident Russian ethnic and linguistic groups coexist in nearly equal numbers. After a century in which the country was occupied for most of its existence by foreign superpowers (Germany and the Soviet Union), Latvians are now trying to reestablish their own existence, to redefine themselves in accordance with their own history and to establish a harmonious and cooperative relationship with the Russian residents.

To this end, Latvia recently began to develop its own serial dramas on national television. A third of these serial dramas makes a conscious effort to incorporate strong, positive characters that invite vicarious identification from both the Latvian and Russian communities of Latvia. The dialogue in this series also incorporates frequent use of the Latvian and Russian languages, each used accurately and in its entirety within given sections of the dialogue.

This program series, *Tas notika Rīgā* (That's Happening in Riga), incorporates Latvian and Russian characters who play roles in which mutual involvement and cooperative effort constitute a substantial portion of the narrative. *Tas notika Rīgā* is a serial drama that explores everyday problems associated with work, family and domestic relations for an early middle-aged working couple where the husband is Russian and the wife Latvian. The couple copes with the daily problems of earning a living, managing an extended family, wrestling with the problems of a bureaucracy and responding to the problems and concerns of neighbors and friends. That setting allows for an exploration (within a dramatic format) of numerous social problems confronting the Latvian and Russian population groups and for mutual interaction in the pursuit of common goals. Each vignette mixes Latvians and Russians at the various social levels, much as the American serial drama *ER* mixes the genders and ethnic groups at each social level of a hospital. This program, partially supported by the European Union, is the first effort by Latvian National Television to incorporate consciously the principle of sensitization in dramatized programming.

Topical Concerns Involved in Minority Media Use

Several topical concerns can be identified in connection with minority group use of the media. The first topic concerns the way that minority groups use the media for themselves. It should be noted that minorities use media in differential ways, depending largely upon their relative degree of integration or assimilation in the society.

A subsidiary area of interest regarding media use by minority groups for themselves concerns the extent to which the media (with a focus on broadcasting) can help a minority group maintain its language and culture. That question is examined here by exploring the institutional role of broadcasting in linguistic and cultural maintenance in the United States. Among institutions that influence linguistic and cultural maintenance, a more prominent role for the media as an influential factor is found than was previously suspected.

Language reinforcement concerns have only a thin foundation in existing theory. Speech and language functions of the media fall within the general purview of meaning construction, and meaning is dependent upon the use of symbols and symbolic interaction (DeFleur & Plax, 1980). Theory suggests that the media establish new words and provide the meaning associated with them; the media enrich our understanding of existing terms by extending their meanings; the media displace former meanings of terms with new meanings; and the media stabilize the meanings of the vocabulary of language.

These components of speech and language concerns within meaning construction theory underscore the fluid nature of our interaction with language. Having an opportunity to interact with the symbols of our native language within a society that uses another language (the use of Lithuanian, for example, within an English-speaking society) not only keeps the linguistic symbols alive and active, but it also allows the dynamic changes of the native language to remain in a state of flux in our minds (as is the case with the primary language of the society, English in this instance).

Linked to the reinforcement concept is the emotional satisfaction that arises from the associations suggested by certain linguistic structures. The use of a grammatically correct, carefully articulated language might suggest a pride in the culture with which that language is associated. Well-spoken language suggests a legitimate status for the culture with which that language is associated. This is generally a minority intragroup concern. Conversely, the use of youth jargon, sentence structures and intonation suggest an acceptance of the user of such linguistic patterns into the particular social subset. Think of the linguistic patterns of youth, jazz musicians or rappers. In short, having a minority language readily available for use by minority linguistic groups reinforces the meaning that the minority culture has for members of that cultural group.

Associated with the question about the extent to which the media can contribute to linguistic and cultural maintenance is the issue about minority group size in linguistic and cultural maintenance. The point made here is that minority group size has only relative significance for cultural maintenance in general and that its significance in linguistic and cultural maintenance is fluid and dependent upon a variety of factors. Although size may provide economic viability for a particular societal subgroup (through small industries and services that support the subgroup), the size of the subgroup is only one factor among many factors affecting the ethnic island (or societal subgroup) in the dynamics of the larger society of which the subgroup is only a part.

Because assumptions are often made—in the United States at least—about the inevitability of assimilation, when minority groups interact with a dominant society over time, a significant issue in the consideration of minority media involves the nature of the relationship of minority societies to the dominant societies of which they are a part and the nature of the evolutionary development of the minority society in relation to the dominant society. Here it is instructive to examine the nature of the relationship of minority societies to the dominant societies in countries other than the United States, as well as to look at the American model. The issue concerns specifically the functions of integration and assimilation and questions whether the two concepts are congruent. The question of whether assimilation is inevitable when majority and minority societies interact over time increases the significance of politics in relation to image. However, a consideration of the media role in societal integration needs to consider the nature of the ultimate relationship between dominant and minority groups.

The question of minority group member assimilation or integration within a society pushes beyond mass communication theory per se. Whereas mass media theories interpret uses, effects, gratifications, and, sometimes, economic and political policies of the media, a bedrock question is often the nature and extent to which minority groups will become integrated or assimilated into the majority society. This question is primarily a social, cultural, and, especially, a political issue that cuts across the disciplines of communication, sociology, economics, and politics. However, because media use is a part of this larger equation, it seems appropriate to examine the integration/assimilation issue within a chapter on minority group media patterns and uses. Consideration of this question seems even more appropriate in light of the considerable interest shown by sociologists and politicians in the nature of the relationships of social groups within a larger society.

Conclusion

This chapter argues that the interrelationship of the media and society plays a significant role in establishing mutual understanding among societal groups and in defining, clarifying and expanding one's own group, thus creating a climate in which tolerance becomes possible. The climate is comprised of dramatic characters, usually (but not necessarily) fictional, exhibiting their physical appearance, their personal mannerisms and acting in accordance with their attitude, opinion, belief and value systems. Such interinvolvement of characters, with their impressions of one another, allows for a cognitive convergence of thought, the essential foundation for intragroup identification and intergroup acceptance. One should also note the fine line that separates real persons and fictional characters, when the fictional characters are cast in a dramatic setting. Within the context of drama, suspension of disbelief virtually eliminates the line between reality and unreality in the receiver's (viewer's, listener's, reader's) mind. The fictional character, in effect, becomes real.

Cognitive convergence of thought applies similarly to nonfictional characters when they are incorporated in a mediated dramatic context. This occurs in a documentary when characters are framed and juxtaposed with other characters and objects to convey a specific idea or feeling.

Attention also converges within the frame of a newscast, as images from the same plane of reference are framed and juxtaposed. Shots of American Abram tanks and Bradley fighting vehicles may be seen moving in a column along a dusty road in the Middle East. Shots of an officer in an American military combat uniform may provide comments of "assurance" as he expresses his opinions in response to a reporter's questions. This shot may be juxtaposed with a shot of an enlisted man operating a piece of equipment or reading the screen of a military computer.

The symbols in the juxtaposed images converge in the mind where they blend together for interpretation. The initial interpretation is based on the available image data. The interpretation for an American would likely be that what he is seeing is "his team" moving "down the field" against the opponent. It is almost impossible to avoid the analogy to American football. The juxtaposition of images allows for a convergence of symbols that is subject to interpretation.

It is instructive to note, however, that the pool of available images is nearly always governed by perspective. And, perspective can provide image data that are subject to wildly different interpretations. For example, when a story is prepared by a reporter embedded with a particular military unit during a war, the viewer has the opportunity to see the conflict from the perspective of a passenger in a car watching the telephone poles and towns go by. The advantage is that it creates sights and, therefore, provides a modicum of insight into a particular road being traversed at a particular time. It provides a vista to the event. The disadvantage is that the vista is equivalent to that of a carpenter ant on a sequoia tree. Asked to define the tree, the ant would describe the long, parallel mountain ridges and deep crevasses around him, occasionally obfuscated by shadows of huge green canopies. The ant's report might be completely accurate and objective, but it would provide an inaccurate idea of what a sequoia tree is like from a human perspective.

It should be noted that shot choice and image juxtaposition may be part of a propagandist's scheme, or they may be completely consistent with a journalist's objective and unbiased report. It is inevitable that one sees the world from one's own unique perspective. However, "shots" chosen for media dissemination provide very different data bases, which may result in very different interpretations of events.

However, in relation to minority media use, perspective—whether intentional or unintentional—creates an image pool that can incline a receiver (viewer, reader) in one direction as opposed to another. The assumption underlying the use of image framing and juxtaposition is that the images will be constructed in response to prosocial motivations.

Regardless of whether the framed characters are fictional or real, the media create a sensory playground in which characters from different social groups interact. Being on that playground, first, creates awareness of the other characters on the playground and, second, allows us to project ourselves into virtual interactions with others. Interaction with others allows us to become accustomed to their patterns of behavior. Becoming accustomed to that behavior is the step preceding smooth, coordinated, cooperative, goal-oriented team interaction. This is the cognitive convergence of thought referred to earlier in this chapter. For ultimate, comfortable acceptance of a person in our field of conscious reality, the idea of a person, first, must be introduced into that consciousness; second, it must allow us to see ourselves in virtual interaction with those others; and, third, it must create a comfortable acceptance of the other in one's field of consciousness.

It should also be remembered that the media format has an impact on the extent to which characters may interact harmoniously within a given field of acceptability. Although any exposure of the image of a person of a particular ethnic group, for example, creates awareness of the characteristics of that person, awareness evolves into understanding only if we see that person interacting with other persons or objects so as to reveal the person's attitudes, opinions, beliefs and values. The media format that creates that opportunity more than any other is the dramatic format.

The strength of the dramatic form is three-fold. First, it allows the viewer to see the ethnic character acting in a manner that reveals his attitudes, opinions, beliefs and values. Revealing these internal characteristics expands exponentially the viewer's depth of insight into the ethnic character.

Second, the dramatic form allows the viewer to see the character as a member of a sympathetic team, working together—each performing his own role—to accomplish a mutually desirable objective (to win the game or to capture the crook).

Third, the dramatic form—more than any other—creates the opportunity for vicarious identification to occur. Vicarious identification occurs when the viewer (or reader) is able to project herself into the psychological mindset of the screen character. Such identification creates the possibility for some transfer to occur of the attitude, opinion, value and belief structure of the screen character to the media user (the viewer, listener, or reader). These abilities, which are a direct result of the type of media format used, give considerable strength to media drama, compared to other forms.

It is also helpful to understand where the lines of influence occur within and among societal groups. Our first area concerns lines of influence among groups. The interest is in creating understanding and empathy between a minority group and the majority group. These are the intergroup media-induced influences referred to in this chapter. The media influences that exist within groups are also important—the so-called intragroup influences of the media. These influences contribute to the sense of community, they strengthen that sense of community, and they help the community define itself.

It is virtually impossible to project media program content without, simultaneously, projecting some image—the image of a person, a country, an ethnic group, a socioeconomic group or some other. The receiver of the mediated image invariably evaluates the representation of the person or ethnic group on the basis of his own attitudes, opinions, beliefs and values. The projection of image at this point is subtle. Research in attitude modification tells us that attitudes are difficult to change. Nevertheless, because they are not impervious to change, images—evaluated in a particular light—may contribute to attitude modification and, by extension, to the modification of opinions, beliefs and values.

Where minority groups are concerned, image is significant in three ways. First, the overall acceptance of a minority group in the larger society of which it is a part depends upon the image of the minority held by the majority. Therefore, the character of the image of a minority group that is projected to the majority will help shape the attitudes, opinions and beliefs held by the majority group of the minority group.

Of equal importance, however, is the image of the majority group held by the minority group. The view of the majority held by the minority will shape the attitude, opinion and belief structure of the minority toward the majority. Such an image can generate a number of cooperation or resistance variables that can facilitate or impede a smoothly functioning society.

A third way in which image projection into a societal group is significant relates to the way in which the image of a group affects the group's self-image. Self-image, of course, has an impact on self-confidence and motivation.

Economic, political and cultural forces also drive the assimilation/integration issue. Powerful economic engines encourage the assimilation/integration process; less powerful engines exert less force in that direction. Political systems that allow for full political participation by minority groups encourage assimilation; political systems that allow for something short of full political participation may encourage integration, but not assimilation. Culture, too, provides variables that facilitate or impede mobility of a minority group member within the dominant society.

Among the numerous mass media theories, three seem to be particularly pertinent to minority group uses of the media. *Social organization* theory stresses the significance of norms, roles, ranking and sanctions and suggests that they are learned through communication in a social setting. One such social setting is dramatized program matter in the media.

Modeling theory also suggests that media can function positively in societal integration. Through identification with characters in a drama, the viewer (or reader) may model his behavior after that of the screen character, which has become a model for the viewer.

Construction of meaning theory helps us understand the relationship of the media and integrative tendencies of society. To know something, we must be able to name it. The name gives shape to the concept and allows descriptions of that content to be shared with other people. Thus, knowledge is formulated and disseminated uniformly. The language symbols and conventions that people agree to (1) deter-

mine our perceptions of both the physical and social world, (2) allow us to interpret the world around us, and (3), ultimately, determine the way we behave toward that world. Image association in media narrative becomes a portion of our sensuous reality. The development of a vocabulary for that reality gives it meaning.

Collectively, social organization theory, modeling theory, and construction of meaning theory suggest that the media can sensitize people to the possibility of coexistence and mutual involvement in societal functions. As the nature of these interactive activities is associated in people's minds, the pattern of the association is remembered. Over time, image relationship suggests that such interactions are not only possible, but also normal.

1. What is the cognitive convergence of thought? Why is it so important in media presentations that have a prosocial orientation?

2. What elements are present in the dramatic form of media presentation? Why is the dramatic form in media content construction important? In what respect do news stories (television, radio or newspapers) resemble the stories in serial dramas or soap operas? What are the differences?

3. What is image? Why is it important in the acceptance or rejection of persons of societal groups different from the majority (e.g., ethnic groups, genders, homosexuals, full-figured persons)?

4. What forces—aside from media images—drive integration and assimilation? What is the relative importance of media images and non-media economic, political, and cultural forces? How are those forces interrelated in the developmental steps leading toward assimilation and integration?

5. Of the three patterning theories discussed in this chapter—social organization theory, modeling theory and construction of meaning theory—which do you think is the most important in promoting societal organization? Why?

Name: _____

Date: _____

1. The author has provided a number of ALANA examples to illustrate communication theory from television programs. Provide your own ALANA examples for the concepts introduced in the eight sections of the chapter. They may be drawn from actual media products depicting ALANA or ones you create yourself.

2. Watch an episode of a currently running television series or a recording of an episode from a previous series. As you watch, make notes on the way that the characters depict the norms, roles, ranking and sanctions of the types of persons shown in that episode. Pick one character and describe the way that she or he complies with the social norms implicit in the situation, the role assumed by that character in society in which she or he exists, how the rank of the character is depicted, and how the character complies with the social sanctions implicit in the dramatic context.

3. Watch an episode of a television series or movie of your choosing. Identify the "hero" character (the one with whom vicarious identification could occur). Describe the characteristics of that person. How do these characteristics allow her or him to overcome the obstacles confronted in the development of the plot line? Why do you find yourself reacting positively to the characteristics that you identify as meaningful to you?

REFERENCES

Bandura, A. (1994). Social cognitive theory of mass communication. In J. Bryant & D. Zillmann (Eds.) *Media effects: Advances in theory and research*. Hillsdale, NJ: Erlbaum.

Bandura, A. (1971). *Psychological modeling: Conflicting theories*. Chicago: Aldine Atherton.

Bandura, A. (1965). Influence of models' reinforcement contingencies. *Journal of Personality and Social Pscyhology, 1*, 589-595.

Baran, S.J. & Davis, D.K. (2003). *Mass communication theory: Foundations, ferment and future* (3rd ed.). Belmont, CA: Wadsworth.

DeFleur, M.L., & Ball-Rokeach, S.J. (1989). *Theories of mass communication* (5th ed.). New York: Longman.

DeFleur, M.L., & Dennis, E.E. (1998). *Understanding mass communication: A liberal arts perspective* (6th ed.). New York: Houghton Mifflin.

DeFleur, M.L., & Plax, T.G. (1980). *Human communication as a bio-social process*. Paper presented at the meeting of the International Communication Association, Acapulco, Mexico.

Littlejohn, S.W. (2001). *Theories of human communication* (7th ed.). Belmont, CA: Wadsworth.

McQuail, D. (2000). *Mass Communication theory: An introduction* (4th ed.). London: Sage.

Severin, W.J. & Tankard, J.W., Jr. *Communication theories: Origins, methods, and uses in the mass media* (5th ed.). New York: Longman.

Tan, A.S. (1986). *Mass communication theories and research* (2nd ed.). New York: Macmillan.

An Examination of Mainstream and Black Media's Influence on the Self-Concept of African Americans[1]

Tamika J. A. Carter and Richard L. Allen

Introduction

African Americans' feelings toward themselves (self-esteem) and feeling toward their groups (group identity) are intimately interconnected. How African Americans feel about the group directly affects how they feel about themselves. This also works in the opposite direction (Allen, 2001; Markus & Kitayama 1991, 1994; Nobles, 1973; Triandus, 1995).

This chapter explains how the media play a role in influencing these feelings in African Americans, who, as a group, have a strong relationship with the media. This precedes a discussion of the effects media have on the African-American self-concept, which can loosely be defined as the degree of closeness one feels to similar others in ideas, feelings and thoughts (Broman, Neighbors & Jackson, 1988, p. 148). The discrepancy between largely negative mainstream media effects (majority print and electronic media) and largely positive Black media effects (Black produced/Black-oriented print and electronic media/content) is also explained.

A brief summary of the historical relationship between African Americans and the mass media sets the stage early in the chapter for discussion of the emergence of a Black press and, later, Black electronic media. The significance of media images as a form of social control is quickly addressed, then developed as it relates to the clash between mainstream media images of Blacks and those of African Americans' own creation. The chapter then describes the structure of the African-American belief system to facilitate understanding of what the findings refer to specifically. Description of the relationship between the self/group constructs and the mainstream versus the Black media follows, and the chapter closes with general conclusions in relation to the findings.

African Americans in the Media

Mainstream image-makers have portrayed African Americans in comedic and degrading ways in the mass media from colonial times onward. These images have projected into the minds of the public that Blacks are frivolous, lazy, inept, uninterested in and unworthy of participating in various social and political activities of larger society.

African Americans in response have tried to create their own media images over time, countering the negative, stereotypical examples put forth by mainstream (White-controlled) media with their own products, which have included African-American culture and values.

Portrayals of African Americans in the mainstream and Black media, then, have effects on audience members. Dates & Barlow (1993) utilize the Gramscian notion of "ideological hegemony" to critically evaluate the nature and consequences of African-American images in the mass media.

Antonio Gramsci argues that ruling class alliances in modern societies maintain their power by cultivating a consensus among subordinate classes; coercion is used only as a last resort. Cultural domination is the best means of achieving consensus, or "common sense" among all sectors of the social order.... Gramsci also argues that cultural domination provokes its opposite, cultural resistance, in subordinate classes.... The dominant culture must constantly strive to expand its hegemony while fending off challenges and interventions from the very classes and groups it seeks to subjugate (pp. 3-4).

The authors also submit that in modern American society, the mass media assist in the justification of class, race and gender inequalities.

In other words, as Davis (1982) concisely stated, "The image is an instrument of social control, and he who controls the image, controls the person" (p. 61). He states that television largely controls the images by which Americans see the world and accordingly determine their action.

Television has been credited with providing the most influential interpretations of social reality of all mass media (Allen, Dawson, & Brown, 1989; Allen & Waks, 1990; Gray, 1989; Pierce, 1980; Signorielli, 1990, 1993). Television images can create problems for children especially, as early visual images and attitudes are much more salient than those developed later in life (Wilson & Gutierrez, 1995). Moreover, television has had a particularly important relationship with African Americans. Aside from watching more television than the general population, African Americans are also heavily dependent on television for information about Blacks and the Black community and tend to use television as a source of information about the world (Dates & Barlow, 1993; Gray, 1995; McDonald, 1983; Poindexter & Stroman, 1981; Stroman et al., 1989-1990).

Alexis Tan (1985, as cited by Wilson & Gutierrez, 1985) found in a 1979 study that steady exposure to television entertainment programs that either ignore Blacks or assign them to low-status roles could lead to low self-esteem among Black viewers. The fact that the study failed to show a cause and effect relationship between television portrayals and low self-esteem among Black adults was attributed to the statistical analysis employed.

The Importance of Black Media

African Americans, troubled by mainstream media's depictions of their group, have developed their own media products and their own means of distributing them. "White domination of mainstream culture inevitably gave rise to African American cultural resistance, splitting the Black image" (Dates & Barlow, 1993, p. 16).

The resulting battle over who would create images of the African American, which is important in molding self-esteem, opinion and public agenda setting, was the catalyst for instituting a Black press (p. 371). Black media (print and electronic) may be seen as a filter of African-American information sources pertaining to the general status of African Americans both as a distinct group and in relation to the dominant society. Thus, the Black media play a significant role in determining the content of Blacks' views of themselves or the content of the African-American racial belief system. In general terms, the Black media, especially the Black print media, have served two basic functions: (a) as an agent of social change and (b) to crystallize Black racial consciousness (Allen, Thornton, & Watkins, 1993).

The research concerning the latter function has varied. For example, Allen and Bielby (1977) found that racial identification was not associated with reading *Ebony*, an established Black medium. However, later research by Allen and Hatchett (1986) that did not classify the type of Black print medium found that there was a positive relationship between exposure to Black media and positive views of African Americans. Therefore, Black print media in general may have an important socialization role in the reinforcement of positive images of African Americans, while any particular source (e.g., *Ebony*) may not show significant results.

In referring to Black media, the emphasis has been primarily on print. Nevertheless, television, by comparison to other modes of mass media, may play a more significant role in the transmission of cultural orientations as shown in previous literature.

Television plays an important role in cultivating the dominant culture (Gerbner, Morgan and Signorielli, 1994) and in continuously activating people's racial attitudes (Devine & Monteith, 1999; Dixon, 2002; Gilliam, Valentino & Beckman, 2002; Valentino, 2001). Unfortunately, as stated earlier, Blacks have been treated in mainstream television as subordinates, relative to Whites, and have mainly been presented in a stereotypical manner (Comer, 1982; Entman & Rojecki, 2000; Pierce, 1980). And while, on the one hand, the number of Blacks on television has increased over time, on the other, several content analyses have provided evidence that images of Blacks as a group are still largely stereotypical (e.g., Coltraine & Messineo, 2000; Dixon, 2000; Dixon & Linz, 2001; Weigel, Loomis, and Soja, 1980).

It is likely then, given the importance of television as a medium and source of ideas, that content relevant to African Americans will be specifically attended to by the group and will be quite influential. Black-oriented television fare in its complexity depicts both truthful and distorted images of African Americans. Thus, its impact on the African-American racial belief system is both positive and negative (Allen, 2001; Allen et al., 1989). To clarify further, African Americans do not necessarily produce or control the content, though it is intended for them. Consequently, the content varies widely in terms of positive and negative representations of Blacks, as well as the degree of accuracy in a given program. Therefore, depending on the nature and source of subject matter in a particular television show, the effects of what are broadly defined as Black-oriented media should vary widely.

The African-American Self-Concept

It is within the context of both African Americans' distinctive relationship with the media and the media's split nature concerning the group that one turns to examining the self-concept of the African American. The literature informs us about both the historical and contemporary assault on the African-American psyche and the strength shown in creating viable alternatives. (In this case, countering mainstream images with Black media images would provide an example.) As many have noted, Blacks have very different experiences from other groups in the United States, and consequently, their view of the world and especially of themselves and of their group would differ in fundamental ways from others' in this country (Akbar, 1981, 1988). DuBois (1964) addressed this issue in terms of an ever-present dilemma—a double consciousness, this sense of always looking at one's self through the eyes of others, of measuring one's soul by the tape of the world that looks on in amused contempt and pity (p. 16-17).

The identity of African Americans in the United States is multidimensional and characterized by tensions and paradoxes that are marks of oppression and exploitation. A wide range of viewpoints and frequently conflicting findings have emerged from attempts to capture the essence of this identity or self-concept (Cross, 1991, 2003; Phinney, 1990, 2003; Porter & Washington, 1979). Some suggest that as an outcome of the historical assault on African Americans, they have internalized the mainstream view and, as a result, have a low view of themselves and their group (see, for example, Clarke & Clarke, 1947; Grier & Cobb, 1968). Other research noting the same forces working against African Americans finds that they tend to have a high view of self and group, particularly relative to Whites (see Cross, 1991, 2003; and Phinney, 1993, for reviews of this literature).

In addition, Phinney, Chavira & Tate (1993) extend similar findings to Latinos. In fact, Markus & Kitayama (1991) found that the independent view of the self (separate from the group identity) is a European American concept that is typically regarded as the standard. On the other hand, the interdependent view of the self is characteristic of African (persons of African descent), Asian, Latino and several Southern European cultures. This suggests that the self is fundamentally social, an inseparable part of a social group (Allen, 2001).

Recent Findings

Allen's work on the African-American racial belief systems[2] begins with a schemata model[3] to explain the development of five important sets of attitudes in this population: (1) negative stereotypical beliefs, (2) positive stereotypical beliefs, (3) Black autonomy, (4) closeness to elite groups, and (5) closeness to mass groups.

Negative and positive stereotypical beliefs were based on Tajfel's (1981) thesis that individuals tend to assign positive attributes to their own group and to reject negative ones. Individuals continually treated on the basis of their race, however, are likely to assign either negative or positive values to their racial group. African Americans, then, find themselves in a position to accept positive group attributes and to reject stereotyping and demeaning images of Blacks portrayed by the dominant culture. This aspect of the belief system helps us understand media effects on African-Americans' self-esteem. Black autonomy is the ideological position that suggests African Americans should build political and social institutions based on the cultural values and interests of the group. Closeness to elites refers to the extent to which an individual acknowledges that his or her political self-worth and that of the group can best be served by supporting African-American leaders. Closeness to masses refers to the emotional bond to one's racial group, which grows out of the perception that African Americans share a similar fate. Together, closeness to masses and closeness to elites help characterize group identity. (More detailed discussion and representations of these dimensions can be found in Allen's 2001 publication, *The Concept of Self: A Study of Black Identity and Self-Esteem*.) African self-consciousness (which generally refers to an awareness of col-

lective consciousness and involvement in activities that both celebrate and preserve African heritage) is another important aspect of the African-American self-construct.

Group identification is an overarching theme in all of the self-concept elements, having been developed historically as a mental shortcut for interchanging individual utility with group utility. Allen and his collaborators (1989, 2000) work to identify the structure of this belief system and the impact of socioeconomic status on it. The authors conclude that as Blacks become more affluent, they are: 1) less likely to adopt a separatist view, while 2) they view themselves as more distant from other groups of Blacks, both elite and mass. Religiosity works in the other direction—as individuals with lower socioeconomic status are more religious, this leads to a stronger positive identification with the Black community in both mass and elite terms. In this work, the hypothesized roles of Black print media, (a) as an agent of social change and (b) to crystallize Black racial consciousness, were generally confirmed. That is to say that Black media seem to live up to their reputation as a positive force. This analysis was extended in Allen et al. (1993) from a measurement perspective.[4]

In much of this research the authors have relied primarily upon survey methods, which have been pushed into the realm of quasi-experimentation.[5] Therefore, the research has gone beyond merely model fitting and provides a firmer foundation for inferences than often found in survey research literature.

PRELIMINARY RESULTS:
GROUP IDENTITY AND SELF-ESTEEM

Some noteworthy results from *A Culturally Based Conception of the Black Self* (Allen, 2001) include the findings concerning differential effects of age, income and religiosity on the Black self-concept and attention to mainstream versus Black media.[6] More specifically, the study revealed that older African Americans are more likely to attend to mainstream television and mainstream print fare, whereas younger people were more likely to attend to Black print and electronic media. As income and education increased, people paid more attention to main-stream media. Greater income also showed a positive influence on attention to Black media, while greater education did not.

Allen found that the African-American's positive view of the group influenced the individual's positive view of himself or herself. Those who had greater self-worth were less likely to embrace negative stereotypes about the group.

Also, to re-examine the group identity and racial belief systems discussed earlier, Allen (2001) found the following relationships between the constructs and media:

Mainstream television had a negative influence on Black autonomy, a negative influence on African self-consciousness[7] and a negative influence on self-esteem. Mainstream print media had a negative influence on self-esteem and a positive relationship with African self-consciousness, which could indicate that those with more African self-consciousness are more likely to attend to print media and not to television, which tends to portray the group more negatively.

Black print media on the other hand exhibited a positive influence on self-esteem, a positive influence on closeness to elites, a positive influence on Black autonomy and a positive influence on African self-consciousness. Exposure to Black television and movies was negatively linked to Black autonomy and African self-consciousness.

The above exemplifies the problematic nature of the concept of Black media. Given the substantial barriers to obtaining ownership, African-American representation in the television industry is largely limited to production and on-screen roles. Pressure from the African-American community to better portray the group has led to some concessions. However, the quality of roles has not expanded to the degree that the quantity available to African Americans has increased over time.

Black-oriented media—intended for Black audiences, but not necessarily written, produced or directed by Black people—varies as far as representation of Black life. As Allen (2001) discussed, "The content may incorporate either a predominately assimilationist, pluralist, or multiculturalist theme. The predominate theme to which an individual pays attention will likely influence his or her sense of self (Gray, 1995, p.174)."

It would be advantageous for future research to assess the producers of programs and the type of content within them to better understand these issues and allow for more confidence in particular findings.

General Conclusions

While the form of the psychological infringement has changed over time, its contemporary impact has been of considerable interest to scholars for many years, and many different hypotheses and various speculations have been submitted. While a substantial body of literature points to group identity and self-worth as two problem areas for African Americans, these results support the idea that how you feel about your group influences considerably how you feel about yourself. Hence the phrase, "I am because we are."

This study assumes considerable importance, recognizing the movements within African-American communities toward increasing positive group representation, and particularly more accurate representation of the group in the mass media. Mass media may prove to play an important role in increasing the individual's self-esteem or self-worth by first increasing the feelings toward the group.

Using the aforementioned studies as a starting point, more research needs to be done to explore the effects of mass media—both mainstream and Black/Black-oriented—on the development of self-esteem, positive group identity and African self-consciousness. Additionally, the intervening effects and the mutual relationship between these constructs and media consumption needs to be looked at more closely. For example, does there exist a negative correlation between mainstream media and the self/group constructs because (1) those with lower self-esteem and a weak sense of African-self consciousness are more likely to attend to mainstream/electronic media or (2) attending to the content within mainstream/electronic media erodes self-esteem and undermines African self-consciousness.

This study is one of a few that has formally investigated the media's link with the self-esteem/group identity relationship, and it uses a number of constructs reflecting the general notion of group identity. A number of caveats, however, should be stated. First, any conclusions regarding cause and effect must be viewed as tentative. While the findings constitute necessary conditions for inferring casualty and eliminating some competing hypotheses, they are not sufficient. To validate these findings, longitudinal studies, replications and quasi-experiments are needed.

Further, it would be useful to explore other causal sequences. Both group identity and self-esteem are dynamic processes that may change dramatically for individuals and for groups, depending on the prominence of particular historical events.

Finally, to the extent that these relationships between the self-esteem of stigmatized groups and other constructs of the ethnic self (as it varies from the European self) are a function of attention to mainstream versus ethnic media, similar studies are needed to analyze whether these findings can be expanded to include other ALANA groups.

Endnotes

1. This paper examines the media's relationship with African-Americans' belief schemata, including self-esteem, positive and negative stereotypes and group identity. This work is a modified, adapted and expanded version of an earlier piece entitled, "The Media, Group Identity and Self-Esteem Among African Americans: A Program of Research" by Richard Allen (1998). It attempts to incorporate more recent work done in the area and suggests ongoing problems to be solved and issues to be addressed.

2. Richard Allen's work on African-American racial belief systems has been developed primarily in the National Survey of Black Americans (NSBA) (Allen et al., 1989; Dawson, Brown, Allen, 1990; Allen & Thornton; 1992; Allen et al., 1993). Allen's work on Whites' beliefs about racial equality has been pursued in the 1988 American National Election Study (Allen & Kuo, 1991). Over the past 15 years, Allen has been involved in two independent data collections in the Detroit metropolitan area, and he has collected data in Venezuela to extend his work comparatively (Allen & Izcaray, 1988; Allen, 1991).

3. This is based upon schema theory, which holds that all knowledge is packaged into units, called schemata. These schemata contain information about how to use this knowledge (Rumelhart, 1980).

4. Here, the invariance of the model across income groups was more strongly established in the case of Black autonomy, positive stereotypes and closeness to mass groups. Moreover, the stronger negative stereotypes and closer attachments to elite groups were confirmed among lower status Blacks.

5. The authors have simultaneously employed comparisons of groups and employed structural equation models with latent variables to test hypotheses.

6. Here, the researchers have examined mutual causation between key attitude constructs. Simultaneity was modeled between self-esteem, on the one hand, and closeness to masses, closeness to elites and positive and negative stereotypes, on the other hand. Each of the constructs was corrected for random error, thereby enhancing interpretation of the results.

7. Allen (2001) adopts Baldwin & Bell's (1985) description of African self-consciousness:

"The major dimension of their self-consciousness construct is exemplified in: (1) an awareness of collective consciousness (or black identity) and African heritage; (2) the recognition of a need for institutions to foster such things as values and practices that affirm African life; (3) involvement in activities that celebrate African dignity, worth, and integrity; and (4) participation in actions that resist onslaughts on the development and survival of African peoples" (p. 132).

Name: _____

Date: _____

1. In what ways can "Black media" be conceptualized?

2. Could various conceptualizations lead to drastically different research results? Explain.

3. What are some different ways one could account for the relationships found between the African-American self/group-constructs and media exposure?

4. In what ways could these results possibly help explain relationships between other ALANA groups and the media?

5. Select another ALANA group and describe what similarities and/or differences you might expect to see in the way the media affect their self-esteem and group identification. Why do you think these differences exist?

Name: _____

Date: _____

1. View an episode of a "Black-produced" television show. Identify a character that you believe is either stereotyped or not stereotyped, and explain why you came to that conclusion. Analyze and discuss (1) how this character exhibits typical or atypical characteristics of Black people you know and (2) whether (and why) you like or dislike this character.

2. Repeat the above exercise, instead viewing a "Black-oriented" show in the same genre (e.g., comedy, drama, action). Analyze and discuss the similarities and differences you observed between the two programs.

REFERENCES

Akbar, N. (1981). Mental disorder among African-Americans. *Black Books Bulletin* 7, 18-25.

Akbar, N. (1988). *Chains and images of psychological slavery*. NJ: New Mind Productions.

Allen, R. L, & lzcaray, F. (1988). Nominal agenda diversity in a media-rich, less-developed society. *Communication Research*, 29-50.

Allen, R. L (1991). Political efficacy and perception of economic relations: The role of communication in a media-rich, underdeveloped society. *Gazette*, 47, 79-105.

Allen, R. L. (2001). A culturally based conception of the Black self-concept. In V. H. Milhouse, M. K. Asante & P. Nwosu (Eds.), *Transcultural realities: interdisciplinary perspectives on cross-cultural relations* (pp. 161-185). Thousand Oaks: Sage Publications.

Allen, R. L. (2001). *The concept of self: A study of Black identity and self-esteem*. Detroit: Wayne State University Press.

Allen, R. L., & Bielby, W. T. (1977). *Blacks' relationship with the print media*. Madison: Institute for Research on Poverty University of Wisconsin.

Allen, R. L, Dawson, M. C., & Brown, R. E. (1989). A schema-based approach to modeling an African-American racial belief system. *American Political Science Review*, 83, 421-441.

Allen, R. L., & Kuo, C. (1991). Communication and beliefs about racial equality. *Discourse and Society*, 2, 259-279.

Allen, R. L., Thornton, M.C., & Watkins, S. (1993). An African American racial belief system and social structural relationships: A test of invariances. *National Journal of Sociology*, 6, 157-186.

Allen, R. L, & Thornton, M. C. (1992). Social structural factors, Black media and stereotypical self characterizations among African Americans. *National Journal of Sociology*, 41-75.

Allen, R. L, & Waks, L (1990). Social reality construction: The evaluation of the status and role of women and Black. *Howard Journal of Communications*, 2, 170-191.

Baldwin, J. A., & Bell, Y. (1985). Psychology of Black Americans. *Western Journal of Black Studies, 9*, 61-68.

Broman, C., Neighbors, H., & Jackson, J. (1988). Racial group identification among Black adults. *Social Forces, 67*(1), 146-158.

Coltraine, S., & Messineo, M. (2000). The perpetuation of subtle prejudice: Race and gender imagery in 1990s television advertising. *Sex Roles, 42*(5-6), 363-389.

Comer, J. H. (1982). The importance of television images of Black families. In A. W. Jackson (Ed.). *Black families and the medium of television* (pp. 19-25). Ann Arbor: University of Michigan, Bush Program in Child Development and Social Policy.

Cross, W. E., Jr. (1991). *Shades of Black: Diversity in African-American identity*. Philadelphia: Temple University.

Cross, W. E., Jr. (2003). Tracing the historical origins of youth delinquency & violence: Myths & realities about Black culture. *The Journal of Social Issues, 59*(1), 67.

Dates, J. L., & Barlow, W. (1993). *Split image: African Americans in the mass media* (2nd ed.). Washington, D.C.: Howard University Press.

Davis, O. (1982). Where are the Black image-makers hiding? In A. Jackson (Ed.), *Black families & the medium of television* (pp. 61-69). Ann Arbor, MI: Bush Program in Child Development and Social Policy.

Dawson, M. C., Brown, R. E., & Allen, R. L (1990). Racial belief system, religious guidance, and African American political participation. *The National Political Science Review*, 2, 22-44.

Devine, P. G., & Monteith, M. J. (1999). Automaticity and control in stereotyping. In S. Chaiken (Ed.), *Dual-process theories in social psychology* (pp. 339-360). New York: The Guilford Press.

Dixon, T. L., & Linz, D. (2000). Overrepresentation and underrepresentation of African Americans and Latinos as lawbreakers on television news. *Journal of Communication, 50*(2), 131.

Dixon, T. L., & Linz, D. (2002). Television news, prejudicial pretrial publicity, and the depiction of race. *Journal of Broadcasting & Electronic Media, 46*(1), 112.

Dubois, W. E. B. (1964). *Souls of Black folks.* New York: Fawcett.

Entman, R. M., & Rojecki, A. (2000). *The Black image in the White mind: media and race in America.* Chicago: University of Chicago Press.

Gerbner, G., Gross, L., Morgan, M., & Signorielli, N. (1994). Growing up with television: The cultivation perspective. In B. Jennings (Ed.), *Media effects: Advances in theory and research* (pp. 17-41). Hillsdale, NJ: Lawrence Erlbaum Associates, Inc.

Gilliam, F. D. Jr., Valentino, N. A., & Beckmann, M. N. (2002). Where you live and what you watch: The impact of racial proximity and local television news on attitudes about race and crime. *Political Research Quarterly, 55*(4), 755.

Gray, H. (1989). Television, Black Americans, and the American dream. *Critical Studies in Mass Communication, 6,* 376-386.

Gray, H. (1995). *Watching race: Television and the struggle for "Blackness."* Minneapolis: University of Minnesota Press.

Grier, W. H., & Cobb, P. M. (1968). *Black rage.* New York: Bantam Books.

Markus, H., & Kitayama, S. (1991). Culture and the self: Implications for cognition, emotion, and self motivation. *Psychological Review, 98*(5), 224-253.

Markus, H., & Kitayama, S. (1994). A collective fear of the collective: Implications for selves and theories of selves. *Personality and Social Psychology Bulletin, 20*(2), 586-579.

McDonald, J. F. (1983). *Blacks and White T.V.: Afro-Americans in television since 1943.* Chicago, Nelson-Hall.

Phinney, J. S. (1990). Ethnic identity in adolescents and adults: Review of research. *Psychological Bulletin, 108,* 499-514.

Phinney, J. S. (2003). Ethnic identity and acculturation. In K. M. Chun & P. B. Organista (Eds.), *Acculturation: Advances in theory, measurement, and applied research* (pp. 63-81). Washington, DC: American Psychological Association.

Phinney, J. S.; Chavira, V. & Tate, J. D. (1993). The effect of ethnic threat on ethnic self-concept and own-group ratings. *Journal of Social Psychology; 133*(4), 469-478.

Pierce, C. (1980). Social trace contaminant: Subtle indicators of racism in T.V. In S. B. Whithey & R P. Abelson (Eds.), *Television and social behavior: Beyond violence and children* (pp. 249-257). Hillsdale, NJ: Lawrence Erlbaum.

Poindexter, P. M., & Stroman, C. A. (1981). Black and television: A review of the research literature. *Journal of Broadcasting, 25,* 103-122.

Rumelhart, D. (1980). Schemata: The building blocks of cognition. In R. Spiro, B. Bruce & W. Brewer (Eds.), *Theoretical issues in reading comprehension* (pp. 33-35). Hillsdale, NJ: Lawrence Earlbaum.

Signorielli, N., & Morgan, M. (Eds.). (1990). *Cultivation analysis: New directions in media effects research.* Newbury Park, Calif.: Sage.

Signorielli, N. (1993). *Mass media images and impact on health: A sourcebook.* Westport, Conn.: Greenwood Press.

Stroman, C., Merritt, B. D., & Matabane, P. W. (1989-1990). Twenty years after Kerner: The portrayal of African Americans on prime-time television. *Howard Journal of Communications, 2,* 44-56.

Tan, A. S. (1985). *Mass communication theories and research* (2nd ed.). New York: Wiley.

Tajfel, H. (1981). *Human groups and social categories: Studies in social psychology.* Cambridge: Cambridge University Press.

Triandus, H. C. (1995). *Individualism and collectivism.* CO: Westview.

Valentino, N. A. (2001). The race card: Campaign strategy, implicit messages, and the norm of equality. *Public Opinion Quarterly, 65*(4), 607.

Wiegel, R. H., Loomis, J. W., & Soja, M. J. (1980). Race relations on prime time television. *Journal of Personality & Social Psychology, 39*(5), 884-893.

Wilson, C. C., & Gutierrez, F. (1985). *Minorities and media: Diversity and the end of mass communication.* Beverly Hills: Sage Publications.

Wilson, C. C., & Gutiérrez, F. (1995). *Race, multiculturalism, and the media: From mass to class communication* (2nd ed.). Thousand Oaks, CA: Sage Publications.

Latina/o Experiences with Images and Their Transformation

II

Looks Like Me? Body Image in Magazines Targeted to U.S. Latinas

Melissa A. Johnson, Prabu David and Dawn Huey Ohlsson

One in five young Hispanic women has attempted suicide, compared to one in ten Anglo-American or African-American female teens.[1] One of the correlates with the mental states that lead to suicide is the negative self-esteem resulting from perceptions among young Hispanic women that they are overweight.[2]

Eating disorders in the United States have been categorized as "White" female diseases. White has been understood to be Anglo-American White, since this is the population that has been the subject of most eating disorder research. Part of the reason eating disorders have been positioned as White woman's diseases is because comparative ethnic studies usually have been conducted with African-American populations. Hispanic women or teens and other ethnic groups have only recently received attention.

However, statistics point to a Latino population that is at risk, if struggles with weight perception are indicators. According to the Centers for Disease Control, although more than one-fourth of U.S. students think they are overweight, 32% of Hispanic students consider themselves overweight. Hispanic teens are most likely to be attempting weight loss (45% compared to 33% of Black teens or 43% non-Hispanic Whites). To lose weight, Hispanic female teens are significantly more likely than Black female teens (11% compared to 4%) to have taken laxatives or vomited. Anglo-American and Hispanic teens are more likely than Black students to take diet pills.

And Anglo-American and Hispanic young women are significantly more likely than their African-American counterparts to have dieted to lose weight (53% and 48% respectively, compared to 32%) (Centers for Disease Control, 1996).

Studies of U.S. mass media's role in body image perceptions point to the ubiquitous waif-like model in general market media as setting the standard for female beauty. But, in addition to attending to mainstream media, Latinas in the United States also view, read and listen to ethnic media designed for them. If ethnic media are designed to provide alternatives, it holds that alternatives might include different standards for body image.

The following study investigates the subject of body image and Hispanic women. The purpose was to describe the images of women in 13 ethnic magazines targeted to Hispanic women in the United States, to analyze whether there were differences among magazines and to analyze differences among various subcategories of these Latina magazines.

Review of the Literature

ETHNIC MEDIA FUNCTIONS

Most ethnic media models state that one key function is to provide a haven from general market media stereotypes for the cultural group. Latino magazines are a large genre of ethnic magazines in the United States, serving the fastest growing ethnic group.[3]

U.S. theoretical perspectives about ethnic media since the 1920s have conceptualized a number of additional functions (although some distinguish immigrant from ethnic media, differentiating between those that serve new immigrants from those that serve longer-term immigrants and ensuing generations). Most separate ethnic media into two categories—those that are assimilation-oriented and those that are pluralistic. Assimilation means giving up one culture and taking on another (Gudykunst & Kim, 1997). Pluralism refers to sustained ethnic differentiation and heterogeneity, implying practice of one culture while participating in the majority society (Subervi-Velez, 1986). In addition to providing comfort and a respite from negative stereotypes, pluralistic functions include: to preserve and transmit native culture and identity by maintaining the language and promoting ethnic pride; to establish a minority news agenda; to announce community events and cover minority social activities (including minority business advertising); to promote the group's political/social interests and motivate them to be socially and politically active; and to serve as collective expressions of anger at injustices (Constantakis-Valdés, 1992; Downing, 1992; Fox, 1996; Gutiérrez, 1977; Huntzicker, 1995; Miller, 1987; Riggins, 1992; Subervi-Velez, 1994).

Assimilation functions of ethnic media are: serving as instruments of social control; maintaining the dominant languages of the host society; maintaining the dominant ideology; borrowing general market media genres; and socializing to "the modern" (Constantakis-Valdés, 1992; Gutiérrez, 1977; Riggins, 1992).

Symbolic empowerment has been another vital function (Riggins, 1992). In other words, just by having one's own large-circulation magazines replete with one's own images, a group symbolically has power. Another recently discussed symbolic function is the unification of subgroups[4] (Flores, 1997; Fox, 1996; Husband, 1994; Rodriguez, 1997). Ethnic media are purported to be the vehicles that will allow Latinos to evolve from a number of subgroup identifi-

ers (such as Mexican-American or Cuban-American) to one Latino identity. Mass media's ability to create a nation of pan-Hispanics out of cultural groups who have distinct identities is a powerful function.

THE CONCEPT OF IDENTITY

Communication researchers have analyzed media's role in identity creation (e.g., Gergen, 1991; Merelman, 1995; Turow, 1997). In particular, the way female readers use the magazines to construct self-identity and socialize to societal norms has received attention (Brown, White, & Nikopoulou, 1993; Ferguson, 1983; Garner, Sterk, & Adams, 1998; McCracken, 1993; Nemeroff, Stein, Diehl, & Smilack, 1994; Simonds, 1996; Wolf, 1991). However, when considering the complexity of comparing one's own body image to images in ethnic media, it is useful for the purposes of this study to explore the concept of identity in the social psychology literature as well.

One long-standing approach to sense of self and acquisition of group identity is *social identity* theory. Social identity is defined as the aspects of an individual's self-image that derive from the social categories to which he perceives himself as belonging (Tajfel, 1978; 1981; Tajfel & Turner, 1986). In other words, an individual is not a stand-alone self. While the cognitive area of social psychology concentrates on individual cognitive processes, social identity focuses on the intersection between self and group. It stresses that individual perception and cognition rely on socially accepted knowledge, methods and categories.

Within the social identity tradition is *self-categorization* theory (Turner et al., 1994), which describes "self" as emerging from the cognitive processes of social comparison and categorization, where the person appraises herself in relation to others. Collective processes and social relationships mediate the cognitive functioning of the individual. In other words, we have two levels of identity—personal self identity (one's definition of individual characteristic relative to one's group) and group identity (membership in group(s) which can range from ethnic groups to professional organizations). Somebody's behavior depends not just on his individual characteristics but on group membership. Identity provides security and a stable sense of self (Rivenburgh, 1997), and self identity and collective identity are linked to self-esteem (Deux, 1992; Liebkind, 1992). This approach is particularly applicable to the social psychology of ethnic groups. If one is a member of a majority culture, one's body image identity is probably individual (I am an overweight person, I am a short person). However, if one is a member of an ethnic group, one might mediate those individual definitions with group norms (I am full-hipped like others in my group; I am short like others of my group). Part of the identification process with a group is the wish to increase whatever similarity has been noted (Liebkind, 1992)—in this case, in the ethnic group. An "imaginary ethnic prototype" can be an inner model to be emulated, without a real counterpart in reality (Liebkind, 1992).

ETHNICITY AS IDENTIFIER

The social groups that serve as comparisons in this study are ethnic groups. We go to "others" for comparison information; in this study the "other" are people portrayed in ethnic media. Ethnicity can be self-identified or placed upon us by others (Oboler, 1995; Padilla, 1985). For instance, someone might self-identify as Mexican American or Puerto Rican, but institutional forces (e.g., government agencies, universities) might categorize that person as Hispanic. The terms Latino and Hispanic are used interchangeably in this paper to refer to a U.S. resident who self-identifies with the indigenous or Spanish-speaking cultures of Mexico, Puerto Rico, Cuba, Central America, or South America. Hispanics are also of European-Spanish origin, and Portuguese-speaking Brazilians may self-identify as Latin-American (although normally not as Hispanic). The feminine form of Latino, Latina, refers to Latin-American women.[5]

One contributor to self-construction is perception of one's physical self. Our study examines how a media genre—women's magazines targeted to Hispanics in the United States—has chosen to display women's physiques.

MASS MEDIA, BODY IMAGE AND EATING DISORDERS

Research has supported the link between body image, eating disorder etiology, and mass media, especially the role of magazines (Anderson & DiDomenico, 1992; Berchmans, 1998; Garner, Garfinkel, Schwartz, & Thompson, 1980; Harrison & Cantor, 1997; Martin & Kennedy, 1993; Nemeroff et al., 1994; Richins, 1991; Silverstein, Perdue, Peterson, & Kelly, 1986; Silverstein, Peterson, & Perdue, 1986; Thomsen, Gustafson, McCoy, & Williams, 1998; Wiseman, Gray, Mosimann, & Ahrens, 1992). Television or combinations of media also have been sources of investigation (David & Johnson, 1998; Downs & Harrison, 1985; Myers & Biocca, 1992; Ogletree, Williams, Raffeld, Mason, & Fricke, 1990; Stice, Schupak-Neuberg, Shaw, & Stein, 1994).

In addition to mass media ideals as sociocultural explanations for the mental and physical disorders related to body image, culture has also been offered as an explanation for variation among eating disorder patterns (Magweth, Pope, Hudson, 1995). However, until recently most of the cultural comparison studies have compared African Americans and Caucasians, or occasionally these groups and Asian Americans (Akan & Grilo, 1995; Averett & Korenman, 1999; Harris, 1995; Striegel-Moore, Schreiber, Pike, Wilfley, & Rodin, 1995). Generally these studies have indicated that Black women adopt a larger ideal body size, have greater body image satisfaction, experience less social pressure about their weight and are more accepting of being overweight. Although these are risk factors for obesity and its related health problems, they are not risk factors for eating disorders.

Recently Latinos have been subjects of study. In a study of body composition of young multiethnic females in Texas, researchers found that even after adjustment for body size, Hispanic females had significantly higher fat mass and percentage of body fat than non-Hispanic White females (Ellis, Abrams, & Wong, 1997). In a bicultural study of anti-fat attitudes, students in Mexico were significantly less concerned about their own weight and more accepting of overweight people than were U.S. students (Crandall & Martinez, 1996).

The drive for thinness could be more intense among Latinas living in the United States, where acculturating to U.S. standards of thinness may have unique challenges. In one study (Woodruff, Zaslow, Candelaria, & Elder, 1997), higher acculturation levels were associated with greater dietary fat avoidance, which could lead to positive nutritional outcomes but also lead to more body image dissatisfaction. In another, researchers found that acculturation and eating disorders were positively associated in Hispanic girls, but not in Asian or European girls living in the United States (Gowen, Hayward, Killen, Robinson, Taylor, 1999). In fact, acculturation to U.S. norms generally has negative influences on many health behaviors. Alcohol use, drug abuse, smoking and sexual relations at an earlier age are higher among more acculturated Latinos (Molina & Molina, 1994; Sabogal, Pérez-Stable, Otero-Sabogal, & Hiatt, 1995). Suicides also are higher among U.S.-born Hispanics, versus those of Latino immigrants now residing in the United States (Sorenson & Shen, 1996).

Suicide attempts among Latinos and others have been linked to the depression resulting from body image or weight dissatisfaction, dieting frequency and eating disorders (Carbonell, 1998; French et al., 1997). Recent research has concluded that Caucasian and Hispanic Americans have shown more body image disturbances than Asian Americans or African Americans (Altabe, 1998). Hispanic girls are as likely as African-American girls to be overweight, but significantly more likely to think they are overweight and consequently diet, vomit, and use laxatives (Field, Colditz, & Peterson, 1996). Also, Hispanic women show more binge eating symptoms than African Americans or Anglo Americans and reported more depressive symptoms than those in the other groups (Fitzgibbon et al., 1998). In addition, although the Latino and Anglo-American women had similar lean body ideals, Hispanic women weighed significantly more in the Fitzgibbon et al. study. In a multiethnic study of 17,545 female students, Hispanics dieted and used laxatives and diuretics more often than Blacks, Caucasians, and American Indians. Along with American Indians, Latinas

were most likely to use intentional vomiting to lose weight (French et al., 1997). In summary, a body of health studies and National Center for Health Statistics data indicate Latinas are a high-risk population for eating disorder etiology. Given these risk factors, we set out to examine the extent to which visual images in the Hispanic media are sensitive in portraying realistic body image ideals for Latinas.

Bandura's *social cognitive* theory, an extension of his social learning theory, suggests that human behavior is affected through cognitive processing of direct and vicarious experiences (Bandura, 1994). The social realities and symbolic modeling visible in mass media are important forms of vicarious experience that are able to transcend previously limited individual environments (Bandura, 1986, 1994). Immigrants or second- and third-generation ethnic groups who are marginalized from majority groups may rely on media more for ideal images of womanhood. The data above suggest that this process may be occurring among some Latinas in the United States.

Latino Women's Magazines: A Profile

The world's largest publisher of Spanish-language magazines is Editorial Televisa, headquartered in Mexico City with U.S. operations in Miami. Newsstands throughout the U.S. and Latin America sell their Spanish-language editions of classics like *Vanidades* (a 37-year-old upscale women's magazine) and *Cristina*, among many others. *Cosmopolitan* has had a Spanish-language edition since 1973, which Editorial Televisa currently publishes via an agreement with Hearst. Other Hearst/Editorial Televisa Spanish-language magazines are *Buenhogar* (Good Housekeeping) and *Harper's Bazaar*. In another business relationship, Editorial Televisa and Marie Claire Album publish *Marie Claire en Español*. The circulations of some of these popular publications range from 25,000 to 400,000 in the United States.

While Editorial Televisa's market has been Spanish-speakers, new publications in the United States have targeted second- and third-generation Latinas who do not necessarily read Spanish. The trade press reports that the magazines and major advertisers are marketing to upscale, educated, acculturated Latinas (Ballon, 1997; Beam, 1996; Fest, 1997; Gremillion, 1996).

Latina Style was founded in 1994 by Anna Maria Arias to provide cultural, business and entertainment news. Arias is a former managing editor of *Hispanic Magazine*. Similar in name is *Latina* — Christy Haubegger's venture published by the company that produces *Essence*. *Latina* started as a bimonthly and in mid-1997 switched to a monthly, enjoying substantial advertising support and a circulation of 200,000. Both publications are in English intermixed with Spanish phrases. *Latina* translates some articles into Spanish. *Moderna* is published by *Hispanic Magazine* in Austin, Texas and has been issued since 1997, although at this writing it is ceasing publication. *Estylo* is published by Mandalay Publications in Los Angeles and began in summer, 1997. Marisol Barrios-Jordan launched *Latina Bride* in winter, 1997. These three publications are bilingual.

Whether in these Latina magazines or in general market media, body images of models or persons in editorial coverage are selected by editors and/or photo editors, given the options available (e.g., celebrity photos submitted by public relations practitioners). Follow-up treatments such as airbrushing or digitized changes are the consequences of gatekeeper choices. Therefore, considering news and feature photographs separately from advertising photographs is useful.

Given the literature on Latinas and body image, the role of magazines in setting cultural standards for body image, and the impact of media on personal identity and ethnic identity, the following research questions were developed:

RQ1: What is the typical body size and muscle tone of women featured in non-advertising photographs in Latina women's magazines?

RQ2: Do body sizes of non-advertising women's photographs in Latina women's magazines differ by magazine?

RQ3: Do body sizes of non-advertising women's photographs in Latina women's magazines differ by origin of publication?

RQ4: Are there differences between fashion magazines and other general interest magazines targeted to U.S. Latinas in the body sizes of non-advertising women's photographs?

Results

Overall, the findings raise concerns about the body images available to readers of Latino women's magazines. More than 80 percent of the images were thin or very thin. More than a third of images were "buff" (highly toned or moderately high-toned) and almost 98 percent were toned. The mean body size was 2.07 (moderately thin, approximately a women's size 4), with a standard deviation of 0.7. The mean muscle tone was 2.64 with a standard deviation of 0.59. In other words, the average woman was thin and mostly smooth-skinned, with some muscle lines showing.

The findings are interesting when analyzed by magazine title (See Tables 2 and 3). For instance, only four magazines had any "very large" images at all — *Cristina la Revista, Latina, Latina Style,* and *Moderna*. And even though "very thin" accounted for 15.9% of images overall, *Latina Bride* had no very thin images, and the highest mean body size (2.88, about a woman's size 12) in the sample. On the other hand, it did not feature any "very large" images, either. Another noteworthy finding was for *Latina Style*. This was the only magazine in which there were more coded images for "moderate" than for "moderately thin." This publication is targeted to professional women and features more "real" women (e.g., politicians, entrepreneurs, social activists) than the fashion magazines or publications that focus on celebrities. It was no surprise that fashion magazines like *Harper's Bazaar* and *Vogue* had high percentages of very thin images. And although *Cosmopolitan* is known worldwide for its sexual content, leading us to believe it would tend toward full-breasted, full-buttocked women, almost a quarter of the women in *Cosmopolitan en*

Español were very thin and 93% were either very thin or thin.

Next we considered data patterns by geographic origin of the magazine. We divided magazine titles into four origin groups: Spain, Mexico, Miami, and elsewhere in the United States. Five hundred and six magazine images from magazines originating in Miami (Editorial Televisa) were grouped separately from 338 images generated from magazines published elsewhere in the U.S. (Los Angeles, Austin, Washington, D.C., and New York City) because of magazine language and ownership differences. Six hundred and fourteen images from magazines published in Mexico (Editorial Televisa) and 291 in Spain formed the remaining two of the four groups.

When we analyzed the magazines grouped by origin, we found that the differences among the four groups for body size were significant F (3, 1704) = 52.19, p < .001. Post hoc tests of origin by body size showed that although the Mexican and Spanish groups did not have significant mean differences between them, Mexico-generated publications significantly differed from the Miami-based publications and other U.S.-generated publications. Likewise, Miami-generated and "other U.S." means differed from each other (See Table 3). The Miami publications (*Cristina*, *Cosmopolitan en Español*, and *Vanidades*) are all in Spanish, and the other U.S. publications are bilingual or in English. The summary of the findings is as follows: While there was no significant difference between magazines from Spain and Mexico, all other pairs differed significantly from one another.

Tests of differences for muscle tone were not significant. Moreover, because our operationalization of muscle tone did not allow for much variance, we discontinued consideration of muscle tone in the rest of the analysis.

The other research questions dealt with format. Given sample sizes, the only magazine format comparison possible (fashion versus general interest/feature) was within the Mexico group. Fashion magazines published in Mexico comprised 58% of the images, and had a mean body size of 1.78. General interest women's magazines comprised 42% of the images in the Mexican group and had a mean of 2.03. Independent

t-test confirmed that body size differences were significant, with t (1, 597) =5.34, p< .001.

To summarize the results: women in Latino magazines were thin; women in Latino magazines based in Mexico or Spain were thinner than those in U.S.-based magazines; and when fashion versus general interest magazines could be compared, women in fashion magazines targeted to Hispanics were thinner than those in Latino general interest magazines. In addition, the mean body weight in *Latina Bride* was significantly different from the other magazines, perhaps due to a conscious editorial effort to feature typical women rather than models.

Discussion

LATINO MAGAZINES, BODY IMAGE AND ETHNIC IDENTITY

Latino women's magazines as a group are not a haven from the unrealistic physical ideals found in other women's magazines. If Latinas are enacting the process of self-categorization theory (and social comparison theory) by appraising themselves in relation to Latina magazine images, most will find wide gaps between their realities and ethnic media ideals. Rather than provide a pluralistic alternative and a refuge from mainstream media, the Latina magazines fulfill an assimilationist function of socializing to the "modern."

However, this may not be a U.S. ideal but a transnational phenomenon of assimilating to a global thin ideal, since many of the thinnest images were found in magazines distributed throughout the Spanish-speaking world. If anything, the new U.S. (the non-Miami-based group) publications are doing a slightly better job of providing a variety of body types that mediate the thin look. Certainly, the Spanish-language women's magazines distributed in the United States are different from the other magazines also categorized as ethnic media. Based on this and other studies (e.g., McCracken, 1992), we can argue that some magazines in this study are ethnic and some are international publications. One explanation of why the newer bilingual and English-language publications have more image variety is that their definition of Latino comes in part from the contrast with the majority culture, unlike the traditional Spanish-language magazines distributed in Latina/o majority cultures.

There are other reasons that English-language and bilingual magazines differ in their portrayals. One could be more editorial sensitivity to body image issues because they have been widely discussed in the United States, or an orientation to middle-class women rather than upper-class women. Another could be periodic U.S. feminists' attempts to sensitize magazine editors about female portrayals. An effort to include all subgroups of U.S. Latinas (Panamanians, Peruvians, etc.) also may propel editors to feature a wider variety of body types in magazine-selected models. In addition, variety should be more prevalent when using photographs of Latinas who are businesswomen, politicians, and the like, instead of mostly celebrities or fashion models. The fashion magazines in this study were the Spanish-language ones published in Mexico and Spain. Although all magazines present image and lifestyle ideals, readers may expect fashion images to be more artistic and less realistic than the images in general interest publications. One cannot deny that a plethora of thin images from all types of sources affects cognitive "others," but readers may expect some genres of images to be closer "others." This study examined only editorial content, suggesting that these women in editorial images might have been more powerful sources of comparison than advertising models whom readers would consider more distant others.

Rather than being mostly a function of ethnicity, body image in Latino women's magazines—especially the ones published in Mexico and Spain—could be a function of class. For instance, mostly upper-class women in Latin American countries have the income and education to make reading these magazines a habit. (Magazines are expensive in Latin America, relative to most countries' average incomes.) In addition, the role of class in maintaining thinness can be significant—from affording hairdressers and leisure-time workout sessions to having the energy to make beauty a priority. As more Latinas in the United States work outside the home in jobs requiring more education, they may desire to be more "professional-looking"—equated with thinner.

MEDIA FUNCTIONS: IMAGES EMPOWERING AND DYSFUNCTIONAL

Will body dissatisfaction and eating disorders be reduced if Latinas read or view more ethnic media than general market media? In some ways, a Latina-controlled average thin image is empowering, because it negates the "fat mamacita" stereotype often conveyed in U.S. mainstream media. Fat also connotes laziness, another negative stereotype in a modern industrial or postmodern technological world. Positive images of Latinas can reduce negative associations with membership in a non-majority culture by creating positive social identities for the group. On the other hand, in creating a "modern" standard, it is dysfunctional in its conveyance of an image that few women can live up to. As in U.S. general market media, a thin ideal creates a social "other" for comparison that can fuel body dissatisfaction and the mental or physical health consequences discussed at the beginning of this chapter.

MEDIA FUNCTIONS: ASSIMILATION AND PLURALISM

Thin images in Latina magazines fulfill pluralistic media functions like empowerment and promoting ethnic pride. They help cement a standard of U.S. Latino identity and beauty that has the potential to unite subgroup ideals of beauty. But in perpetuating the thin ideal, Latina magazines also are assimilationist in that they replicate a standard for Anglo-American women that has been promoted in U.S. general market media. In the case of body image, assimilation encoding is visual.

ROLE OF COMMERCIAL LATINO MAGAZINES

No magazine industry observer would suggest that editors begin to feature mostly unattractive or obese women (or men) in their publications. These media are, after all, commercial media, vehicles for presenting ideal lifestyles. The publications recognize their role in featuring consumer goods as part of those lifestyles. Body image dissatisfaction triggers consumption of fashion and beauty products, in addition to contributing to eating disorders. Given the U.S., Latin American and Western European media systems, commercial women's media in part depend on creating needs for beauty products. This sets up a tension between dysfunctional and functional consequences of ethnic media.

However, it is sensible for publishers to accurately portray a group who spends a higher percentage of their income on consumer goods. There are 11 million Latinas in the United States and 5 million Latinas aged 16 or over in the U.S. workforce (Byerly & Deardorff, 1995). Latinos in the United States have a purchasing power of $348 billion (Nuiry, 1997). Each year, Hispanic women spend 17 percent more of their income on cosmetics, fragrances, and personal-care products than non-Hispanics. And because Latinos have bigger households and are younger than national averages, they spend a bigger portion of their income on household items, supplies, food and clothing. Ethnic magazines need to balance their desire to deliver this attractive consumer market to advertisers with their editorial responsibility to provide a variety of possible "others" to U.S. Hispanic women, who are increasingly at risk for eating disorders.

Not enough time has been spent in ethnic media studies concentrating on the role of the visual in creating and cementing personal and group identities, particularly ethnic identity. Existing ethnic media models may be more idealistic than realistic about some of the ethnic media functions related to identity, chiefly because they have been based on Spanish-language broadcasting and/or newspapers. Future ethnic media studies and body image studies need to separate magazine genre when considering reader gratifications or effects. The role of the visual in personal and group identities deserves more study as we consider all forms of media in the new millenium.

Endnotes

1. Centers for Disease Control (1996). *Youth risk behavior surveillance — United States, 1995.* http://www.cdc.gov/epo/mmwr/preview/mmwwrnum/00043812.num

2. Discussion with Josefina Carbonell, President, National Coalition of Hispanic Health and Human Services Organizations (COSSMHO), Miami, Florida, June 24, 1998.

3. Byerly, E. & Deardorff, K. (July, 1995). Bureau of the Census, Current Population Reports: National and State Population Estimates 1990 to 1994. http://www. census.gov/prod/1/pop/p25-1127.pdf

4. In this paper, subgroups refer to individual Latin American cultures such as Mexican American, Puerto Rican, Dominican.

5. The use of these broad terms for the purposes of this article does not mean to slight the ethnicity of Latinos who are more apt to self-identify in relation to a country or indigenous group (e.g., "I am Puerto Rican, I am Dominican, I am Quechua"). "Latino" is used when the group members are both male and female. Anglo-American and European-American are descriptors for Caucasians whose ancestry is European. Black or African-American are terms used to describe persons of African ancestry.

6. New publications like *Glamour en Español* and *Latingirl* were not in this sample.

TABLE 1

Body Size and Muscle Tone in 13 Women's Magazines Targeted to U.S. Latinas

Body Size	Frequency
Very thin	15.9%
Moderately thin	65.3
Moderate	15.0
Moderately large	3.0
Very large	0.7
	99.9%*

n=1,708
*due to rounding

Muscle Tone	Frequency
High tone	3.6%
Moderate-high tone	30.6
Moderate tone	63.7
Moderate-low tone	2.0
Low tone	0.1
	100.0%

n=1,006

TABLE 2

Distributions of Body Size Among 13 Women's Magazines Targeted to U.S. Latinas

Magazine Name	Very Thin	Moderately Thin	Moderate	Moderately Large	Very Large
Buenhogar (n=62)	14.5	69.4	11.3	4.8	—
Cosmopolitan En Español (n=173)	23.7	68.8	6.9	0.6	—
Cristina La Revista (n=158)	3.8	62.7	25.3	4.4	3.8
Elle en Español (n=210)	20.5	73.8	5.2	0.5	—
Estylo (n=83)	3.6	79.5	14.5	2.4	—
Harper's Bazaar (n=140)	35.7	61.4	2.9	—	—
Latina (n=64)	9.4	57.8	23.4	6.3	3.1
Latina Bride (n=47)	—	53.2	29.8	17.0	—
Latina Style (n=33)	3.0	36.4	39.4	12.1	9.1
Marie Claire En Español (n=187)	15.0	69.5	13.9	1.6	—
Moderna (n=101)	8.9	44.6	36.6	8.9	1.0
Vanidades (n=166)	14.5	60.8	20.5	4.2	—

TABLE 3

Mean Body Size in Latina Magazines by Publication Origin

USA English-language or Bilingual Magazines (Group M = 2.44)

	M
Estylo	2.16
Latina	2.36
Latina Bride	2.64
Latina Style	2.88
Moderna	2.49

USA Spanish-language (Miami-based) (Group M = 2.13)

Cosmopolitan en Español	1.84
Cristina	2.42
Vanidades	2.14

Mexico Spanish-language (Group M = 1.89)

Buenhogar	2.06
Elle	1.86
Harper's Bazaar	1.67
Marie Claire	2.02

Spain Spanish-language

Vogue España	1.95

APPENDIX 1

Magazines, Publishers, and Estimated U.S. Circulation by Group

Magazine by Group	Publisher	Est. U.S. Circulation*
U.S. English-language or Bilingual Magazines		
Estylo	Mandalay Publications	50K
Latina	Essence Publications	175K
Latina Bride	THINK Publications	new
Latina Style	Latina Style, Inc.	150K
Moderna	Hispanic Publishing Corp.	150K
U.S. Spanish-language		
Cosmopolitan en Español	Editorial Televisa/Hearst	36K
Cristina	Editorial Televisa, Miami	80K
Vanidades	Editorial Televisa, Miami	70K
Mexico Spanish-language		
Buenhogar	Editorial Televisa/Hearst	26K
Elle	Hachette Filipacchi Presse	30K
Harper's Bazaar	Editorial Televisa/Hearst	25K
Marie Claire	Editorial Televisa/Marie Claire Album	20K
Spain Spanish-language		
Vogue España	Condé Nast	25K

* Unaudited circulation as of 1997

Sample

The intent was to include all magazines targeted to Latinas in at least the major markets of the United States. To be included in the sampling frame, magazines had to have a U.S. circulation of at least 20,000 and be available on newsstands or via subscription in the United States. (If a reader was required to write to Mexico or Spain for a subscription, for instance, the publication was not included.) Regional publications and organization-specific publications were excluded. [6]

The sampling period was July 1997 through June 1998. Magazine publishing schedules ranged from biweekly to quarterly, so the sampling frame was composed of each of the four quarterly magazines during the period, plus a randomly selected issue from each quarter for the nine titles published monthly or biweekly (Riffe, Lacy, & Fico, 1998). The quarterly *Latina Bride* did not begin publication until the winter of 1998, so only three issues were coded. This resulted in 51 magazine issues. Appendix 1 lists magazines, publishers and estimated U.S. circulations at the time of data collection.

A pretest of three magazines with different origins, language and length was conducted to determine an appropriate procedure for selection of images to code. Based on the time needed to code each magazine and the desire for a manageable sample size, every other female editorial image of at least one inch square was selected for coding. All advertising was excluded, as were illustrations. Both individual and group photos were selected, with every other woman coded in a group photo. In order to be included, a woman's body had to be visible at least to the waist.

Measures

We coded body image in two ways: body size and muscle tone. The pretest indicated that the magazines did not present many large women, so this study's body size choices have less range and smaller intervals than scales that would be constructed for use in a study of Latinas in the general U.S. population. The Likert scale categories for body size ranged from "1" for very thin (about a woman's size 2) to "2" for moderately thin, "3" for moderate (sizes 8-10), "4" for moderately large, and "5" for very large (about a women's size 16 or more). The coding for muscle tone was: "1" for obvious muscle throughout the body; "2" for some muscle lines visible on the legs, arms, and/or stomach; "3" for not visible muscles but skin that had an overall smoothness; "4" for some visible loose skin; and "5" for lots of loose skin. In order to maintain coder consistency, photo samples of body size and body tone were used by the coder along with the code sheet. One student coder analyzed all of the images.

When a random sample of seven percent of the images from the 13 magazines was double-coded, intercoder reliability was 80% for body size and 83% for muscle tone. There was no pattern in the differences between coders, except that the coder who analyzed the original images was less likely to record "can't tell."

Coding every other person in 51 magazine issues resulted in 1,749 images. The percentage of images from each magazine ranged from 2.2 % to 16.6 % of the total sample (See Table 1). Some images did not allow for both characteristics to be coded because of bulky clothing, photographic angle, etc. Therefore, only 1,708 images were coded for body size and 1,006 images were coded for muscle tone. Analyses were conducted using the Statistical Program for the Social Sciences (SPSS).

Name: _____

Date: _____

1. According to the authors, what are some of the roles of ethnic media?

2. What are the main findings of the study?

3. Do the authors believe that magazines published for Latinas can protect them from general market media pressures to be thin?

4. Do you agree with the authors' speculation that notions of thinness might be connected with ideas about what is modern?

5. What other aspects of ethnic media body image besides thinness should researchers study? When you look at human images in magazines, what else do you notice?

6. Who are the people in the magazine industry that could change the way women and/or men are portrayed in ethnic media?

7. Is it important for ethnic groups to have their own magazines? What in this study would support that notion? What in this study would lead you to believe ethnic media do not serve an important role?

8. How do these findings compare with other readings about ethnic media content?

1. This research studied editorial images in magazines. These were photographs that the magazine staff chose to use, and the magazine staff had control over their placement in the publication. However, advertisers and their advertising agencies select the images that appear in magazine advertisements. Working with a classmate, procure two different ethnic magazine issues—perhaps varying by gender targeted, ethnicity targeted or type of magazine. Choose 10-20 advertisements and study how body image is portrayed in the advertisements. What are some of the similarities and differences? How would these affect college students' self-identities if they were comparing themselves to these pictures?

2. Procure an issue of a magazine targeted to an ethnic audience. Choose five or six images that you believe represent a variety of body image portrayals. Write a sentence or two about each image and paste the photo next to it. Which, if any, of these images might be classified as pluralistic? Which, if any, could be classified as assimilationist? What other ethnic media functions do the images seem to fulfill?

REFERENCES

Akan G. E., & Grilo C. M. (1995). Sociocultural influences on eating attitudes and behaviors, body image, and psychological functioning: A comparison of African American, Asian American, and Caucasian college women. *International Journal of Eating Disorders, 18*(2), 181-187.

Altabe, M. (1998). Ethnicity and body image: Quantitative and qualitative analysis. *International Journal of Eating Disorders, 23*(2), 153-159.

Anderson, A. E., & DiDomenico, L. (1992). Diet vs. shape content of popular male and female magazines: A dose-response relationship to the incidence of eating disorders? *International Journal of Eating Disorders, 11*(3), 283-287.

Averett, S., & Korenman, S. (1999). Black-White differences in social and economic consequences of obesity. *International Journal of Obesity, 23*(2), 166-173.

Ballon, M. (1997, September). Start-up mambos to beat of booming market. *Inc* 19, 23.

Bandura, A. (1986). *Social foundations of thought and action.* Englewood Cliffs, NJ: Prentice-Hall.

Bandura, A. (1994). Social cognitive theory of mass communication, in J. Bryant & D. Zillman (Eds.), *Media effects: Advances in theory and research.* Hillsdale, NJ: Lawrence Erlbaum.

Beam, C. (1996, September 1). The Latina link in two languages. *Folio: The magazine for magazine management, 25,* 23-24.

Berchmans, B. M. (1998). Consumption of teen magazines by adolescent Italian girls: Reading patterns and motives. Paper presented to the Magazine Division of the Annual Convention of the Association for Education in Journalism and Mass Communication, August 5-8, Baltimore, MD.

Brown, J., White, A.B., & Nikopoulou, L. (1993).Disinterest, intrigue, resistance: Early adolescent girls' use of sexual media content. In B.S. Greenberg, J.D. Brown, & N. Buerkell-Rothfuss (Eds.), *Media, sex, and the adolescent* (pp. 177-195). Cresskill, NJ: Hampton Press.

Centers for Disease Control (1996). *Youth risk behavior surveillance—United States, 1995.* http://www.cdc.gov/epo/mmwr/preview/mmwwrnum/00043812.num

Carbonnell, Josefina (June 24, 1998). Presentation at the National Association of Hispanic Journalists conference, Miami, FLA.

Constantakis-Valdés, P. (1992). Toward a theory of "immigrant" and "ethnic" media: The case of Spanish-language television. Paper presented at the annual convention of the International Communication Association, Miami, FL.

Crandall, C. S., & Martinez, R. (1996). Culture, ideology, and antifat attitudes. *Personality and Social Psychology Bulletin, 11,* 1165-1176.

David, P. & Johnson, M.A. (1998). The role of self in third-person effects about body image. *Journal of Communication, 48*(4), 37-58.

Deux, K, (1992). Personalizing identity and socializing self. In G. M. Breakwell (Ed.), *Social psychology of identity and the self concept* (pp. 9-33). London: Surrey University Press.

Downing, J. D. H. (1992). Spanish-language media in the greater New York region during the 1980s. In S. H. Riggins (Ed.), *Ethnic minority media: An international perspective* (pp. 256-275). Newbury Park, CA: Sage.

Downs, A. C., & Harrison, S. K. (1985). Embarrassing age spots or just plain ugly? Physical attractiveness stereotyping as an instrument of sexism on American television commercials. *Sex Roles, 13*(1/2), 9-19.

Ellis, K. J., Abrams, S. A., & Wong, William W. (1997). Body composition of a young, multiethnic female population. *American Journal of Clinical Nutrition, 65*(3), 724-731.

Ferguson, M. (1983). *Forever feminine: Women's magazines and the cult of femininity*. London: Heinemann.

Fest, G. (1997, October 27b). Speaking the language, *Adweek, 38*, 25-30.

Field, A. E., Colditz, G. A., & Peterson, K. E. (1996). Racial/ethnic and gender differences in concern with weight and in bulimic behaviors among adolescents. *Obesity Research, 5*(5), 447-454.

Fitzgibbon, M. L., Spring, B., Avellone, M.E., Blackman, L.R., Pingitore, R., Stolley, M.R. (1998). Correlates of binge eating in Hispanic, Black, and White women. *International Journal of Eating Disorders, 24*(1), 43-52.

Flores, J.(1997). The Latino imaginary: Dimensions of community and identity. In F. R. Aparicio & S. Chávez-Silverman (Eds.), *Tropicalizations: Transcultural representations of Latinidad* (pp. 183-193). Hanover, NH: University Press of New England.

Fox, G. (1996). *Hispanic nation: Culture, politics, and the constructing of identity*. Secaucus, NJ: Birch Lane Press.

French, S. A., Story, M., Neumark-Sztainer, D., Downes, B., Resnick, M., & Blum, R. (1997). Ethnic differences in psychosocial and health behavior correlates of dieting, purging, and binge eating in a population-based sample of adolescent females. *International Journal of Eating Disorders, 22*(3), 315-322.

Garner, D. M., Garfinkel, P. E., Schwartz, D., Thompson, M. (1980). Cultural expectations of thinness in women. *Psychological Reports, 47*(2), 483-491.

Garner, A., Sterk, H. M., & Adams, S. (1998). Narrative analysis of sexual etiquette in teenage magazines. *Journal of Communication, 48*(4), 59-78.

Gergen, K. J. (1991). *The saturated self: Dilemmas of identity in contemporary life*. USA: Basic Books.

Gowen, L. K., Hayward, C., Killen, J. D., Robinson, T. N., Taylor, C. B. (1999). Acculturation and eating disorder symptoms in adolescent girls. *Journal of Research on Adolescence, 9*(1), 67-83.

Gremillion, J. (1996, June 10). Young, gifted, & 'Latina.' *Mediaweek, 6*, 34.

Gudykunst, W. B., & Kim, Y. Y. (1997). *Communicating with strangers: An approach to intercultural communication*. 3rd edition. New York: McGraw-Hill.

Gutiérrez, F. (1977). Spanish-language media in America: Background, resources, history. *Journalism History, 4*(2), 34-41.

Harris, S. M. (1995). Family, self, and sociocultural contributions to body-image attitudes of African American women. *Psychology of Women Quarterly, 19*, 129-145.

Harrison, K., & Cantor, J. (1997). The relationship between media consumption and eating disorders. *Journal of Communication, 47*(1), 40-67.

Huntzicker, W. E. (1995). Chinese-American newspapers. In F. Hutton and B. S. Reed (Eds.), *Outsiders in 19th–century press history: Multicultural perspectives* (pp. 71-92). Bowling Green, OH: Bowling Green State University Popular Press.

Husband, C. (1994). General introduction: Ethnicity and media democratization within the nation-state. In C. Husband (Ed.), *A richer vision: The development of ethnic minority media in Western democracies* (pp.1-19). Paris: The United Nations Educational, Scientific, and Cultural Organization.

Liebkind, K. (1992). Ethnic identity—Challenging the boundaries of social psychology. In G. M. Breakwell (Ed.), *Social psychology of identity and the self concept* (pp.147-185). London: Surrey University Press.

Magweth, B., Pope, H. G., Jr., & Hudson, J. I. (1995). Bulimia nervosa in two cultures: A comparison of Austrian and American college students. *International Journal of Eating Disorders, 17*(4), 403-412.

Martin, M. C., & Kennedy, P. F. (1993). Advertising and social comparison: Consequences for female preadolescents and adolescents. *Psychology and Marketing, 10*(6), 513-530.

McCracken, E. (1993). *Decoding women's magazines: From Mademoiselle to Ms.* Houndmills. UK: Macmillan.

Merelman, R. M. (1995). *Representing Black culture: Racial conflict and cultural politics in the United States.* New York: Routledge.

Miller, S. M. (1987). *The ethnic press in the United States: A historical analysis and handbook.* New York: Greenwood.

Molina, C. W., & Aguirre-Molina, M. (1994). *Latino health in the U.S.: A growing challenge.* Washinton, D.C.: American Public Health Association.

Myers, P. N., & Biocca, F. A. (1992). The elastic body image: The effects of television advertising and programming on body image distortions in young women. *Journal of Communication, 42*(3), 108-133.

Nemeroff, C. J., Stein, R. I., Diehl, N. S., & Smilack, K. M. (1994). From the Cleavers to the Clintons: Role choices and body orientation as reflected in magazine article content. *International Journal of Eating Disorders, 16*(2), 167-176.

Nuiry, O. E. (1997). Cashing in on Latinas. *Latina Style, 3*(4), 23-33.

Oboler, S. (1995). *Ethnic labels, Latino lives: Identity and the politics of (re)presentation in the United States.* Minneapolis: University of Minnesota.

Ogletree, S. M., Williams, S. W., Raffeld, P., Mason, B., & Fricke, K. (1990). Female attractiveness and eating disorders: Do children's television commercials play a role? *Sex Roles, 22*(11/12), 791-797.

Padilla, F. M. (1985). *Latino ethnic consciousness: The case of Mexican Americans and Puerto Ricans in Chicago.* Notre Dame, IN: University of Notre Dame Press.

Richins, M. L. (1991). Social comparison and the idealized images of advertising. *Journal of Consumer Research, 18*(1), 71-83.

Riffe, D., Lacy, S., & Fico, F. G. (1998). *Analyzing media messages: Using quantitative content analysis in research.* Mahwah, NJ: Lawrence Erlbaum.

Riggins, S. H. (1992). The promise and limits of ethnic minority media. In S. H. Riggins (Ed.), *Ethnic minority media: An international perspective* (pp. 276-288). Newbury Park, CA: Sage.

Rivenburgh, N. (1997). Social identification and media coverage of foreign relations. In A. Malek (Ed.), *News media and foreign relations: A multifaceted perspective* (pp. 79-91). Norwood, NJ: Ablex.

Rodriguez, A. (1997). Cultural agendas: The case of Latino-oriented U.S. media. In M. McCombs, D. L. Shaw, & D. Weaver (Eds.), *Communication and democracy: Exploring the intellectual frontiers in agenda-setting theory* (pp. 183-194). Mahwah: NJ: Lawrence Erlbaum.

Sabogal, F., Pérez-Stable, Otero-Sabogal, R., & Hiatt, R. A. (1995). Gender, ethnic and acculturation differences in sexual behaviors: Hispanic and non-Hispanic White adults. *Hispanic Journal of Behavioral Sciences, 17*(2), 139-159.

Silverstein, B., Perdue, L., Peterson, B., & Kelly, E. (1986). The role of mass media in promoting a thin standard of bodily attractiveness for women. *Sex Roles, 14*(9/10), 519-532.

Silverstein, B., Peterson, B., & Perdue, L. (1986). Some correlates of the thin standard of bodily attractiveness for women. *International Journal of Eating Disorders, 5*(5), 895-905.

Simonds, W. (1996) All consuming selves: Self-help literature and women's identities. In D. Grodin & T. R. Lindlof (Eds.), *Constructing the self in a mediated world* (pp. 15-29). Thousand Oaks, CA: Sage.

Sorenson, S. B., & Shen, H. K., (1996). Youth suicide trends in California: An examination of immigrant and ethnic group risk. *Suicide and life-threatening behavior, 26*(2), 143-154.

Stice, E., Schupak-Neuberg, E., Shaw, H. E., & Stein, R. I. (1994). Relation of media exposure to eating disorder symptomatology: An examination of mediating mechanisms. *Journal of Abnormal Psychology, 103*(4), 836-840.

Striegel-Moore, R. H., Schreiber, G. B., Pike, K. M., Wilfley, D. E., & Rodin, J. (1995). Drive for thinness in Black and White preadolescent girls. *International Journal of Eating Disorders, 18*(1), 59-69.

Subervi-Velez, F. A. (1986). The mass media and ethnic assimilation and pluralism: A review and research proposal with special focus on Hispanics. *Communication Research, 13*(1), 71-96.

Subervi-Vélez, F. A. (1994). Mass communication and Hispanics. In Padilla, F., N. Kanellos & C. Esteva-Fabregat (Eds.), *Handbook of Hispanic Cultures in the United States: Sociology* (pp. 304-357). Houston, TX: Arte Publico Press.

Tajfel, H. (1978). *Differentiation between social groups: Studies in the social psychology of intergroup relations*. London: Academic Press.

Tajfel, H. (1981). *Human groups and social categories: Studies in social psychology*. Cambridge: Cambridge University Press.

Tajfel, H. & Turner, J. C. (1986). The social identity theory of intergroup behavior. In S. Worchel & W. G. Austin (Eds.), *Psychology of Intergroup Relations* (2nd ed.) (pp. 7-24). Chicago: Nelson Hall.

Thomsen, S.R., Gustafson, R. L., McCoy, J. K., & Williams, M. (1998). Beauty and fashion magazine reading and anorectic cognitions as predictors of dieting behavior in college-age women. Paper presented to the Magazine Division of the Association for Education in Journalism and Mass Communication, August 5-8, Baltimore, MD.

Turner, J. C., Oakes, P. J., Haslam, S. A., & McGarty, C. (1994). Self and collective: Cognition and social context. *Personality and Social Psychology Bulletin, 20*(5), 454-463.

Turow, J. (1997). *Breaking up America: Advertisers and the new media world*. Chicago: University of Chicago.

Whisler, K., Nuiry, O., & McHugh, S.R. (1997). *The 1997 national Hispanic media directory*. Carlsbad, CA: WPR Publishing.

Wiseman, C. V., Gray, J. J., Mosimann, J. E., & Ahrens, A. H. (1992). Cultural expectations of thinness in women: An update. *International Journal of Eating Disorders, 11*(1), 85-89.

Woodruff, S. I., Zaslow, K. A., Candelaria, J., & Elder, J. D. (1997). Effects of gender and acculturation on nutrition-related factors among limited-English proficient Hispanic adults. *Ethnicity and Disease, 7*(2), 121-126.

Wolf, N. (1991). *The beauty myth: How images of beauty are used against women*. New York: Anchor Books.

Latina Stereotyping and New Mestiza-Womanism in Rosie Perez Films

Diana I. Rios

Introduction

Over the past few years the general public and academics alike have witnessed increased interest in Latino male and female talent in popular culture. No one has recognized this more than artists of Spanish-language backgrounds, whether they be from the United States, Latin America or Spain, since it appears that Latino-styled actors are finding broadened opportunities. U.S. Latino audiences are seeing more images, sounds and styles that are unmistakably Latino. This current fascination is more lasting today than previous waves of cultural and political fashion because of enormous Latino population increases and, thus, Latino consumption. In the past, the allure of and curiosity about Latino exoticism were fed by Hollywood industry actions that were in alignment with the Good Neighbor policy with Latin America. Latino music in dance halls, on recordings, and on the radio helped fuel general market interest in those things Latino during the 1940s and well into the 1950s. Furthermore, bandleader star Desi Arnaz, the first Latino to star in a prime time television show, brought Latinos to national attention, beginning in the 1950s.

The goal of this essay is to critique the film roles of Rosie Perez, using film videos that were available for public consumption between 1989 and 2000. This research differs from previous writings about Perez's image that use critical and cultural theory and focus on only particular aspects of representation (Vargas 1996; 1999;

Valdivia, 1998). This overview research describes and critiques Perez's film roles and characters by referencing common Latina media archetypes and exercising a new framework created by Chicana-Latina and African-American feminists.

Perez, a Puerto Rican heritage actor from New York, played roles that were typical for Latinas in the twentieth century and are still commonplace at the beginning of the twenty-first century. Her personal style is candid and often brazen. When speaking about the development of a new dance and performance show for the Home Box Office (HBO) cable channel, she is quoted as saying, "I don't want any commercialized, watered-down, bullshit acts on my show" (McAdams, 1993, p. 23). This stylistic tendency is often repeated in interviews and reflected in most of the roles she plays. Since her debut in Spike Lee's *Do the Right Thing* (1989), Perez has made several large-budget Hollywood films as well as lesser-known independent films. She tends to be cast in earthy, gritty roles where her personal urban and working class experiences are emphasized in speech style, movement and dress.

Given the overwhelming tendency of popular media to recycle character types in general, and ethnic character types in particular, this research will illustrate that Perez is too often in roles that are recreations of old, tried, and not-so-true Latina image types. On the other hand, Perez is also cast in some roles that are refreshing and new. These latter roles would be more in alignment with mestiza and womanist perspectives (Walker, 1983; Anzaldua, 1987; Reid, 1993; Sandoval, 1998; Carstarphen, 1999; Rios & Carstarphen, 2001; Carstarphen & Rios, 2003). These perspectives, developed by feminists and women-of-color scholars, envision women as multi-faceted human beings capable of positive expression, creativity and love of self and their communities. Women also embody other characteristics that challenge negative qualities typically assigned to women of color.

This work will begin with a selected overview of Latinas in U.S. film in order to establish their common renderings in popular media. Much is drawn from foundational film research on Chicano and U.S. Latino film imagery written by Berg (2002), Keller (1994) and other investigators. The mestiza-womanist framework is a working guide that will be used to discern new elements in the construction of a new Latina image. The core of this essay will be the description, critique and evaluation of the character traits and character types played by Perez. This research is driven by a concern with the injurious distortions of Latinas that have continued for decades in literature and mass media (Lester, 1996; Pettit, 1980), especially in the social and economic contexts of Latino chic. More now than ever before, the communication field needs research on communities of color. It is hoped that the analytic framework used here, and its interpretive application, will assist other scholars in their assessments of twenty-first century Latina images and the representations of other women of color.

The Latino Image in Hollywood

Much has been written about the Latino image in mass media (Woll, 1980; Pettit, 1980; Berg, 2002; Noriega, 1992; Fregoso, 1993; Keller, 1994; Wilson & Gutierrez, 1995; Lester, 1996). Research has demonstrated how negative literary and visual representations are continuously regurgitated. Complex and diverse representations of Latinos are few and far between.

Woll, Berg and Keller have each categorized Chicano (Mexican-American) and other Latino images that have been recycled through the past century. Common female types, and their varia-

tions, include but are not limited to: the half-breed harlot, the dark lady, the cantina girl, the vamp or temptress, the female clown or buffoon, the faithful, moral or self-sacrificing señorita, and the suffering mother. Overall, images of Latinas are distortions that are mostly oversexed, immoral or ignorant. The half-breed harlot is sexually available and psychologically confused. Her biethnic or biracial heritage makes her an unwanted misfit. Her loose morals add to her social isolation. The dark lady is a mysterious woman who is most likely of questionable character. The cantina girl is a loose woman who works in bars. The vamp or temptress is a selfish, manipulative beauty. The female clown or buffoon provides comedic relief. At another extreme of sexuality and morals are the faithful, moral, or self-sacrificing señorita (single, young lady) or *señora* (older woman or married lady), and the suffering mother. The women can be overly spiritual to the extent of appearing ignorant and backward. They carry the burdens of the world on their shoulders.

Berg explains that the consistent and repeated attribution of negative qualities of ethnic and racial groups reflects European-American society's repressed desires and frustrations. This type of racism is aggravated in the fast-paced nature of media production. In the end, viewers, readers and listeners are left with cookie-cutter representations that they have witnessed before and will be exposed to again.

In addition to this, Hollywood has long held the practice of muddling characters into indiscernible ethnic backgrounds or converting them into more palatable European Americans whenever possible. Today's example of ethnic erasing tendencies is the packaging of actor Jennifer Lopez. Her Latina ethnicity is erased in well-marketed films like *Anaconda* (1997), *No Way Out* (1999), *The Cell* (2000), *Angel Eyes* (2001) and *The Wedding Planner* (2001). There are so few Latinas that have been allowed to appear on screen that the precious few that exist have potential to challenge old images and replace them with something new.

Focusing on the cultural factors involved in Latino audience media use, Rios (1996; 1999; 2000) conducted field research in several Chicano-Latino communities in the southwest and northeast. This audience research describes how women and men experience ease of consumption as well as struggle to find cultural fulfillment in both mainstream and Spanish-language media. One consistent complaint voiced by visual and print media audiences is that Latino representations in entertainment and news are distorted or absent.

A Mestiza and Womanist Framework

Mestiza and womanist perspectives (Anzaldua, 1987; Sandoval, 1998; Walker, 1983; Thomas, 1998-99) have been necessary feminist-of-color responses to needs for culturally relevant frameworks for analysis of popular texts as well as for other kinds of socio-cultural action. Recently, communication scholars have used one (Reid, 1993, pp.109-124; Carstarphen, 1999) or both (Rios & Carstarphen, 2001; Carstarphen & Rios, 2003) of these perspectives in media analyses. These perspectives, like others described in Shohat and Stam (1994), offer infusions of cultural pluralistic thought into the more common European-American centered approaches in the study of popular culture. Writings by Jane Gaines (1994), bell hooks (1990) and Rosa Linda Fregoso (1993) discuss the longstanding need for feminist analysis in popular culture to treat race/ethnicity as a substantial issue.

The mestiza-womanist framework used in this work constitutes a melding of streams of thought established in U.S. third-world feminist criticism in the 1970s. As described by Sandoval (1998), feminists of color wanted a mode of analysis for creative writings and research that was more culturally and racially inclusive. Hurtado (1999) has called for dedication to a multicultural feminism for practical and theoretical work across disciplines and social classes. Gloria Anzaldua (1987) articulated a writing and research approach for Chicanas (Mexican Americans), Latinas and women of color in the classic volume titled *Borderlands/La Frontera: The New Mestiza*. Anzaldua presents a broad, flexible theory of a new mestiza perspective and consciousness. It is the duty of additional schol-

ars to develop and use the new mestiza mode of analysis across disciplines. According to Anzaldua's philosophy, the new mestiza's life is informed by complex cultural experiences as an ethnic minority woman living in the White-majority United States. Furthermore, the *Borderlands* describes a space of multicultural existence and way of life. This borderlands existence can be positive since a location in the borderlands makes the Chicana Latina flexible, resilient and capable of divergent thinking. On the road of survival and success, "The new mestiza copes by developing a tolerance for contradictions, a tolerance for ambiguity. She learns to be an Indian in Mexican culture, to be Mexican from an Anglo point of view. She learns to juggle cultures" (p.79).

Black feminist author Alice Walker (1983) describes a woman-of-color perspective called *womanism* in the landmark volume *In Search of Our Mothers' Gardens*. A womanist is a Black feminist or feminist of color. Also, a womanist "appreciates and prefers women's culture, women's emotional flexibility (values tears as natural counter-balance of laughter), and women's strength" (p. xi). Some of the qualities that distinguish a womanist are her appreciation of all things female, a love for herself, commitment to the survival and wholeness of all in her community and a universal embrace of all cultures (p. xi). Womanism's goal for cultivating Black female pride and striving for cultural diversity parallels mestiza objectives.

Mestiza is the feminine form of the word *mestizo*. Mestizo people are the post-colonial mixed-blooded people described in writings by philosopher Jose Vasconcelos. They are "*la primera raza sintesis del globo,*" or the fifth "cosmic" race composed of the four major races of the world (cited in Anzaldua, p.77; also see discussion on "*la raza cosmica* versus the melting pot" by Fernandez, 2000, p.63). Vasconcelos' strengthening words about Latinos of all the Americas counters racist colonial and internal colonial writings about Latinos as being expendable, mixed-blooded mongrels. Acknowledging mixed blood, and seeing it as an asset, creates an avenue for Latinos to negate classist, racist claims of White-European racial purity. It also helps to erase racial superiority claims that some

Latinos believe they have over other people of color because of a lighter skin tone (Latinos come in all colors) and other qualities that might garner them privileges in White societies. By acknowledging *mestizaje*, the state of mixed blood, Latinos begin a freedom from "isms" and begin embracing the heritage of all peoples.

Womanist and mestiza worldviews offer a theoretical and methodological compass (Sandoval, 1998) by which scholars of color may conduct critical analysis. Scholars use multicultural points of reference, with an emphasis on the contributions and strengths of their people-of-color communities. The mestiza-womanist approach, employed here, envisions women as multi-faceted. In this perspective, women are assured, self-respectful, caring of others, and embody other characteristics that contrast with the pejorative qualities historically assigned to women of color. The mestiza-womanist approach is a cross-disciplinary project informed by gradual accumulation of policy-action documents, literary writings and media analyses by ethnic minority scholars.

Vast theoretical development of mestiza-womanism is too tremendous a task within the confines of a single work. Therefore, this paper will select relevant pieces from Chicana-Latina and African-American feminism in what will be called mestiza-womanism. This research extends mestiza-womanist analysis initiated by Carstarphen and Rios (2003). The mestiza-womanist approach, concomitant with assessments of Chicana-Latina images in Chicano-Latino film research, will be used to appraise character portrayals and character traits. It is expected that most Latina characters will be replications of detrimental Latina archetypes of the past, but that some will be part of a new, advantageous Latina image in popular culture. Given the potential for social impact of mass media—on the perceptions, attitudes and opinions of new generations of cinema attendees, cable television viewers and video watchers—it is hoped that Perez will be able to secure intriguing, multidimensional, and dignified roles beyond the years surveyed.

The Films of Rosie Perez

Perez is among the few Latinas to successfully break into film. She has averaged more than one film per year between the years 1989 and 2000 (see Table 1). She has accomplished much, though she must regularly challenge racism in the entertainment industry. She states, "The racism, the sexism, I never let it be my problem," and, "It's their problem. If I see a door comin' my way, I'm knockin' it down. And if I can't knock down the door, I'm sliding through the window. I'll never let it stop me from what I wanna do" (Meyers, 1993, p. 36).

Perez's film career began in 1989 when Spike Lee cast her as the main protagonist's love interest in the film *Do the Right Thing*. This hard-hitting independent film about Black-White race relations in inner city New York gave Perez the film exposure she needed to launch her career. Vargas (1999) describes how Perez was discovered on stage while competing in a "butt" contest (p.120). Spike Lee writes that he discovered Perez when she was dancing at his birthday party in a Los Angeles club (Lee with Jones, 1989). Highly sexualized, spitfire roles have been most prevalent in Perez's career thus far (see Table 1 for overview). Better roles for Perez are clearly difficult to secure.

In *Do the Right Thing*, Perez was cast as a loud, foul-mouthed, hypersexual girlfriend named Tina who has an undependable boyfriend named Mookie. Mookie is a young pizza deliveryman. Scenes showing Mookie and Tina together illustrate that their relationship is primarily founded on sex. Nude scenes focus on Tina's body during lovemaking and present Tina as a voluptuous sexpot, with few other assets. Her child by Mookie is a little boy who does not receive much attention or monetary support from his father. Tina lives with her mother in a cramped apartment, unable to afford to live on her own as a young, single mother. In several scenes, she appears to be overwhelmed with her life's limitations and is frustrated by her emotional dependence on Mookie, the absentee partner and father. Throughout the film—from the famous shadowboxing introduction where Tina is not effectively fighting the White power structure, to sex scenes with Mookie, to scenes where she appears in the neighborhood—she does not have much authority and control in her life. Life's problems run Tina over.

This film is clearly a Black film, showcasing several African-American artists. However, the character Tina is not Black per se, she is *mestiza* and specifically a Puerto Rican with Afro-Caribbean features. Vargas (1996; 1999) describes her as a Black *Puertorriqueña*. In his film journal about the making of *Do the Right Thing,* Spike Lee writes about discovering Perez, "Her name is Rosie Perez. Not only is she from Brooklyn, she's from Fort Greene, my neighborhood. Help me Jesus. I'm seriously considering her for the role of Tina. She's definitely what I'm looking for: a fine young ghetto babe. Rosie is Puerto Rican, but she looks Black"(p.75). Tina's mother has common Latina physical characteristics, with her dark hair and olive skin. We also hear Puerto Rican-style Spanish spoken in Tina's household. In anger Tina tells Mookie off by calling him *pendejo*, a Spanish-language word for idiot or dummy. She is indeed playing a Latina character, a mestiza with prominent Black markers.

Overall, Tina's character appears to repeat the all too common qualities found among Latina and African-American representations of a rough, hot-tempered harlot. She is a loud, cussing, Latina spitfire, barely making ends meet. If one were to apply an African-American aesthetic (Jones, 1991) to Tina, she acts like a "bitch" (loud mouthed) and a "ho" (highly sexed). Unfortunately the prominent character traits that Tina exhibits are repeated often in other roles Perez plays.

Using a mestiza-womanist lens to see the character Tina, and her behaviors, one can extract a view that is more understanding of single motherhood among women of color. The director Lee makes it clear that Tina and Mookie are unable to gain fulfilling employment or a living wage. They are both examples of working poor. Tina keeps a job, but her options in life are delimited by her lack of advanced education and a specialized trade or skill. Her anger and other demonstrations of high emotion, in a mestiza-womanist analysis, can be interpreted as appropriate responses to closed opportunities in work and education. She should dance with joy or be comedic about her difficulties.

As explained by Anzaldua (1987) regarding the state and development of mestiza consciousness, Tina's expressions of extreme discontent are indicative of the inner struggles among mestizas who must navigate between their Latina culture and the dominant White culture. Tina's frustrations, related to low social class and economic instability, add layers that Tina must challenge. Unfortunately, she has not yet arrived in a personal space where she understands herself enough to make personal changes. Nor does she understand the dominant society well enough to navigate successfully within it. She needs personal and practical tools to save herself from forever "floundering in uncharted seas" (p.79). Tina's "outrageous, audacious, courageous or willful" (Walker, p. xi) behaviors are not all bad. Tina is not silenced. She speaks her womanly mind, whether people like what she says or not.

In the independent film *A Brother's Kiss* (1996), the character Debbie echoes a more mature and straight-pathed Tina. Where Tina in *Do the Right Thing* is a hopeless, angry, loud single mom, Debbie is more thoughtful. She can become angry, but also strategizes to improve her situation. This youthful, gritty, working-class woman is more aware and more motivated about what she wants for her life and the life of her baby girl. Unlike Tina, Debbie's maturity allows her to break away from a previous boyfriend and later from the main protagonist of the film.

The father of her child is a tall, charismatic, Anglo man who shares her working-class experiences. Debbie meets him when he is a straight-laced school bus driver but is forced to break with him when he takes a job as drug shop worker and becomes an addict. In a touching and sad scene toward the end of the film, Lex inadvertently meets Debbie and baby while walking down the street. He is dirty, homeless and strung-out on drugs. Debbie lends a caring ear and a stern voice as he tries to convince her that he does not have anything to do with drugs. When they exchange pleasant good-byes, we the audience are sure that Debbie has no intention of allowing him back into their lives. Mother and baby have a difficult but positive future together.

The fact that Debbie is a single mother and woman of color in the film is reminiscent of previous images of working-class women of color where they have many children, no husband and live at the mercy of society. However, in *A Brother's Kiss*, the character Debbie is not tragic. She does not know all the answers to life, but is as self-directed and self-sufficient as she can muster. Though she has many medical expenses because of her chronically ill child, she is not shown walking into a welfare office for help. She seeks the help of family and extended family with her unforeseen burdens.

The film takes advantage of Perez's reputation for sexpot characters by presenting lovemaking scenes and showing Debbie's sensual body. However, in this film, Debbie's sexuality does not overshadow her other characteristics. The character describes herself as a good person. "I'm good," she plainly states in a conversation with a new boyfriend. We the audience believe her to be a good and decent human being.

Debbie's humanistic and more positive qualities are more in line with the qualities for a woman of color according to the mestiza-womanist perspective. Debbie is in a more advanced state of personal development than Tina. "The new mestiza copes by developing a tolerance for contradictions, a tolerance for ambiguity...She learns to juggle cultures" (Anzaldua, 1987, p.79). She is learning to juggle events in her socio-cultural environment. Debbie, like Tina, is not silenced, but she is more contemplative. This introspective quality allows for more careful decision-making and more cautious words.

We see a hot-tempered, foul-mouthed spitfire character in a segment of the independent film, *Night on Earth* (1991), and an over-sexed character in a segment of *Subway Stories* (1997). Both appearances by Perez are short but potent. In *Night on Earth*, Perez delivers a concentrated performance as an outrageous woman named Cindy. In the middle of the night, her boyfriend spots her walking swiftly to some destination. He tries to convince her to ride along with him in a taxicab. When she refuses, he resorts to picking her up and shoving her into the cab as she kicks, screams and curses in protest. A mestiza-womanist perspective would focus on Cindy's self-assuredness and independent nature. She appears to define her own path in life. Cindy is "willful," "audacious," and could even be called "courageous" (Walker, p.xi). Cindy walks boldly and quickly in the night, ready to conquer that which impedes her—even if it's a boyfriend.

Perez plays a nameless, voiceless, hyper-sexual professional in a segment in *Subway Stories* called *Love on the A Train*. Dressed in business-class grey and muted tones, her character discretely masturbates against the clasped hand of a male passenger. The male professional, also on his way to work in Manhattan, clutches the subway train pole every morning for a month of anonymous titillation. The woman professional is a repackaged harlot type in conservative dress and pearls. A mestiza-womanist perspective might say that the woman is in charge of her own sexuality, but the story is no more than Hollywood-style sexual exploitation.

We see foul-mouthed spitfires in *Somebody to Love* (1994) and *Dance with the Devil* (1997). *Somebody to Love* is a small film with two big names in its ranks, Harvey Keitel and Anthony Quinn. Perez plays Mercedes, a Los Angeles taxi dancer. She works in a bar where tickets are sold to men, who may choose from a selection of women and transvestite dancing partners. This character is the sexy "cantina girl," complete with rough edges. Mercedes is not completely streetwise, since we see her often deceived by her lover (played by Keitel) and an alleged movie agent.

Mercedes is an aspiring actress. At home, she practices Anglo-American diction and straight posture. She relentlessly shows up for casting calls only to be disappointed that she is either too tall, too short or has too heavy of an accent. While attending one casting call, she reads the description for the type needed. She mumbles excitedly, "mid-twenties, dancer, New York, Spanish." She becomes infuriated when a "Barbie doll" is hailed out of the crowd. She yells at the man in charge who selected the extremely tall, White, blond haired woman, and is almost thrown off the lot for being boisterous and contradictory.

A mestiza-womanist assessment of Mercedes sees her as more confident and goal-oriented than the characters Tina from *Do the Right Thing* or Debbie from *A Brother's Kiss*, though she still has far to go. Like most other characters played by Perez, Mercedes is willful and audacious. Appropriately, Mercedes, like many women of color working outside the home, is challenging life. She is constantly looking for the right break and desperately focuses on her goal of becoming a screen actress.

Dance with the Devil (1997) presents the most extreme characterization of a streetwise, hypersexual harlot that Perez has ever played. Perez plays Perdita Durango in this internationally produced independent film. The Spanish-sounding word "*Perdita*" is derived from the word "*perdición*," which means perdition, outrage and ruination. The unusual name itself is revealing about the character, her life and her future. Perdita is an itinerant opportunist who displays gratuitous sexuality and severe violence. The film showcases the ultimate in negative typing of Latinas and other women. The destructive nature of the content places it outside the boundaries of consideration in a positive mestiza-womanist framework. Perdita is an ever lost mestiza of the U.S.-Mexico borderlands with no base and no signs in sight for directions.

In addition to hot-tempered sexpots, Perez's characters are especially greedy in the Hollywood films *White Men Can't Jump* (1992) and *It Could Happen to You* (1994). Even in the Disney animated feature *Road to El Dorado* (2000), Perez's illustrated character is a greedy, buffoonish harlot. In *White Men Can't Jump*, Perez appears with actors Woody Harrelson and Wesley Snipes. The three form a Brown, White, Black conglomerate with general-market audience appeal and ethnic minority interest. To the general market, the film title may be a curiosity and a challenge. Some might say that the title-statement is an insult because it publicly declares a shortcoming of White men—those same men who lead our patriarchal society.

In *White Men Can't Jump*, Perez plays a fascinating character named Gloria Clemente who we see sitting in bed surrounded by books. She and her boyfriend live in a cheap hotel room. She spends her days memorizing trivia and studying history in hopes of being a contestant on the game show Jeopardy. Gloria watches television all day, vicariously competing with the other contestants. She is high-strung, foul-mouthed and sensual. She is the Latina vamp once again, with a difficult personality. We wonder why Gloria is not using her intelligence and ambition to gain formal credentials. Looking more closely at Gloria, we see that she has set her goals on those things that she has exposure to and knowledge about—and she certainly has a great deal of exposure to popular media. Everyone has her specialty, and Jeopardy is the niche in which Perez chooses to excel.

When Perez is pulled to contestant stardom on Jeopardy, she makes the decision to break off with her dim boyfriend and any basketball pick-up game schemes he and his buddy are brewing. This female character demonstrates independence and self-assuredness. She sets careful sail in her uncharted seas of daytime television. From a mestiza-womanist perspective, Perez is on a path where she can fulfill her own ambitions. What Gloria does not show are characteristics of generosity and love for community once she has new wealth. Contrary to the mestiza-womanist worldview, which places importance in loving and helping the collective, Gloria is not balancing her self-centered desires with supportive behavior toward any community.

The most individualistic character played by Perez is Muriel in *It Could Happen to You*. In this film, Perez is teamed with bigger box office attractions Nicolas Cage and Bridget Fonda. It is unfortunate that the Latina character of the film, with whom Latino audiences and audiences of color might expect to identify, is a greedy, scheming, hot-tempered vamp. Early in the film, the character is understandably upset that her White husband Charlie promised half of his lottery winnings to a diner waitress when he was short of cash to give her a tip. However, Muriel's continuous fits of anger during interactions with her sweet, too-honest cop husband make her quickly unsympathetic. The conflicts between the greedy wife and husband contrast sharply with the soft flirtations between the husband and waitress. The generosity of the waitress and husband contrasts with Muriel's greedy behavior. It is all too clear that Brown and White are a mismatch and that the compassionate, honest, White male is better coupled with the nice, hard-working, White female.

Throughout the film, a slow death is bequeathed upon the Latina character through symbolic annihilation and character assassination. Consistently and repeatedly, the despicable vamp rears her head and triggers a symbolic slap in the face to Latino audiences. By the end of the film, Perez's character has not undergone personal development for the better using constructive mestiza-womanist strategies. In fact, she appears as vampish and self-serving as ever. She is punished when her husband and the waitress end up with love, money and happiness in a magical hot air balloon exit from the land of Oz. In this instance, the tripartite combination of love, money and happiness works for nice people of the majority culture, not for greedy, selfish people of color. Audiences of color are left with great disappointment.

In contrast with the academic critique of her role in *It Could Happen to You*, Perez sounds audaciously proud about the forceful character she plays. She is quoted as saying, "I'm the woman you love to hate," and, "I make everybody's life misery. I was so nasty, the audience applauded during the test screening when I got mine" (Pearlman, 1994, p. 14). Furthermore, when asked whether this role could define her in the future, she is quoted as saying, "It's a lot of fun to go to work, be a bitch, and get paid for it" (Pearlman, 1994, p. 14).

In the film-length children's cartoon called *Road to El Dorado* (2000), Perez lends her voice to a comedic, indigenous woman named Chel. Chel symbolizes the pre-mestiza mother of "*la raza cosmica*," historically called *La Malinche*, the translator for Spanish conquistador Hernán Cortez. *Road to El Dorado* and many other animated features by Disney have been highly criticized for distorted and pejorative representations of people of color (Woll, 1980; Guerrero, 1993; Shohat & Stam, 1994; Cripps, 1993; Martin-Rodriguez, 2000). *Road to El Dorado* mangles the European conquest of the New World and warps images of indigenous peoples. Chel is a jungle-wise, native woman who seizes opportunities to gain riches while assisting and fulfilling the sexual desires of a pair of buffoon-ish European conquistadors. In short, Chel is a clever, thieving harlot. This character is spunky, and may even have an independent nature, but she does not exhibit other mestiza-womanist qualities.

Perez tones down characterizations of the sexpot and vamp in the Home Box Office (HBO) movie called *Criminal Justice* (1990), in the Hollywood features *Untamed Heart* (1993) and *Fearless* (1993), and in the independent film called *The 24-Hour Woman* (1999).

In *Criminal Justice*, Perez is teamed with actor Forest Whitaker. The character Denise Moore is down-and-out, jobless, poor, unskilled and addicted to drugs. Denise has a limited future and her highest goals are related to obtaining more drugs to satisfy her habit. Unlike previous Perez characters, however, Denise of *Criminal Justice* is more contemplative, though she makes poor decisions. In a mestiza-womanist view, Denise is appropriately angry and frustrated at being robbed, assaulted and relegated to the underclass. Her expression of anguish is normal for those circumstances. But, Denise demonstrates womanly strength by appearing in court to confront her alleged assailant. Her sheer presence, in a loose T-shirt and jeans, intimidates the alleged criminal. Overall, Denise's dark qualities, all too commonly found among Latina archetypes, overshadow her other promising qualities.

Perez plays a minor role as Cindy, a diner waitress, in the tragic love story *Untamed Heart* (1993). The subsidiary role to Christian Slater and Marisa Tomei's characters leaves little room for development. We learn she is doing her best in a dead-end job. She is simply a friendly, hardworking "cantina girl," or domestic type. She does not appear in sex scenes nor does she look sensual in her prim pink waitress uniform. She can speak her mind, and her verbal style and heavy Brooklyn accent make her sound street smart. Unlike other Perez characters, Cindy is not overbearing.

Perez has important roles in *Fearless* (1993) and *The 24-Hour Woman* (1999). She was nominated for an Academy Award for *Fearless* and was named best supporting actress by film critic organizations. *Fearless* also boasted cinema stars Jeff Bridges and Isabella Rossellini. Perez plays an airplane crash survivor, Carla Rodrigo, who is traumatized by her inability to save her infant from death. Carla is a moral, self-sacrificing, suffering mother, but there is more to her character.

Working-class Carla befriends another airplane passenger, Max Klein, a White male played by Jeff Bridges. Carla and Max cross ethnic and class boundaries while helping each other cope with being survivors. But Perez's character is no sexual temptress or vamp. Though there is an attraction on both sides, Carla and Max maintain a friendship.

At home, Carla and her husband maintain both traditional and new Latino traditions. Their home is adorned with common cultural artifacts and religious icons. When misused and misunderstood by Hollywood, this decor would look cultish and backward. However, in the context of this Latino-Catholic household, ethnic and religious adornments and rituals appear to be appropriate expressions of mestizo culture and spirituality. The director is said to have rewritten the role of Carla to fit Perez's look and accent (Gregory, 1993, p. 48). Perez explains, "He listened to everything I told him about Latin households," and, "I told him that there had to be café *Bustelo* in the kitchen and a shrine in honor of dead loved one[s] and that my character had to be attend[ing] a Catholic Church with a Spanish-speaking priest" (Gregory, 1993, p.48). Carla is not a deferential *señora* of the house. She is a contemporary, working class mestiza in emotional turmoil. Regardless of her emotional crisis, she has a clear personal and cultural compass for living.

Using a mestiza-womanist perspective, Carla is one of the most multi-faceted characters Perez has ever played. The shift from vampy sexuality to the emotional and personal journeys of Max, Carla, and their respective families is refreshing. Carla is a suffering mother but not a tragic character—clearly a different character type for Perez. Perez explains, "It was so uncomfortable slipping into the character… because she was weak. Even when I watched it in the screening, I didn't relate to her" (Meyers, 1993, p. 36). Mestiza-womanism acknowledges the need for women to express themselves, to shed tears, not as a sign of weakness, but as a quality of humanity.

The 24-Hour Woman is a simple, critically acclaimed film. It has been analyzed in depth by Carstarphen and Rios (2003) and Rios and Carstarphen (2001), who examine the roles of African-American women and Latinas. The most notable aspect of this film is that the lead Latina character, Grace, is not a cantina girl, vamp, sexual temptress or domestic. Similar to many of Perez's other characters, Grace is highly vocal and emotionally expressive. Grace may even be called a spitfire because of her high energy level. However, Grace is not the sexpot of *Do the Right Thing, Dance with the Devil, Somebody to Love, Subway Stories,* and *Road to El Dorado.* She is not greedy as we see in *It Could Happen to You* and *White Men Can't Jump.* Nor is Grace cursing a lover as in *Night on Earth, Do the Right Thing, White Men Can't Jump* and *Dance with the Devil.* She is not the cantina girl of *Untamed Heart* and *Somebody to Love.* She is not the jobless drug addict of *Criminal Justice.*

Grace is an over-worked media professional and an over-stressed mom, trying to make her contemporary Latino marriage, family, extended family and multicultural friendships work. From a mestiza-womanist perspective, Grace is constructively negotiating in the borderlands of motherhood and career. She should not be silent during her professional and personal struggles. Overall, despite an odd twist in the narrative, Grace demonstrates many of the characteristics needed in the creation of a new Latina for mass media.

The odd twist in the film (that is simply Hollywood sensationalism) comes when Grace is pushed over the edge and shoots at her husband. These scenes resurrect the streetwise, hot-tempered, spitfire types that Perez often plays. As described in Rios and Carstarphen (2001), a small group of seminar students provided oral and written responses to this film for a class exercise. Among many supportive statements about the film, they criticized the gun scenes as stupid. However, these students, the majority of whom were women, did not want to condemn Grace for having this emotional breakdown because they sympathized with her burdens at work and home.

The 24-Hour Woman seemed to hit a special chord with Perez's life. Perhaps it is the relevancy to the mestiza experience that allowed Perez to bring Grace to life for mainstream and ethnic minority audiences. She is quoted as saying that all the stress the character endured, "Made me even more sure about the fact that I want to have children," and that her biological clock was about to go off (Zeide, 1999, p.28).

Conclusions

There is an inescapable surge of public interest in Latinos in popular culture. Latinas and Latinos have a stronger presence in general market media in this current era than in previous years. Perez, a talented performer, has had a consistent film presence between 1989-2000. Unfortunately, in spite of the need for more fully developed Latina characters, old stereotypes are too often repeated. Perez is a high-quality actor who needs access to excellent roles. When asked in an interview if she was concerned about "be-ing stereotyped as a feisty, foul-mouthed, working-class Latina," she answered, "All the time, all the time" (Applebome, 1999). She explains more fully, "You have to understand the racism in Hollywood. The majority of Latin actresses in Hollywood were always playing either spitfires or maids. Now here is a woman who comes in and does leads opposite White people and Black people and other Spanish people, and she's comfortable in her skin? Gasp! How dare she?"(Rodriguez, 2003, p.40).

Perez challenges the entertainment industry with her strong presence. Despite this fact, this research has shown that not many of Perez's characters can be easily placed within a mestiza-womanist perspective. The desire for a more sophisticated mestiza-womanist character is a reasonable ideal. Latino audiences deserve renderings of themselves that contrast with the negative qualities typically assigned to people of color. A logical component of future media analyses of this kind is to conduct Latina audience response research to a wide variety of Rosie Perez films.

TABLE 1

The Films of Rosie Perez: Old & New Character Traits

Title	Old Character Traits	New Character Traits
Do the Right Thing (1989)	streetwise, hot-tempered spitfire, harlot	
Criminal Justice (1990)	streetwise drug addict	contemplative independent
Night on Earth (1991)	streetwise, hot-tempered spitfire	independent
White Men Can't Jump (1992)	streetwise hot-tempered, greedy spitfire	independent
Fearless (1993)	emotional, religious, suffering mother	loyal friend dedicated, monogamous wife
Untamed Heart (1993)	streetwise, "cantina girl"	loyal friend
It Could Happen to You (1994)	streetwise, greedy, hot-tempered spitfire; buffoon	independent
A Brother's Kiss (1996)	sensual	dedicated mother, honest contemplative
Dance with the Devil (1997)	extremely violent, hot-tempered spitfire, harlot	independent
Somebody to Love (1997)	streetwise, "cantina girl," spitfire, harlot	ambitious, sensitive
Subway Stories (1997)	harlot	working professional
The 24-Hour Woman (1999)	hot-tempered spitfire	ambitious professional & working mom, independent
Road to El Dorado (2000)	thieving, clever, harlot, buffoon	spunky

Name: _____

Date: _____

1. If you had the power to create new and improved imagery of U.S. Latinas, what would these images look like?

2. What cultural differences might you find among Latina, African-American, Asian-American, or Arab-American women who all watch the same Rosie Perez film?

3. Compare and contrast the journey that Rosie Perez's characters take with the real life journeys of women of color and women in today's world.

4. In your own words, describe the mestiza-womanist framework used here. What are the strengths and limitations of this interpretive framework?

5. How may women-of-color media talent (actors, writers, producers) have more (or may not) opportunities to create new images within our information society?

1. Discover three U.S. Latina television actors who appeared during the past three decades. For example, find one actor for 1990s, one for the 1980s, and one for the 1970s. Report their personal biographies to the class.

2. Discover three U.S. Latina film actors from the past three decades. Gather critical film reviews, from national news sources, about a movie that each actor appeared in. Discuss the role and character type played by the actor. Report to class.

3. Pick a film where Rosie Perez has a substantial role. Watch the entire film and conduct a cursory mestiza-womanist analysis on your own. An individual or team of two may do this assignment. Report to class.

4. Pick a film featuring any woman of color in a substantial role. Apply a mestiza-womanist interpretive framework. Write up your research. This written assignment may be done by an individual or a team of two.

REFERENCES

Anzaldua, G. (1987). *Borderlands: The new Mestiza*. San Francisco, CA: Spinsters/Aunt Lute.

Applebome, P. (Feb. 14, 1999). Trying to shake a stereotype but keep on being Rosie Perez. *New York Times*, Sunday late edition, section 2, p. 11. [available on Lexis Nexis]

Berg, C.R. (2002). *Latino images in film: Stereotypes, subversion, resistance*. Austin, TX: University of Texas.

Carstarphen, M. G. & Rios, D. I. (2003). Brown and Black women in Nancy Savoca's *The 24-Hour Woman*. In D. I. Rios & A. Mohamed (Eds.), *Brown and Black communication: Latino and African American conflict and convergence in mass media*. Westport, CT: Praeger.

Carstarphen, M. G. (1999). Gettin' real love: Waiting to exhale and film representations of womanist identity. In M. Meyers (Ed.), *Mediated women: Representations in popular culture* (pp.369-382). NJ: Hampton.

Cripps, T. (1993). *Making movies Black: The Hollywood message movie from World War II to the Civil Rights Era*. NY: Oxford.

Fernandez, C. A. (2000). La raza and the melting pot: A comparative look at multiethnicity. In Rosenblum, K. E. & Travis, T. C. (Eds.), *The meaning of difference: American constructions of race, sex and gender, social class, and sexual orientation* (pp.62-70). Boston: McGraw-Hill.

Fregoso, R. L. (1993). *The bronze screen: Chicana and Chicano film culture*. Minneapolis, MN: University of Minnesota.

Gaines, J. (1994). White privilege and looking relations: Race and gender in feminist film theory. In D. Carson, L. Dittmar, J. R. Welsch (Eds.), *Multiple voices in feminist film criticism* (pp.176-190). Minneapolis: University of Minnesota.

Gregory, D. (1993). Rosie Perez: The actress is turning Hollywood out! *Essence*. October, 24, 6, p. 48.

Hurtado, A. (1999). *The color of privilege: Three blasphemies on race and feminism*. Ann Arbor: University of Michigan.

Jones, J. (July-October, 1991). The new ghetto aesthetic. *Wide Angle*, 13, 3-4, 32-43.

hooks, b. (1990). *Yearning: race, gender, and cultural politics*. Boston, MA: South End Press.

Keller, G. D. (1994). *Hispanics and United States film: An overview and handbook*. Tempe, AR: Bilingual/Review Press.

Lee, S. with Jones, L. (1989). *Do the right thing*. [companion volume to the Universal Pictures film] NY: Simon and Schuster.

Lester, P. M. (1996). *Images that injure: Pictorial stereotypes in the media*. Westport, CT: Praeger.

Martin-Rodriguez, M. M. (2000). Hyenas in the pride lands: Latinos/as and immigration in Disney's *The Lion King*. *Aztlan*, 25, 1, 47-66.

McAdams, J. (1993). Perez ridin' high with new HBO show. *Billboard*. January 16, 105, 3, p.23.

Meyers, K. (1993). *Entertainment Weekly*. November 5, p. 36.

Noriega, C. (1992). *Chicanos and film*. MN: University of Minnesota.

Pearlman, C. (1994). Evil woman. *Entertainment Weekly*. March 4, p. 14.

Pettit, A. G. (1980). *Images of the Mexican American in fiction and film*. College Station, TX: Texas A&M.

Reid, M. A. (1993). *Redefining Black film*. Berkeley, CA: University of California.

Rios, D. I. (1996). Chicano cultural resistance with mass media, in R. De Anda, (Ed.), *Chicanas and Chicanos in contemporary society*. Boston, MA: Allyn and Bacon.

Rios, D. I.(1999). Latina/o experiences with mediated communication. In A. Gonzalez, M. Houston, and V. Chen (Eds.), *Our voices*. Los Angeles, CA: Roxbury.

Rios, D.I. (2000). Chicana/o and Latina/o gazing: Audiences of the mass media. In D. R. Maciel, I. D. Ortiz, and M. Herrera-Sobek (Eds.), *Chicano renaissance: Contemporary cultural trends*, (pp.169-190). Tucson, Arizona: University of Arizona.

Rios, D.I. & Carstarphen, M. G. (2001). Latinas and African American women in the film *The 24-Hour Woman*. Paper presented at the annual convention of the Association for Education in Journalism and Mass Communication (AEJMC), August.

Rodriguez, R. (2003). Broadway Rosie. *Hispanic*. March, pp. 36-38, 40.

Sandoval, C. (1998). Mestizaje as method: Feminists-of-color challenge the canon. In C. Trujillo (Ed.), *Living Chicana theory* (pp. 352-370). Berkeley, CA: Third Woman Press.

Shohat, E. & Stam, R. (1994). *Unthinking eurocentrism: Multiculturalism and the media*. NY: Routledge.

Thomas, L. E. (Winter,1998-99). Womanist theology, epistemology, and a new anthropological paradigm. *Cross Currents*, vol. 48, 4, 488-99.

Valdivia, A. N. (1998). Stereotype or transgression? Rosie Perez in Hollywood film. *The Sociological Quarterly*, 39, 3, 393-408.

Vargas, J. A. G.(1999). Who is the Puerto Rican woman and how is she?: Shall Hollywood respond? In Meyers, M. (Ed.), *Mediated women* (pp. 111-132). Cresskill, NJ: Hampton Press.

Vargas, J. A. G. (1996). A case study of Hollywood's constructed Puertorriqueña identity. *Studies in Latin American Popular Culture*, 15, 2-19.

Walker, A.(1983). *In search of our mothers' gardens*. New York: Harcourt Brace Jovanovich.

Wilson, C. & Gutierrez, F. (1995). *Race, multiculturalism, and the media*. Newbury Park: Sage.

Woll, A. L. (1980). *The Latin image in American film* (revised edition). Los Angeles: University of California.

Zeide, E. (1999). Can New York women balance both kids and a career? *The New York Post*. p. 28.

A Multidisciplinary Approach to Cultural Competence in Film and Television

*Gloria Ruiz, Beatriz Robinson, Susan Angulo,
Gary Feinberg, Judy Bachay and Edward Blackwell*

The debate concerning television and film's depiction of the ethnic and racial makeup of the United States is reaching new heights as the population becomes increasingly diverse. Further energizing this debate, the nation is experiencing an important paradigm shift in its race and ethnic relations. The assimilationist theme that shaped our social and legal policies regarding the treatment of immigrants and minorities during much of the 19th and 20th centuries has given way to a new theme in these relations known as pluralism. As we begin the 21st century, we have come to recognize and celebrate diversity in minority and cultural relations. The many "hyphenated" Americans are conceived as having unique cultural qualities that need and deserve to be recognized, preserved, and respected. Taken together, they now are understood to form a patchwork quilt, each contributing to the strength, beauty and successful functioning of the whole.

Correspondingly, the media industry today faces the challenge of attracting multicultural audiences who are proud of their traditions, desire to have them showcased, and who also enjoy increased purchasing power and amplified confidence in their rights and privileges as consumers. Indeed, it is not an easy task. To remain enterprising, the media need to produce products that appeal to broad audiences. Producers must provide programming interesting to mainstream audiences, select audiences and mixed markets (e.g., multigenerational families whose members represent varying levels of acculturation).

As such, independent filmmakers are acutely aware of the potential conflict between creating authentic multicultural product and creating product that puts the proverbial *"butts in seats."* The organizers of the Brazilian Film Festival in Miami, Florida, June 2-9, 2002, declared that the number one challenge shared by both Brazilian and U.S. independent film producers is how to express the cultural diversity of the regions and peoples of the Americas, yet still create a viable, successful product for the global marketplace.

The Brazilian Film Festival held in Miami Beach on June 5, 2002, included a seminar focusing on cultural diversity and films. At the seminar, Andre Lee, Marketing Director of Urban World Entertainment, noted that his company, which sponsors the largest Black film festival in the world every August in New York City, was initiated because, of the four billion dollars spent on entertainment in the world, 50 percent is spent by Latinos and Blacks. Providing a venue that reflects a world that is a great deal larger and a great deal more complex than the mainstream U.S. is an imperative. Lee believes that in the last year the audience has changed significantly and that people are ready to have their thinking and beliefs challenged by cinema. Diversity, thus, can be normalized and snapshots of cultural representations can be palatable.

Sergio Giral, Cuban film director of the film *Maria Antonia* among other recognized productions, also attended this conference. He believes there is a tremendous need for filmmakers to approach the reality of diversity from an *emic* approach; in other words, to represent cultures with an insider's perspective (as opposed to *etic*, which is a perspective from outside a culture). While most of his movies have been produced in Cuba, where politically imposed boundaries and limitations had an impact on authentic cultural expressions, he holds sacred the need to express a culture's unique identity through film. He contends that language is crucial to identity. For example, subtitles must be used rather than inauthentic accents. Both Lee and Giral concur that, despite one's desire to reach the United States film market, filmmakers must be true to their own cultures.

What is called for, then, are balanced and realistic productions that demonstrate acceptable levels of *cultural competence*. We use the term cultural competence to suggest that valuable representations of diverse groups reflect realistic, thoughtful and nuanced (as opposed to stereotypical) portrayals. Still, with few minorities in key positions (such as writers, producers and network executives) there is an apparent lack of both will and knowledge for creating authentic programming (Center for Media and Public Affairs, 1999; National Association for the Advancement of Colored People, 2001; National Rainbow Coalition, 2003; Collins, 2000; Writers Guild of America, 1998).

This paper identifies global questions to help film/television producers and critics discern if productions are culturally competent. We expect they can serve as a critical tool that film and television professionals can use to measure their success in adequately depicting diverse communities. We have used an interdisciplinary approach, including the fields of communications, psychology, linguistics, and liturgical practice, to serve as a foundation for our guidelines.

The concept of developing global questions for determining cultural competence in film and television originates in South Florida, an area whose multicultural communities expect to be adequately represented and respected. Not only is South Florida culturally diverse, but it is also experiencing a noticeable growth in the film and television industries. As of 1999, a state sponsored study of South Florida's film and entertainment industries found they generate over $2 billion, with 13,740 employees and 2,885 establishments (MGT of America Inc., 2000).

We focus our discussion of media appropriateness and effectiveness on Hispanics to provide our readers with a specific context for understanding the questions used to determine cultural competence. While our examples are taken from Hispanic realities, we suggest these guiding questions can serve to determine cultural competence for any ethnic group. First, we review how Hispanics have been portrayed in the media. Next, we explore the effects of inauthentic representations and their relationship to identity development and consumer choice. We follow that review with an examination of the characteristics and issues concerning Hispanics as an illustration of the relevance of, within and among group differences to legitimate media portrayals. Then, using linguistic depictions as an example, we consider current media concerns voiced by Hispanics in the Miami area.[1] Finally, using the "production" philosophy of the Catholic Church as a springboard, we present specific guidelines for cultural competence in media.

Rather than a didactic set of instructions for determining cultural competence, we structured the guidelines in a question format. The questions take into consideration that, while particular groups of people share specific characteristics, all groups have common concerns about how they are represented to others. For example, we assume all groups are concerned with the appropriate and respectful representation of their language and its usage. In this way, the guiding questions are applicable to any ethnic group, though they are illustrated herein through the Hispanic culture.

The guidelines encourage reflection on the possible existence of stereotypical portrayals and patterns in media productions. We define stereotypical portrayals as those limited in both breadth and depth, thus leading to skewed representations. For example, stereotypical depictions do not account for within group variety of language, color, socioeconomic status, physicality, geography, vocation and other cultural markers such as religion, political orientations and ceremonial customs. Stereotypical portrayals also can exist if certain group members (e.g., women, gays, lesbians) are consistently omitted. Furthermore, stereotypical representations tend to lack in contextual bases and are typically time-bound in their depictions (e.g., the vixen with long wavy hair, heavy make-up, long painted nails, costumed in tight skirts with high heels; or the silent housewife/domestic worker who is fearful, knows her place and is practically invisible).

Hispanic Hollywood

Hollywood and the television industry maintain an unimpressive record when it comes to the authentic representation of Hispanics. From the early days of silent films, Hispanic male characters have been, for the most part, lovers, buffoons, drunken and sleepy villains, charming Cisco Kid-*caballeros*, drug dealers and addicts, juvenile delinquents or other types of criminals or *bandidos*.

Stereotypical female characters also include buffoons along with vamps, spitfires, harlots, maids and the indigent (Kanellos, 1997, pp. 587-608; Barquin, 1998; Ramirez Berg, 2000). Some of the more notable films with these stereotypical depictions include *Bronco Billy and the Greaser* (1914), *The Four Horsemen of the Apocalypse* (1921), *Flying Down to Rio* (1933), *Mexican Spitfire* (1939), *the Mark of Zorro* (1920, 1940, 1974), *The Gang's All Here* (1943), *My Darling Clementine* (1946), *West Side Story* (1961) and *The Young Savages* (1961). Despite the growth and diversification of Hispanics in the U.S., stereotypical depictions have continued in later films such as in *Raiders of the Lost Arc* (1979), *Romancing the Stone* (1984), *Scarface* (1983), *Eight Million Ways to Die* (1986), *Colors* (1988), *Falling Down* (1993), *Clear and Present Danger* (1994), *Desperado* (1995) and *Six Days, Seven Nights* (1998), to name a few (Barquin, 1998; Ramirez Berg, 2000).

Historically, the Hollywood studios have forced many Hispanic actors to change their Spanish names to Anglo names. Directors and agents told them that they would not succeed in show business unless viewers saw them as non-Hispanic. Thus, Spanish-American Margarita Carmen Cansino became Rita Hayworth; Bolivian-American Raquel Tejada, Raquel Welch; Mexican-American Martín Estévez, Martin Sheen; and Cuban-American Rocky Echevarria, Steve Bauer. Fortunately, those days are over, and now most young Hispanic actors including Andy García, Cameron Díaz, Emilio Estévez, Jennifer López, John Leguizamo and others are able to keep their Spanish names and succeed in Hollywood.

Likewise, mainstream English language television has a history of portraying stereotypical Hispanic characters. Hispanic advocacy groups such as Children Now and the National Latino Children's Institute point out that Latino characters shown on television are mostly maids, janitors, drug lords or gang members, and serve as background to offset other main characters (The National Latino Children's Institute NLCI, 1997; Children Now, 2000). The few times Hispanic women appear on the screen or television, they continue to be stereotyped as exotic ladies or sexy spitfire women of loose morals who usually try, unsuccessfully, to conquer nice Anglo males who remain loyal to their Anglo wives or girlfriends. To explain this characterization strategy, Victoria Thomas (1998) suggests that Latin lovers were used in movies to appeal to non-Latino audiences. Examples in today's television programs (2002) include characters such as Rosario, the maid, in the television comedy "Will and Grace" (NBC), Fez in "That Seventies Show " (Fox) who is constantly marginalized because he is a "foreigner," and the spitfire reporter Lucía Rojas-Klein, a self-centered Cuban-American co-host in "Good Morning Miami" (NBC). This continued stereotyping brings to mind the question, "Where are the male and female Hispanic leaders, heroes and professionals on mainstream and prime time television fare who could offset these negative representations?"

Additionally, Latinos of color suffer further minimalization (i.e., a "double jeopardy" of exclusion based on ethnicity and race). Presently Spanish themed programs are relegated to Spanish language television. Through 1999, there were no English language television shows about an Hispanic family, even though there are more than 34 million Hispanics in the nation. Today, one can see *Resurrection Blvd* and follow the lives of a Mexican-American family, but only if one pays the premiums for cable television. For comedy shows about Latino families such as "Greetings from Tucson!" (WB) or the "George Lopez Show" (ABC), the jury is still out. One would hope that, as the networks develop Hispanic themed programs, they would integrate rather than block-schedule Hispanic programs, as are most African-American themed television programs.

Although Spanish language television networks such as Telemundo have attempted crossover programming, English-speaking television networks have not. Advertisers, however, perhaps more savvy regarding the Hispanic market, have begun to run minimally bilingual commercials to their sales advantage.

Traditionally, Hollywood producers and directors feared making movies about Hispanics because they thought they would lose money. That situation, too, is beginning to change as some "crossover movies" (movies that appeal to broad audiences) about Latinos, seen by Latino and non-Latino audiences, have had success at the box office. Among the more recent feature films are *A Walk in the Clouds* (1995), *Selena* (1997), *Dance with Me* (1998), *The Mask of Zorro* (1998), *Gabriela* (1999) and *Tortilla Soup* (2001).

To ensure this progress continues employment behind the cameras needs to improve. Even so, organizations such as the National Council of La Raza have denounced both the movie and television industries for failing to hire Latinos, not only as actors, but also as writers, directors and producers. According to a survey by the NAACP, of the 839 writers working on primetime television shows, 11 are Latino (Jackson, 2000). Coupled with the Screen Actors Guild (SAG) reports that the number of Hispanic members (4,852) is minimal compared to the 73,358 non-Hispanic Whites (Pachon, et al., 2000), we can see there is a significant need for improvement in Hollywood's hiring practices for key decision makers in film and television programming. Additionally, film schools themselves are not diverse in faculty or student popu-

lations, decreasing the likelihood that minorities are "in the pipeline" for significant media positions.

Finally, communications researchers such as Federico Subervi-Vélez (1999) find there is an insufficiency in sophisticated research analyzing portrayals and employment of Hispanics in the media. He calls for both in-depth and longitudinal studies that address Hispanics and media representation. Comprehensive studies such as *Don't Blink, Hispanics in Film and Television* (1994) need to be funded for analysis of film and television to address this lack of information and to understand trends in programming as it relates to Hispanic portrayals.

Negative Stereotypes, Media Invisibility, Inauthenticity, and Identity Development

Stereotypes themselves are not inherently inaccurate or socially dysfunctional. They often do contain an element of truth, simplify a complex world and make it possible to identify important predictors of people's actions. In addition, they help us to interpret ambiguous behavior and to provide readily available explanations for why certain people behave in a characteristic manner. They also are useful in evaluating members of different groups. Simply stated, stereotypes are cognitively efficient. When situations are complicated, involve multiple tasks or allow limited time for interpretation and resolution, as is often the case in media character portrayals, stereotypes offer readily available and cognitively inexpensive solutions, much as they do in real life. However, the mechanism by which stereotypes work includes ignoring differences among those in the outgroup while inflating similarities of those belonging to the in-group. Correspondingly, stereotypes oversimplify and exaggerate, thereby often causing serious harm.

This is especially problematic where members of the audience have a strong need to simplify their world (i.e., to structure it). Such individuals tend to ignore the situational forces that may affect a person's behavior and attribute that behavior instead to their innate nature (Kenrick,

Neuberg & Cialdini, 2002). Aggravating the dysfunctions of stereotyping even further is the fact they are affected significantly by the emotional state of the audience. Generally speaking, where the audience's emotions are highly aroused (e.g., when it is frightened, angered or elated) limited cognitive resources become taxed and recourse to the simple solutions offered by stereotyping are more likely to occur. At the same time, as Kenrick, Neuberg and Cialdini (2002) observe, almost every racial, ethnic or religious group has both negative and positive attributes that may be articulated into a stereotype. The perceiver's emotional mood can very much affect the quality of the stereotype constructed (i.e., whether it is favorable or unfavorable). For example, Esses and Zanna (1995) found that where a group of Canadian students were made angry they were more likely to view Native Indians, Pakistanis and Arabs unfavorably, and to devalue stereotype traits (e.g., dark skin) typically associated with these ethnic groups. Given that the mass media, and especially the film industry, often manipulate both the cognitive and emotional state of their audience when creating a character or constructing a story line, their attention to the negative consequences of stereotyping becomes all the more important.

Indeed, when minorities are repeatedly portrayed in limited stereotypic ways, they likely affect how the general public comes to perceive them in real life. This is especially true where the public's exposure to members of the minority group is restricted to media characterizations. Social psychologists Langley, O'Neal, Craig, and Yost (1992), among other researchers, observe that such portrayals go a long way in cultivating and perpetuating inaccurate and undesirable beliefs and feelings about minority groups. As sociologist Stephen Schaefer (2000) explains, the mass media are a powerful source for introducing stereotypes into everyday life. They create labels that take on such significance that people ignore facts that contradict those labels. A 1998 survey of boys and girls ages 10-17 asked, "How often do you see your race on television?" Over 70% of the White children responded "very often," compared to only 42% of African Americans, 22% of Latinos, and 16% of Asian Americans. Even more troubling, generally these young people view the White characters as affluent and well educated, while they view minority characters as "breaking the rules," "being lazy," and "acting goofy" (Children Now, 1998).

There is a vast body of scholarly literature generated by behavioral scientists that identifies and elaborates the many negative consequences of stereotyping as well as the mechanisms through which they operate. Stereotypes influence how people feel about themselves and, equally important, how they interact with others. In their research, Sigelman and Tuch (1997) found that if people feel others hold incorrect, if not also extremely disparaging, attitudes, it would invariably make it difficult to have harmonious relations. Similarly, psychologists Claude Steele and Joshua Aronson (1995) have conceptualized the term "stereotype vulnerability" to denote an observed phenomenon where members of minority groups fail to live up to their potential and actually play into the negative stereotype. Minorities are not as productive as they can be when they are aware of a negative stereotype due to the fear they inevitably will prove the stereotype.

To illustrate, Steele and Aronson (1995) found an experimental group of African-Americans who believed a test they were given measured psychological factors scored just as well as a comparative White cohort. However, those African-Americans who thought the test measured core abilities and limitations scored significantly lower than their White counterparts. Alternatively, White participants scored equally well regardless of their beliefs about what the test measured. Other examples of stereotype vulnerability abound. Shih, Pittinsky, and Ambady (1999) found women score more poorly on math tests when they thought they were competing with men than when gender was not made salient. Similarly, Aronson et al. (1999) observed White American males performed worse on a math test when they thought they were competing with Japanese males than when ethnicity was not specified.

Related to the dysfunctions of stereotype threat is the fact that negative stereotypes over time can cause groups to dis-identify with certain otherwise socially desirable or rewarded behavior. To illustrate, at least one study has found the self-image of Black children in the tenth grade is less tied to academic achievement than in the eighth grade, a pattern not evidenced for White children (Osborn, 1995). It has been suggested that this rejection of school performance as significant to one's self-image is really a protective adaptation, helping young Blacks maintain a positive self image when confronted by negative stereotyping (Kenrick, Neuberg, & Cialdini, 2002). In the long run, however, it is highly dysfunctional, leaving them ill prepared to succeed in a world where intellectual skills are so crucial.

Other indirect negative consequences of stereotyping include the huge economic and social costs of maintaining an underclass, a diminished ability to make accurate predictions and assessments of specific others, loss of potential friendships and the like. Also, the targets of negative stereotypes can never be certain about why they are being treated either well or badly. Is it because of something they have or have not done (i.e., their achieved performance), or because of who they are (i.e., some ascribed group membership they hold)? Being able to gauge these reactions of others as a form of social feedback is crucial to one's self-image, self-evaluation and self-esteem.

William Isaac Thomas (1923), a sociologist, developed the concept of "wish fulfillment prophecy" to explain the fact that a person or group described as having a particular set of characteristics begins to display the very traits attributed to them. In effect, it predicts what happens to them in life. Thus, if Mexican-American women are seen as lazy and quick tempered as Weitz (1992) found, it should not be surprising to find that they may come to lack motivation and self-control in real life. This is especially likely where such a negative stereotype is the most salient and consistent image they see of themselves in the media. Still, the situation certainly is not hopeless. It logically follows that more positive, realistic and subtle portrayals of Hispanics and other minorities in the media should help reduce stereotyping and prejudice (Evuleocha & Ugbah, 1989; Donovan & Leivers, 1993).

Lastly, there is a note of caution with respect to any media effort at reducing negative stereotyping by simply highlighting more positive traits of the minority group. Sometimes, including more flattering characterizations of the minority group along with the negative ones only serves to make the negative ones seem more authentic, while at the same time allowing the portrayer to be *perceived* as unbiased and honest in the characterization created.

For many years, media researchers have debated the psychological effects of film and television. What we do know is that (a) visual media construct reality, present ideologies and give value messages (Silver, 1993), and that (b) people learn from modeled behavior (Bandura, 1986). In the case of Hispanics, role models in film and television are few and usually negatively stereotyped. Conversely, in those rare cases where Hispanics appear assimilated and have minimal Hispanic characteristics, they are portrayed as good, law abiding, intelligent, productive and attractive. In essence, it appears less Hispanic is "better."

Keeping in mind learning occurs from imitation and modeling, the content of film and television productions can provide a rich contextual field that fosters healthy psychological development. Given that much of film and television is geared toward adolescent audiences (Corliss, 1998; Leo, 1998; Rapping, 1993; "Demo Derby," 2000) and that Hispanics are the second largest consumers in the nation (Bannon, 2000), it is important to understand how Hispanic teenagers, and similarly other ethnic groups, develop a sense of self-identity and how this self-identity may be affected by media models. Indeed this should be a pertinent question for media producers and critics as identity greatly affects choice and behavior, including consumer choices.

The meaning of any given concept or experience is not universal for all associated individuals. Even the most common of constructs contains, for us as individuals, connotations unique to our personal psyches and experiences. Thus, meaning-making is a complex process requiring an examination of its component parts, with particular emphasis on the element of personal identity. People understand the world vis-à-vis their own identity; it is the dominant lens by which we make sense of the images around us. Identity formation deals with the central questions "Who am I?" and "Why am I here?" These questions merge during the turbulence of adolescence, seeking immediate resolution. Resolution includes conscious examination of all the integral areas of one's life such as the development and acceptance of an ethnic identity essential to the development of a healthy self-concept (Phinney & Rotherham, 1987). In this way ethnicity is central to the development of identity formation, as are gender, sexuality, religion and socioeconomic status. This process of self-definition becomes particularly challenging when the host culture is exclusionary.

Minority adolescents must confront and resolve two salient issues in order to commit to a secure self-identity. One issue is exploring and taking a stand with regard to their status as minority group members. The primary source of stress for these adolescents is ignorance and stereotyping at one end of a continuum, prejudice and discrimination at the other end. A second issue is living with different sets of norms and values; those applying to the ethnic native culture and those applying to the majority values. If adolescents do not have the opportunity to explore their ethnicity in a positive light, they can lose their sense of heritage and become alienated from both their native culture and the host culture (Phinney, 1990).

Discussing current media depictions of Hispanics, a 16-year-old female first generation North American originally from Argentina stated, "Hispanics are not in any of our television shows (e.g., Ally McBeal, Dawson's Creek, 90210) and Jennifer López isn't taken seriously as an actress." Another 19-year-old Nicaraguan said, "Whose media? Yours [English], or mine [Spanish]?" (personal interviews). As these comments suggest, the acculturated first generation Hispanic may not be able to identify with or relate to either the "Spanish" or the "American" depictions of self and experience.

Spanish language programming, such as Univision's Mexican-based *Despierta America,* provides an example of programming with positive Hispanic role models. The program shows

that even in a news format, positive representations of Hispanics are possible. Independent films also can offer examples of authentic representations, presenting both positive and less constructive aspects of culture, ultimately arriving at legitimate, nuanced portrayals. The idea of balanced depictions is key.

What message does the negative characterization of Hispanics convey to media audiences? Undoubtedly, audiences can assume Hispanics, at best, should be accepted only when they lose their ethnic qualities. We question the unfortunate trend of not casting Hispanic actors in varied ethnic roles in film and television productions. Just as Al Pacino played a Cuban in *Scarface,* why are Hispanics (and by extension, other ethnic actors) not cast as characters of varied ethnic origins and walks of life? This unfortunate bias tends to deny the diversity within U.S. society and the talent of ethnic actors.

But who are Hispanics? Are Latinos, or other ethnic minority groups, a monolithic, homogeneous group portrayed authentically through a limited number of stereotypes? To understand the significant nature of within- and between-group differences and the importance of incorporating such differences for authentic media productions, we use the Hispanic culture as a model for analysis.

Hispanics: A Model for Understanding Group Similarities and Differences

Currently, with a population of 37 million (www.census.gov), Hispanics are the fastest growing minority group in the United States today, and within the next few years they will be the largest ethnic minority group in the U.S. By 2020, one in five U.S. children will be of Hispanic origin, and by 2050 Hispanics will comprise 25 percent of the U.S. population. The increase of Hispanics in the U.S. population is one of the most dramatic demographic shifts in American history (Robinson, 1998). They are a young and burgeoning group of consumers who are attracting the attention of businesses and marketers.

Clearly Hispanics are a diverse group for whom simple labels are inadequate in addressing their differing needs, realities and identities. The very term "Hispanic" fails to convey their diversity. Nationally, the term "Hispanic" is often a source of confusion and debate. Some peoples of Spanish-speaking descent adamantly reject the label "Hispanic" since it is viewed as a label created by the United States government (Davis, 1994). Other Latinos reject the term as a symbol of Spanish colonialism. The term "Latino" is one that emerged largely from the southwest area of the U.S. and thus not adopted by eastern Hispanics (Davis, 1994). Most Hispanics, however, prefer to be addressed in terms of their national origin, for example, Mexican or Mexican-American (Ortíz, 1993). The Latino National Political Survey revealed that most Hispanics do not identify themselves as members of a "pan-ethnic group—Hispanic or Latino—but as members of their specific national group" (Marger, 1997, p. 314). Many Hispanics use the word "Hispanic" only to distinguish themselves from "Anglos" (American Federation of Labor and Congress of Industrial Organizations, 1989, p. 104), but not to describe themselves among themselves. Unlike the "mix and merger" that took place among European immigrants to the United States, the various sub-groups of Hispanics have retained a strong sense of cultural and national identity.

The complexity of the "Hispanic" or "Latino" label warrants caution in imputing a common psyche to members of the group. This is because the word "Hispanic" includes people of European, African, Asian, Native-American and mixed ancestry who differ in culture, nationality, religion and historical relationship to the United States. As Oboler explained:

"The term Hispanic fails to recognize the extremely rich ethnic and racial diversity of Latin Americans, for example, Argentines of Italian, German, or French descent, Mexicans of Irish or Japanese ancestry, Cubans with Spanish, Lebanese, African or Chinese forebears; Peruvians of English, Russian-Jewish or Inca lineage; Venezuelans of Polish or Uruguayan stock; Brazilians of Korean or Greek heritage—the

varieties go on and on. And, of course, there are those many Latin Americans who are entirely or partly of African or American Indian ancestry with some of the above thrown in" (1995, p. 15).

We cannot assume all members (e.g., Mexicans, Puerto Ricans, Cubans) of a group, in this case, Hispanics, relate equally to a global group identity. Racial and/or ethnic minorities' attitudes may vary from wanting to assimilate totally into the host culture to rejecting it totally (Atkinson, Morten, & Sue, 1998).

Social researchers, however, have found six variables—race, language, time of arrival in the United States, national origin, minority status, and class — that divide the Hispanic population into distinct subpopulations (Sullivan, 1985; Oboler, 1995). A review of several of these variables highlights the great heterogeneity among Hispanic sub-groups.

NATIONAL ORIGIN

The term Hispanic attempts to label homogeneously peoples of 30 different countries who live in the U.S. As noted earlier, the three largest Hispanic groups in the U.S. are persons of Mexican, Puerto Rican and Cuban origin. They represent 60, 12, and 5 percent of the Hispanic population, respectively (Garza, 1994). The experiences of these groups and others in this country are quite different generally because of their past histories, economic opportunities, education and level of bilingualism (The Federal Glass Ceiling Commission, 1995).

Geographical concentration within the U.S. has a great impact on the experiences of the national subgroups of Hispanics: Mexican Americans live primarily in the Southwest, most Puerto Ricans live in the Northeast, while most Cuban Americans live in Florida (American Federation of Labor and Congress of Industrial Organizations, 1989). Based on such variables, Hispanics of differing national origins have assimilated differently. For example, Cuban women demonstrate higher levels of education and employment and are much more prone to exogamy (marriage outside one's group).

RACE

With regard to race, Hispanics in the U.S. include people who are descendants of the original Caucasian-Spanish colonists, of native Indians and of African slaves (Sullivan, 1985). In the 1990 census, 51.7 percent of Hispanics identified themselves as White, while 42.7 percent self-identified as another race. As the Ford Foundation (1984) report on Hispanics declared, "It [the Hispanic population] is multiracial, containing Blacks, Browns, and Whites" (p. 6). This reality can be demonstrated easily just looking at the three largest Hispanic subgroups in the United States: Mexicans, Puerto Ricans and Cubans. While Mexicans can be either basically European or Indian, *mestizos*, a physical type combining European and Indian traits, overwhelmingly dominates the Mexican population. Puerto Ricans' racial background is primarily European and African, but also includes Native-American ancestry. While Puerto Ricans run the color spectrum, most are "racially 'intermediate'" (Marger, 1997, p. 283), sometimes referred to as mulatto (Atkinson et al, 1998; Moore & Pachon, 1985). Cuban Americans are the most racially homogeneous of the three main Hispanic subgroups, with most Cuban Americans labeled as White.

> "Cuba itself is a racially variegated society, however, suggesting that the Cuban immigration has been racially selective... The majority of early Cuban immigrants were of higher social status in Cuba and hence whiter in color, whereas many of the more recent immigrants have been of lower class origins and of darker color" (Marger, 1997, p. 284).

LANGUAGE

Hispanics vary widely in racioethnic ways and language as well. Not all Hispanics speak Spanish as their primary language (Castex, 1998; Oboler, 1995; Sullivan, 1985). Certainly, this is true for many Hispanics in the United States. A survey of approximately 5,000 Hispanic youngsters in Miami-Dade County, Florida, revealed that 88 percent preferred English ("Kids of Cuban," 1998). In fact, Hispanics from their various countries of origin speak five major European languages: Spanish, Portuguese, French, Dutch and English. Some Hispanics also speak Native-American languages including Quechua, Mayan, Aymara and Guarani. Thus, for many Hispanics, Spanish may be their second language. Additionally, Hispanics speak a variety of regional Spanish dialects (Castex, 1998).

Despite their differences, there are substantial similarities uniting Hispanics. These similarities can be used as the basis for study and comparison, ultimately arriving at a better understanding of the subgroups of Hispanics and of the overall population. The literature on Hispanics demonstrates their strong traditional value system. "The Hispanic culture is filled with 'old fashioned' virtues such as devotion to God, family, and work" (American Federation of Labor and Congress of Industrial Organizations, 1989, p. 105). Hispanics especially value their traditions. Even the often negatively stereotyped concept of "machismo" is rooted in positive traditional values. Within the Hispanic community, the term often refers to one who is a good and responsible provider for his family (Knouse et al.,1992).

In a meta-analysis of literature on Hispanics, the University of South Florida (Gurba & Briscoe, 1989) identified shared cultural characteristics of many Latinos. These traits include:

1. Loyalty to family group
2. Non-assertive behavior and acceptance of authority figure
3. Cultural pride and respect for Hispanic heritage
4. Mutual interdependence
5. Age and gender as determinants of role and status
6. Emphasis on Spanish language

Vázquez et al. (1991) described three cardinal values common to Hispanic subgroups: *respeto* (respect), *personalismo* (a value on personal contact) and *obligación a la familia* (priority given to the needs of the family unit over those of the individual). In addition, others have found that despite distinct permutations found among Hispanics, language, religion and cultural background serve as common ground for them

(Acosta-Belén & Sjostrom, 1988; Ford Foundation, 1984; Kanellos, 1997; Moore & Pachon, 1985).

Because Hispanics have retained their culture to a greater extent than other immigrants to the U.S., they have been able to preserve and enhance that culture, passing on knowledge, beliefs, values and customs from one generation to the next (Atkinson, Morten, & Sue, 1998). Nevertheless, despite the growing number of Hispanics, many misconceptions about the group remain.

Spanish Language: An Illustration of Current Concerns

As an example of current Hispanic concerns related to the media, we present the significant issue of language depiction. The Hollywood film industry must recognize that the demographic changes occurring in the nation are changing the linguistic sophistication of their audience. The U.S. Hispanic market of 37 million includes the second and third generation young, urban, bilingual and professionally successful Hispanic. The "generation ñ" is linguistically and culturally sophisticated and not impressed by blatant ignorance of their language and culture.

We do not have to go far to find examples of at least two types of linguistic incompetence. They include miscasting and incorrect translations. First, there is miscasting roles with actors having a non-native pronunciation of a language to play a native. For example, the movie, *The Perez Family*, a Samuel Goldwyn Co. production (1995), was directed by a native of India and featured non-Latino actors with Marissa Tomei in the lead role. The movie was short-lived. In part, this failure can be attributed to the poor linguistic portrayals.

Successful Latino themed programming is likely related to the extent to which the production includes Latino talent, both on and off camera. Even then, producers must be careful not to use actors who speak dialects other than the one called for in a particular role. A 1998 independent film from Texas, *Conección Cubana*, tried to enter the Miami market in 2001. This produc-

tion initially engendered interest until the film was previewed in Miami. The actors playing Cubans were Mexicans speaking Spanish with a Mexican accent. Not surprisingly, commentary such as, "You mean to say that there are no Cuban-born actors in Texas? Can't Mexican actors learn a Cuban accent and lexicon? Should I take this as a personal insult?" resounded during the preview (Hispanic Film Festival Selection Committee preview of film October 1998).

The language used by a character that creates a stereotype puts into question the credibility of the character. Audiences no longer know who or what the character is supposed to represent. Of interesting note, the *faux pas* is not limited to Hollywood.

The Spanish film industry has been dealing with the varieties of Spanish for decades. In order to sell Spanish films in Latin America, they had to address the influence of indigenous and Black dialects, Italian and even English. The document titled "Palabras equívocas o malsonantes en España, HispanoAmerica y Filipinas" published by Radiotelevisión Española (1970) guides Spanish film and television producers in developing programs that use language that is accepted in the Spanish speaking world. It offers 63 pages of words to be avoided and lists alphabetically common mistakes that will sound an alarm in the viewer's mind. For example, words like *culo* or *coger*, part of normal speech in Spain, have vulgar meanings in Latin America.

While this effort is commendable, it is important for linguists to continually revise these references. A case in point is how Spanish language usage has changed for post-Castro Cubans. *Ajiaco* (a Cuban vegetable soup) is now referred to as *caldoza*. Thus a film representing today's Cuba would appear implausible, particularly to audiences living on the island, should the dated word *ajiaco* be used.

The second example of linguistic incompetence is blatantly incorrect translations. Just imagine Spaniards anxious to see their own Antonio Banderas in a Hollywood film. Antonio had finally made it big and the film is about...what? The English title was translated into "Desperado," but the supposed Spanish translation used a nonexistent word. (Perhaps the translators meant *Desesperados*.) While English speaking U.S. audiences may recognize the word *desperado* and assume it refers to a villain, this word has no meaning in Spanish.

The considerable effort that goes into researching historical accuracy should extend to researching linguistic accuracy. As the U.S. film industry tries to communicate in a multilingual, multicultural mode to reach wider audiences, it should draw on the body of work educators have produced in cross-cultural communication. Educators believe cross-cultural miscommunication can be avoided by understanding the powerful differences separating people. The field of education is interested in breaking down stereotypes and teaching factual information about cultural and linguistic differences such as personal space, patterns of touching, etiquette and ritual, expressions of emotions, ideas about edible and delicious food, gestures, courtship and speech patterns.

U.S. producers do not have to look very hard for accurate information,[2] with such significant Hispanic presence in the United States. It is a matter of fundamental respect, integrity in dramatic representation and skillful practice in film and television production, to understand the nuances, differences and similarities among Hispanics.

The following section reviews how the Catholic Church has developed liturgies that resonate with Hispanics. As evocative, multi-sensory productions, liturgies can be likened to other media productions and demonstrate culturally competent ways of communicating with audiences.

The Catholic Church and Multicultural Outreach: A Culturally Competent Model for Film and Television

The Roman Catholic Church has been engaged in dialogue with the media since the publication of the *Decree on Social Communications* (Flannery, 1980). At the national level, the United States bishops have established the Office of Film and Television. It could be, however, that the Church's work in relation to its religious ceremonies may be the most helpful for this conversation.

One of the outgrowths of the Church's reforms affecting religious observances has been the concern for full and active participation of the congregation. When the assembly comes from different countries or ethnic communities, the task of creating a worship experience that includes everyone becomes challenging. Like good film making, good ceremonies involve local leaders and planners, asking the most helpful questions about the content of the celebration (comparable to a film) and the assembly (comparable to the stars and supporting cast).

Before the 1960s, the Roman Catholic Church addressed diversity by using Latin as a common language for its services and established parishes that addressed special needs of church members who could not be addressed through the use of Latin. In the United States, the Irish, Germans, Italians, Poles and other groups found comfort in their "own" parishes that provided culturally familiar activities. Nonetheless, with the declining use of Latin in the liturgy and the shifting demographic patterns in the United States, parish leaders needed other solutions to care for the spiritual needs of ethnically diverse congregations.

In 1998, the Federation of Diocesan Liturgical Commissions published *Guidelines for Multicultural Celebrations* (Guidelines). To understand the effectiveness of parish celebrations (or productions), the Federation suggested leaders and planners ask three broad questions about how the words and gestures of each liturgy are selected. The questions are: (1) Who makes the selection? (2) How are the words and gestures for each liturgy selected? and (3) How is the liturgy enacted? As with all good communications, these questions and their corresponding answers focus on the audience or, in the case of liturgical planning, on the congregation.

The most important consideration is the extent to which the leadership involved in the planning and execution of the celebration represents the various cultures found in the local community. While a diverse team leadership does not guarantee absolute cultural representation, it is a good start. Such diverse leadership ensures that the cultural requirements of the parishioners are considered, thereby encouraging fuller participation in the ceremonies.

When planning liturgies (staging the event), the planners (producers) need to consider carefully both the verbal and nonverbal elements. A diverse congregation (the cast and audience) experiences and understands color, decoration and liturgical objects in a variety of ways. For example, an African liturgy may incorporate the banana tree, since in parts of Africa the banana tree is used as a symbol of welcome at liturgies. Another example is the use of native musical instruments in musical performances of the celebration. For selecting effective language, careful consideration of vocabulary and word choice is critical to a successful celebration.

Next, the appropriate cast of characters needs to enact the celebrations. It is deemed important that representatives from the different communities are visible at a liturgy. In this case, the celebrant (the star) and the other liturgical celebrants and staff (supporting actors) should represent members of their audience.

The broad questions and specific recommendations of the *Guidelines* represent the best thinking of the Roman Catholic Church in the United States to provide active and full participation in the liturgy for multicultural communities. Indeed, there are many similarities between the concerns of TV and film executives and liturgical planners. Both must deal with the hopes and dreams of increasingly diverse populations. Both must stay focused on their primary message while respecting the variety of ways in which a message can be communicated and received. The three broad questions raised by the Federation's *Guidelines for Multicultural Celebrations* can provide an ideal beginning for TV and film executives and their staff to address diversity in TV and film.

Our discussion of Hispanics and the media herein is presented to serve as a model for pre-production research, ultimately leading to authentic casting and storytelling. Stereotypical portrayals discounting differences of national origin, socio-economic status, geography, physicality, linguistics and other nuances of culture (e.g., food and political world-views) will only continue to alienate the growing number of Hispanics and other racioethnic minority media consumer groups.

Guiding Questions to Address Cultural Competence

As we have suggested, a culturally competent communications industry requires accurate depiction of the human experience in their authentic and unique expressions. Although this article focused on Hispanics for the purpose of illustrating salient issues, we have formulated the guiding questions in a global manner so they can be used for determining the *cultural competence* of a film or television production with regard to any cultural group.

Guidelines

GUIDELINE 1

(Invisibility/under representation) - Media producers should ensure that minorities are proportionately represented in all aspects of production. (e.g., writing, producing, directing, acting and scheduling of programs).

■ **Are reliable sources or consultants sought for information about the cultural groups portrayed?** There is a varied pool of consultants available from which to choose. These include well-trained media professionals who are intimately knowledgeable with the major cultural groups. These consultants can be either indigenous or persons who have studied media, anthropology, sociology or popular culture, and who know the argot of a culture along with the social, cultural ways and artistic values of a group, including the ways of dress, music, and fashion. The consultants should be knowledgeable in the history of the culture and the language in addition to being attuned to its contemporary dimensions. Moreover, they should be sensitive to the racial issues and prejudices within the culture. Therefore, a team of consultants can best fulfill this mission.

The full complement of production workers from the producer to the stage manager, including screen writers, casting agents and directors, should understand that the differences within group members are far greater than differences between cultural groups. While Latinas may typically have brown hair and eyes, a sophisticated production worker could determine that a blonde and green-eyed Latina may be more appropriately cast and that such Latinas do exist. It is important that production workers seek out a support staff that has had experiences with various cultural groups both professional and personal. Such experiences should result in a greater sensitivity of the many ways in which diversity can manifest itself within any one cultural group. The nationality of a consultant does not guarantee that one is fully versed in the nuances that characterize that cultural group. Simply stated, being American does not make a person an expert in American culture. Similarly, being Cuban does not make a person an expert in Cuban culture. It is even worse to assume that, for instance, because one is Mexican, he or she therefore knows or can represent all Hispanic cultures.

■ **Do storylines and character portrayals include significant representation of minority groups?** The elements of significance include that cultural groups have major speaking parts and contribute to the story line such as in lead roles or critical supporting characters. In 2050, one in four Americans will be of Hispanic descent. At minimum, media professionals should be working toward that kind of proportional representation in the media. Furthermore, program producers should look beyond national population averages and consider the indigenous population of a region. A proportional representation of the minorities in the region should be reflected in a production. This does not mean that minorities cannot play bit parts, as the industry saying goes, "There are no small parts, just small actors." The problem arises when minorities are relegated to small parts and are not given opportunities to play starring roles or strong supporting characters. Providing abundant opportunity for the former in no way com-

pensates for a dearth of opportunities for the latter. Likewise, a series of leading roles as negative characters (i.e., a vixen, murderer or gangster), must be balanced by similar opportunities to play positive roles such as professionals, positive leadership roles, or conforming mainstream characters.

■ **Are culturally diverse workers actively sought and employed in all aspects of the production?** Behind-the-camera positions also contribute to how representations are defined. Positions ranging from director to camera technician can make an important difference in how a particular group is portrayed. Therefore, it is important that the range of positions within a production include professionals who are knowledgeable and respect the featured group.

■ **Are culturally competent television and film productions scheduled during optimal times to achieve maximum exposure?** To avoid marginalization and limiting viewership, television programs should be scheduled during prime time viewing hours, and films released during appropriate seasonal schedules. For example, Christmas themed films should not be shown in the summer. Moreover, summer is considered blockbuster debuts for films and fall season is the debut of television fare.

GUIDELINE 2

(Authenticity) Productions should be accurate in their depictions of cultural groups.

■ **Do the images depict the complexity of the cultural group represented? Are certain group members consistently omitted?** In other words, productions that account for within group variety with respect to aspects of personal identity (e.g., age, socioeconomic status, vocation and political orientation) gay, lesbian, single professional women, racial diversity, economic diversity, age, weight, differently-abled, and class achieve more veracity in their depictions.

■ **Are actors well trained in the accent used to represent a particular group?** As with any film or television production, accurate representations of accents are a necessary ingredient to give portrayals authenticity. Accent reflects ethnicity, social class and the historical period of the story. Anything less than authentic accents demeans the Hispanic culture that is represented and loses credibility among audiences. Yet, actors with Mexican or Columbian accents are often used to represent the more than 33 Hispanic nationalities, and non-Hispanic actors do not receive sufficient training in accent reduction and pronunciation. Non-Hispanic actors as well as Hispanic actors of differing nationalities must receive sufficient training regarding specific accents because the linguistic interference of the native accent can make the representation incomprehensible or absurd.

■ **Do vocabulary and grammar reflect the language used during the represented time of the group portrayed?** To ensure the historical authenticity of the lexicon or its timeliness for the film, the linguistic features of that era should be researched.

■ **Is the grammar correct?** Scripts need to follow patterns of universal language acquisition. For example, a native speaker would not make the same mistakes as a second language speaker.

■ **Are translations accurate?** It is not acceptable to merely add a letter or syllable to an English word as adding an 'o' to indicate Spanish is being spoken or to create non-existent words that sound Spanish. In addition, literal translations can diminish the authenticity of a script. A literal translation as simple as the use of the possessive can invalidate a line. In Spanish, the possessive differs from English usage when referring to the body. Thus, where English speakers say *my* hand, Spanish speakers say *the* hand.

■ **Are portrayals lacking in contextual basis or are they time bound in their depictions?** In the case of Hispanics, Latinas are still portrayed mainly as submissive housewives, domestic workers, or sexual vixens. A balanced reality needs depictions of Hispanic women/Latinas who are doctors, lawyers, teachers, business women, and other professionals. Latinas' personality characteristics include women who are aggressive, demure and sexual. In other words, a full range of personalities, educational levels, occupations, religious preferences, moral practices and lifestyles would best reflect the Latina reality.

GUIDELINE 3

(Negative stereotyping) - Media producers should ensure negative stereotypical portrayals are not the predominant patterns for describing cultural groups in dramas, including historical depictions.

■ **What messages do the portrayals convey about the cultural groups?** Within programs there should be recognition of more centrist and positive characters. Equally important, across productions, positive portrayals should counterbalance negative portrayals in the cultural images communicated throughout various productions. For example, Latino characters can be portrayed as achievers, successful in business and family life, wholesome, civically involved, sound parental models, highly reflective rather than emotional and the full panoply of human potentiality.

■ **Do elements of the productions such as language use and physicality offer an alternative to commonly found stereotypes in film and television?** In the case of Latinas, women alternative portrayals of thoughtful and powerful people (without being hypersexualized) can counteract the submissive, oppressed and emotionally driven Latina character.

■ **What responses or reactions might audiences undergo in relation to the media representations of the portrayed group?** Producers need to consider whether the representation of the minority culture incites violence and leaves the audience with inaccurate and negative images and beliefs. Indeed, audiences are best left with a better understanding of the reality of diversity and an enhanced view of minorities. Producers also need to consider the response of minority viewers who may internalize external definitions of self as portrayed and communicated through the visual media. Even flawed characters, when presented as complex and multidimensional, can reduce the negative response of the audience. Ideally, producers should seek to balance portrayals in a production. If negative portrayals are needed for the story line, then these should be balanced with positive representations of the same cultural group with which the audience can positively identify.

- **How might audiences' worldview be influenced by the portrayals represented in the production?** Presentations can expand the audience's appreciation for diversity or they can lead to a type of xenophobia and reaffirm pre-existing prejudices. For example, in the film *A Walk in The Clouds*, the Hispanic father played by Giancarlo Giannini is represented as a hot headed macho man who destroys his own farm because of his inability to control his temper, which contrasts with the film *Guess Who's Coming to Dinner*, in which Sidney Poitier plays a level headed kind and professional man who eventually wins the acceptance of his resistant and prejudiced Anglo father-in-law.

- **Does the humor used in the production make a social commentary that is offensive or stereotypical?** Offense is often considered a necessary ingredient for social comment that humor sometimes addresses. Nonetheless, when no redeeming quality is conveyed in the commentary, the humor can become mean spirited. A good example of how humor can be used to lessen the negative effects of biting social comments can be found in the award winning show *Bernie Mack*. Bernie Mack, the main character, uses humor to comment on his experiences and perspective on raising children. His comments could be considered offensive, but through his use of humor, he redeems himself, as audiences understand his love and compassion for children.

Endnotes

1. In part, the Academic Roundtable, "Cultural Competence in the Film Industry," April 24, 1999, these authors coordinated at the 1999 Miami Hispanic Film Festival, gave us a comprehensive view of the issues faced by producers of Hispanic film.

2. The web address http://www.hispanicfilm.com and e-mail address jangulo@hispanicfilm.com provides the names and addresses of participants in the Miami Latino Film Festival including producers and directors of Hispanic films, academics and film critics who specialize in Hispanic culture and media. We encourage film and television professionals to contact this organization along with other experts to insure they obtain a broad based perspective for their projects.

Acknowledgements

We thank our readers, Dr. Phil Shepardson, Dr. Tony Fernandez and Dr. Raul Fernandez-Calienes, for their support and feedback.

Name: _____

Date: _____

1. If you were conducting a research project on the impact of negative stereotypes on an audience, discuss the elements you would be looking for and how different audiences might be affected.

2. Discuss some of the benefits of using positive and negative stereotypes in television or the movies. What are some of the negative consequences that should concern us?

3. What is the impact of the media on the spaces in which we live? How do the media impact our neighborhoods, the way in which we interact within our living communities?

4. How do the media contribute to the way that we make meaning about our purpose in life, and how do the media help us resolve universal questions about the meaning of life and death.

5. How would you begin to create a conscious awareness of the impact of media with respect to your own personal world view? Where and how do you start?

1. If you were producing a movie about a Cuban-American political candidate running for office whose Argentinian-born wife was abducted by a group of Columbian terrorists seeking to influence drug trafficking policy, how would you go about locating your talent to ensure that it is authentic, culturally competent and intelligible to an American audience?

2. Select any film you have recently seen which has at least one member of a minority group as a principal character. What are some of the things you would point to that would suggest the film was discriminatory and/or prejudicial with respect to that character?

3. Procure an issue of a television advertisement targeted to an ethnic audience. Choose two or three images that you believe represent a variety of portrayals. Write a sentence or two about each image. Which (if any) of these images might be classified as pluralistic? What other media functions do the images seem to fulfill?

4. Create a comparative rubric by collecting data from two hours of broadcast television. Describe the portrayals, including stereotypes and positive characteristics, the content and the type of program such as reality, sitcom, drama or news. Based on the data, identify which programs in what time slots emphasize negative portrayals or insufficient portrayals of diverse groups.

REFERENCES

American Federation of Labor and Congress of Industrial Organizations. (1989). *Workers kaleidoscope: 2000.* Washington, DC: Author.

Acosta-Belén, E., & Sjostrom, B.R. (Eds.) (1988). *The Hispanic experience in the United States contemporary issues and perspectives.* New York: Praeger.

Aronson, J., Lustina, M.J., God, C. et al. (1999). When White men can't do math: Necessary and sufficient factors in stereotype threat. *Journal of Experimental Social Psychology, 35,* 29-46.

Atkinson, D.R., Morten, G., & Sue, D.W. (1998). *Counseling American minorities.* Boston: McGraw-Hill.

Bandura, A. (1986). *Social foundations of thought and action: A social cognitive theory.* Englewood Cliffs, NJ: Prentice Hall.

Bannon, L. (2000, April 6). Latin translation: Is the country ready for a Hispanic 'Rocky'? *The Wall Street Journal,* A1.

Barquin, N. (1998, September 23). The Latin lover and the Latina vamp. Retrieved November 15, 2002, from the World Wide Web: http://www.trincoll.edu/~nbarquin/latin@s.htm

Castex, G. M. (1998). Providing services to Hispanic/Latino populations: Profiles in diversity. In D. R. Atkinson, G. Morten, & D. W. Sue (Eds.), *Counseling American minorities* (pp. 255-267). Boston: McGraw-Hill.

Center for Media and Public Affairs. (1999, Jan-Feb). Women and minorities still knocking on network anchor doors. Retrieved April 2001, from the World Wide Web: http://www.cmpa.com/pressrel/divers98.htm

Children Now. (1998). *A different world: Children's perception of race, class and the media.* Oakland, California: Children Now.

Children Now. (September 2000). Latinowood and TV: Primetime for a reality check, Retrieved May 18, 2002 from the World Wide Web: http://www.childrennow.org/media/fall-colors-2k/fc3-2k-latino.pdf

Collins, G. (2000 September 18). Minority job share doubles in pubcasting, but still lags behind progress of women. *Current Online.* Retrieved July 25, 2002, from the World Wide Web: http://www.current.org/pb/pb017min.html

Corliss, R. (1998, August 3). The class of '98. *Time, 152,* 66.

Cox, T. (1990). Problems with research by organizational scholars on issues of race and ethnicity. *Journal of Applied Behavioral Science, 26,* 5-23.

Davis, K. (1994, May). The Hispanic shift: Continuity rather than conversion? *Journal of Hispanic/Latino Theology,1,* 68-79.

Demo derby. (2000, February 21). *Variety, 378,* 29.

De Varona, F. (1999, May 2). Lesson plan: Hispanics in stage and screen. Unpublished document.

Donovan, R.J., & Leivers, S. (1993). Using paid advertising to modify racial stereotypes. *Public Opinion Quarterly, 57,* 205-218.

Esses, V.M., & Zanna, M.P. (1995). Mood and expression of ethnic stereotypes. *Journal of Personality and Social Psychology, 69,* 1052-1068.

Evuleocha S., & Ugbah, S. (1989). Stereotypes, counter stereotypes, and Black television images in the 1990's. *Western Journal of Black Studies, 13,* 197-205.

Federal Glass Ceiling Commission. (1995). *Good for business: Making full use of the nation's human capital.* Washington, DC: U.S. Government Printing Office.

Flannery, A. (1980). *Vatican Council II: The conciliar and post conciliar documents.* Northport, NY: Costello Publishing Company.

Ford Foundation. (1984). *Hispanics: Challenges and opportunities.* (Working Paper No. 435). New York: Ford Foundation.

Francis, M. (1998). *Guidelines for multicultural celebrations.* Washington, DC: Federation of Diocesan Liturgical Commissions.

Garza, H. (1994). *Latinas: Hispanic women in the United States.* New York: Franklin Watts.

Gurba, C., & Briscoe, D. B. (1989). *Capitalizing on culture: A practitioner's resource book.* Tampa, FL: University of South Florida.

Jackson, J. (2000, January/February). Anything but racism: Media make excuses for "whitewashed" TV lineup. *Extra!* Retrieved September 2, 2002, from the World Wide Web: http://www.fair.org/extra/0001/tv-racism.html

Kanellos, N. (Ed.), (1997). *The Hispanic American almanac.* (2nd ed.). Detroit: Gale.

Kenrick, D.T., Neuberg, S.L., & Cialdini, R.B. (2002). *Social psychology: Unraveling the mystery.* (2nd ed.). Boston: Allen and Bacon.

Kids of Cuban immigrants score poorly. (1998, March 21). *The Miami Herald,* p. A1.

Knouse, S. B., Rosenfeld, P., & Culbertson, A. L. (1992). *Hispanics in the workplace.* Newbury Park, CA: Sage.

Langley, T., O'Neal, E.C., Craig, K.M. Craig, & Yost, E.A. (1992). Aggression consistent-inconsistent, and irrelevant priming effects on selective exposure to media violence. *Aggressive Behavior, 18,* 349-356.

Leo, J. (1998, February 2). Raging hormones on TV. *U.S. News & World Report, 124.* 9.

Marger, M.N. (1997). *Race and ethnic relations: American and global perspectives* (4th ed). Belmont, CA: Wadsworth Publishing.

MGT of America Inc. (2000, December 31). An economic assessment of the Florida film and entertainment industry, State of Florida sponsored study.

Moore, J., & Pachon, H. (1985). *Hispanics in the United States.* Englewood Cliffs, NJ: Prentice-Hall.

National Association for the Advancement of Colored People. (2001, August 15). NAACP television report shows diversity remains unfulfilled goal. *NAACP News.* Retrieved August 22, 2002, from the World Wide Web: http://www.naacp.org/news/releases/tvdiversity081601.shtml

National Rainbow Coalition, Fairness in the Media Facts. Retrieved January 15, 2003, from the World Wide Web: http://www.inmotionmagazine.com/rainbow1.html

National Latino Children's Institute. (Summer 1997). Who's on the air? Latino representations in the media, in *El Futuro Newsletter.* Retrieved November 12, 2002, from the World Wide Web: http://www.nlci.org/press/Past%20articles/whosontheair.htm

Oboler, S. (1995). *Ethnic labels, Latino lives: Identity and the politics of (re) presentation in the United States.* Minneapolis, MN: University of Minnesota Press.

Ortíz, M. (1993). *The Hispanic challenge: opportunities confronting the church.* Downers Grove, IL: InterVarsity Press.

Osborn, J.W. (1995). Academics self-esteem and race: A look at the underlying assumptions of the disidentification hypothesis, *Personality and Social Psychology Bulletin, 21,* 449-455.

Pachon, H.P., DeSipio, L., de la Garza, R.O., & Noriega, C.A. (2000). Missing in action: Latinos in and out of Hollywood, a study by the Tomás Rivera Policy Institute. In C.A. Noriega, (Ed.), *The future of Latino independent media: A NALIP sourcebook* (pp. 15-18). Los Angeles, CA: UCLA Chicano Studies Research Center.

Phinney, J.S. (1990). Ethnic identity in adolescents and adults: Review of research. *Psychological Bulletin, 108,* 499-514.

Phinney, J.S. & Rotherham, M.J. (Eds.). (1987). *Children's ethnic socialization: Pluralism and development.* Newbury Park, CA: Sage.

Radiotelevisión Española, Dirección de Relaciones Internacionales. (1970). *Palabras equívocas o malsonantes en España, Hispanoamerica y Filipinas*. Madrid: Radiotelevisión Española, Dirección de Relaciones Internacionales.

Ramirez Berg, C. (2000). Stereotyping and resistance: A crash course on Hollywood's Latino imagery. In C.A. Noriega (Ed.), *The Future of Latino independent media: A NALIP sourcebook* (pp. 3-13). Los Angeles, CA: UCLA Chicano Studies Research Center.

Rapping, E. (1993, February). The year of the young. *The Progressive, 57,* 36.

Robinson, L. (1998, May 11). 'Hispanics' don't exist. *U.S. News and World Report 124,* 26-32.

Schaefer, R.T. (2000). *Racial and ethnic groups* (8th ed.) Englewood Cliffs, N.J.: Prentice Hall.

Shih, M., Pittinsky, T.L., & Ambady, N. (1999). Stereotypes susceptibility: Identify salience and shifts in quantitative performance. *Psychological Science, 10,* 80-83.

Sigelman, L., & Tuch, S.A. (1992). Metastereotypes: Blacks; perception of Whites stereotypes of Blacks. *Public Opinion Quarterly, 61,* 87-101.

Silver, R. (Ed.). (1993). *Media and values,* no. 62-63, Los Angeles, CA: Center for Media and Values.

Steele, C. (1992). Race and the schooling of Black Americans. *The Atlantic Monthly, 267,* 68-78.

Steele, C., & Aronson, J. (1995). Stereotype threat and the intellectual test performance of African Americans. *Journal of Personality and Social Psychology, 69,* 797-811.

Subervi-Vélez, F. (1999). The mass media and Latinos: Policy and research agenda for the next century. Paper presented at the Communications Workshop, Center for Communications and Community, November 12-13, 1999. Retrieved September 23, 2002, from the World Wide Web: http://www.sscnet.ucla.edu/issr/ccc/toolkit/subervi.html

Sullivan, T.A. (1985). A demographic portrait. In P.S.J. Cafferty & W.C. McCready (Eds.), *Hispanics in the United States: A new social agenda* (pp. 7-32). New Brunswick, NJ: Transaction Books.

Thomas, V. (1998). *Hollywood's Latin lovers: Latino, Italian and French men who make the screen smolder.* Los Angeles, CA: Angel City Press.

Thomas, W. I. (1923). *The unadjusted girl.* Boston: Little Brown.

Vázquez, C. I., Caro, Y., & Clavijo-Passik, A. M. (1991). The integrated cultural influence protocol (CICI): Relevance of culture in clinical work with Hispanics. *Winter Roundtable Proceedings of the Institute for Cross Cultural Counseling* (pp. 50-57). New York: Columbia University Press.

Weitz, R. (1992). College students' images of African American, Mexican American, and Jewish American women. Paper presented at the Annual Meeting of the American Sociological Association, Pittsburgh, PA.

Writers Guild of America (1998). The 1998 Hollywood writers' report overall trends. Retrieved September 28, 2002, from the World Wide Web: http://www.wga.org/manual/Report/minority.html

III

African-American Experiences with Images and Their Transformation

CHAPTER

6

Hollywood's Distortions of Women of Color and Their Stories

Brenda Cooper

"It is only when women fashion their own stories, set their own agendas and tell truths about their own lives that women will be seen clearly."

Caryl Rivers [1]

When novelist Isabel Allende saw Bille August's film translation of her international best seller, *The House of the Spirits* (1982/1986), she found it difficult to relate to the film: "The fiction of the film is 10 times bigger than the fiction of the book.... I say this is not my movie; it is Bille August's movie" (cited in Simpson, 1994, p. 7). It was the same for Alice Walker, who said she had to get used to "seeing my expression taken out of context, rearranged, distorted" (1996, p. 23) when Steven Spielberg adapted her Pulitzer-prize winning novel, *The Color Purple* (1982), to film. And for singer Tina Turner, the pressure to streamline her autobiography, *I, Tina* (1986), into a "puff piece" for Disney resulted in her rarely visiting the set of *What's Love Got To Do With It* (Chapin, Krost, & Gibson, 1993) and not seeing the film for some time after its release (Walker, 1993, p. 5).

These complaints exemplify a primary question in adapting books to film—which parts of the original survive and which do not? Often, what is lost in such translations is literature's capacity to illuminate complicated social, moral and political issues, which are often compro-

mised by filmmakers' need to offer audiences "fast-moving narratives, glossy settings, rich costumes, spectacle and famous faces" (Reynolds, 1993, p. 10). Some scholars have argued (e.g., Henderson, 1973/1974) that the relationship between which parts of the story are lost and which parts survive in the production process always has ideological implications. Indeed, Cheyfitz (1991) asserts that any translation is an appropriation, because of the power the translator exerts over the original author, authors and their voices may be lost, or at best become constructs of the translator. For instance, translators often represent their own ideas in the form of first-person narrative, which functions to obscure their role in creating a new story from the original. Further, in their role as translators, film directors often depict cultural views and ideals that the authors would not share. What is particularly problematical in this process is that the narratives of mainstream Hollywood films often function "to reproduce patriarchal order" (Cartwright & Fonoroff, 1994, p. 125). Thus, the goal of my research is to examine critically how, in the film translations of three books written by women of color—Isabel Allende's *The House of the Spirits* (1982/1986), Alice Walker's *The Color Purple* (1982) and Tina Turner's *I, Tina* (1986)[2]—their resistance to patriarchy and its inherent White privilege is marginalized and

From "Hegemony and Hollywood: A Critique of Cinematic Distortions of Women of Color and Their Stories," *American Communication Journal* 2.2, www.acjournal.org, by Brenda Cooper. Copyright © 1999 by American Communication Association. Reprinted by permission.

negated by the films' directors, Bille August, Steven Spielberg and Brian Gibson, respectively.

Strategies of Patriarchal Resistance and Containment

Scholarly interest in the translation of literature into film has resulted in a large body of interdisciplinary research.[3] Recent research in this area indicates that questionable choices are made in order to fit women's stories to the ideological structures that dominate mainstream Hollywood films. One example is found in Sydney Pollack's adaptation of Isak Dinesen's autobiography, *Out of Africa*. Although both the book and the film versions are based on the years Dinesen lived on a farm in Kenya during the early 20th century, they represent very different accounts of Dinesen's experiences (Cooper & Descutner, 1996). Significantly, the parts of Dinesen's autobiography that resist patriarchal and dominant political ideals of race, gender and religion are omitted from the film, while the parts that survive distort Dinesen's unconventional stories in ways that reinforce patriarchy and White privilege, thus conforming to conventional American ideologies.

The major themes of Dinesen's autobiography are her criticisms of colonialism and her deep affection for Africa and the native Kenyans she lived and worked with for nearly 20 years (Cooper & Descutner, 1996). When Pollack brought Dinesen's story to the silver screen, however, her autobiography was transformed into a romantic drama highlighting Dinesen's relationships with her husband, Bror Blixen, and her lover, Denys Finch Hatton. In fact, the Kenyans' pain and the European settlers' bigotry that are major themes in Dinesen's book are nonexistent in Pollack's film version, replaced with narratives that glorify rather than criticize the European colonists. In her stories, Dinesen poignantly expresses her grief over the changes the European settlers had forced on Kenyans and their culture, and her compassion for their struggles to maintain their identity and dignity. In the film, however, Dinesen is recast as one of the "offending European settlers, forcing her will on the native people without any

sensitivity to their wishes or culture" (Cooper & Descutner, p. 240). Further, Dinesen's compassion for the country and its people are appropriated in the film by the leading male character, Denys Finch Hatton. Although the real Finch Hatton was committed to the colonial effort, in the film he is represented as Dinesen's moral superior, grieving over the changes colonialism has brought to Kenya and chastising Dinesen for her role in them. Explaining why he changed Isak Dinesen's story so dramatically for his film, Pollack remarked, "For film purposes, it seemed...[that] invention was much more economical than the facts and dramatically much better" (Luedtke & Pollack, 1987, p. x).

This metamorphosis is not limited to the case of Isak Dinesen. Analysis of the film adaptation of Alice Walker's *The Color Purple* also shows that Walker's story of a Black woman's evolution to self-empowerment over sexism and racism is reframed by director Spielberg into a film that "imposes a patriarchal interpretation" onto a text that significantly challenged the ideals of patriarchy (McMullen & Solomon, 1994, p. 171). Critics argue that such adaptations not only marginalize women in Hollywood, but also are emblematic of the industry's reluctance to produce films that express diverse viewpoints. And even when women write the screenplays, they may feel pressure from producers and directors to fit their narratives and characters to prevailing patriarchal standards and traditional Hollywood conventions (Seger, 1996).

This chapter further explores the issues surrounding film translations of women's writings. Specifically, I am interested in the ways in which film translations of stories written by women of color can be interpreted through an investigation of the "hegemonic devices" (Dow, 1990, p. 264) used in film narratives to support dominant ideological ideals and interests. In this context, I use hegemony to refer to the "various means through which those who support the dominant ideology in a culture are able continually to reproduce that ideology" in media, in subtle ways that discourage scrutiny or criticism (Dow, p. 262).[4] Hegemonic devices, in turn, represent the specific narrative strategies used in media texts to contain and suppress challenges to the dominant ideals of a culture. For example, Dow's (1990) examination of *The Mary Tyler Moore Show* illustrates how hegemonic devices are used to encourage viewers to think that demands for women's equality issues are being addressed by the television series, while in reality these issues are trivialized through the series' plots and characters. As Dow explains, the central character, Mary Richards, is a single career woman, a portrayal that seems to respond to women's demands for equality in the workplace and in relationships. Mary's career and single lifestyle, however, are represented in the series within traditional frameworks of family and gender relationships that marginalize or negate altogether the character's untraditional roles. Thus, hegemonic devices refer to the ways in which media narratives *seem* to be responding to demands for social change—such as women's equality—while in fact are legitimizing dominant ideologies such as patriarchy (Gitlin, 1982), a concept Chantal Mouffe (1979) refers to as expansive hegemony.

In the case of film adaptations of women's stories, one way to document how hegemonic devices may be used to contain patriarchal challenges made by women writers is to identify the "women's discourse" (Gledhill, 1994, p. 118) in their own narratives and to compare these discourses to those found in the films. The concept of a woman's discourse can be understood by considering how women are socially positioned differently from men. Because women experience their social roles—parenthood, work, family and sexual relations, for example—in gender-specific ways that "frequently contradict patriarchal construction" (Gledhill, p. 118), a woman's voice emerges in authors' writings that disrupts traditional ideological discourses, such as the discourses of male violence and women's empowerment. This is the case in the stories of Isabel Allende, Alice Walker and Tina Turner.

A variety of discourses comprise a film text, but since Hollywood films have been dominated by patriarchal discourses, one result of film translations of women's stories that depict patriarchal resistance is a struggle among competing discourses. Obviously, filmmakers must choose what to include and what to exclude from the literary source material, as well as what to high-light or what to downplay. The result of these choices is potentially profound. The most powerful player in the process of translating novels to films is the director, who can manipulate the stories and images from the books and present them to viewers "in a context that is the director's own" (Redding & Brownworth, 1997, p. 4).[5] Spectators thus become "inextricably connected" to the director's version, and, consequently, the images and narratives depicted in films become the "text and subtext of...how we view the world" (Redding & Brownworth, pp. 4-5).

In short, there is ample evidence to suggest that people from outside the prevailing Hollywood power structure must fight an uphill battle to get their perspectives, values and voices reflected in an industry that is predominantly White and male. And although male authors such as Tom Clancy and John Irving also have complained about film adaptations of their books (Parkes, 1995; Svetkey, 1998), research indicates that it is women's stories in particular that are altered to fit patriarchal ideals that marginalize women and their life experiences (Cooper & Descutner, 1996; McMullen & Solomon, 1994). While men's stories tend to conform to existing patriarchal structures, women's stories often challenge these structures (Gledhill, 1994). It is precisely these challenges that often do not survive the film adaptations. The implications are profound: "[T]he industry has substantial power to influence our public discussion of important social issues. This power is especially troublesome when it is exerted not according to some broad political position—liberal or conservative—but rather to silence or diminish usually marginalized voices" (McMullen & Solomon, p. 171).

This case study expands on previous research by explicating the women's discourses in the writings of Allende, Walker and Turner, as well as the common modes of appropriation in the film adaptations of these stories by women of color.[6] Specifically, I examine the directors' depiction of the ideological challenges underlying each woman's story, noting the clear discrepancies between the film translations and the original works to explicate the hegemonic devices embedded in the films' texts. Thus, a comparison of the original women's discourses in

Allende's, Walker's and Turner's narratives to those found in the film adaptations suggests the questions: "What is being said about women here? Who is speaking? And for whom?" (Gledhill, 1994, p. 119). But before we examine these questions, let us review the background of each woman's work.

Background of Authors

Before discussing the ideological challenges that form the major discourses of the books and the hegemonic devices used in the films to contain these challenges, it is important to provide a context for each woman's writings. All three based their stories on personal life experiences and the experiences of their various family members and friends, constructing their narratives in ways that illustrate Gledhill's (1994) argument that the social and cultural conditions of women's experiences often contradict patriarchal construction and result in a woman's discourse that resists dominant patriarchal and cultural ideologies. Allende's and Walker's books represent the novelization of personal and family experiences, while Turner's is an autobiography (co-authored with Kurt Loder).[7] The links between the books' themes and the women's lives are discussed next.

Isabel Allende and
The House of the Spirits

The House of the Spirits (1982/1986) is an epic historical novel set in South America that follows the lives of three generations of women: Clara, whose clairvoyant powers underlie the mystical themes of the novel; her daughter, Blanca; and Alba, Blanca's daughter. Clara's marriage to Esteban is first filled with joy, and they welcome the birth of their daughter, Blanca, and twin sons, Nicolás and Jaime. But as the marriage progresses and political unrest rocks the country, Esteban's bigotry, cruelty and sexism become major obstacles for the women in his life to overcome. Esteban rapes and impregnates numerous peasant women who live near his hacienda, he tries to kill Pedro, Blanca's peasant lover, and then forces her into a loveless marriage with a perverted aristocrat when he

learns Blanca is pregnant with Pedro's child. He schemes against the revolutionaries who oust his corrupt political party from power, while the women in Esteban's life risk their lives to work clandestinely with the revolutionaries. Throughout the novel, women are depicted as morally and intellectually superior to the male characters, free-thinking and active women who use their own strengths to triumph over the many abuses of patriarchy.

Allende began *The House of the Spirits* (1982/1986) as a spiritual letter to her 100-year-old grandfather, who was dying in the Santiago mansion where Allende had spent much of her childhood and where she sets her novel (Fussell, 1993).[8] For Allende, writing *The House of the Spirits* was "about the desire to recover everything I lost" in Chile (cited in Boudreau, 1993, p. 1). Her uncle, Salvador Allende, was president of Chile and was killed during a CIA-backed military coup in 1973. The coup ended 150 years of democracy in Chile and the new dictatorship committed acts of violence and torture similar to those described by Allende in her novel.[9] After the coup and her uncle's assassination, Allende's parents escaped to Buenos Aires, where an assassination attempt was made on their lives. Allende worked with the underground movement in Chile for two years, participating in resistance activities similar to those of her Alba character in *The House of the Spirits*: "Finding asylum for some, safe houses for others, smuggling information out of the country" (cited in Fussell, p. 80). When her own life was threatened, she moved her family to Venezuela, where they lived in exile for 13 years.

Allende equates her experience in writing *The House of the Spirits* with "slitting my wrists and letting the blood flow out" (cited in Griggs, 1996, p. E5), as many of the novel's characters are so entwined with her life and her family that she reports she often cannot "draw a line between imagination and reality" (cited in Fussell, 1993, p. 52). For example, Clara, the main protagonist, is patterned after her grandmother, a spiritualist who Allende describes as the "crazed soul of the house" who could move ashtrays without touching them and had a three-legged table that spirits moved (cited in Fussell, 1993, p. 80). Her grandfather, who she explains was "a very mean sort of guy" (cited in Hernández, 1996, p. 4) who "killed everything that brought joy" (cited in Fussell, p. 80), was the model for Esteban, but not solely in the terms of the violent, cruel nature of the book's character. It was also her grandfather's place in Chilean society and his reaction to her grandmother's death—he dressed in black for eight years and painted the furniture black—that helps Allende develop Esteban's character (Fussell), as well as the love she felt from her grandfather (Hernández). Nicolás, one of Clara's twin sons in the book, is named after Allende's own son. And Jaime, the other twin son, is based on an uncle who convinced Allende as a child that the characters in his books "escaped their pages and roamed the house at night. When the lights went off, I could hear them—bandits, courtesans, princes, witches, tyrants" (cited in Boudreau, 1993, p. 1).

Before becoming an author at 39, Allende was a journalist, well-known for her outspoken feminist views. Allende explains that she resented the patriarchal culture of Chile and had "wanted to be a man since she was five years old" because, in watching her grandparents' interactions, she realized "what a terrible disadvantage it was to be a woman. I saw how powerful my grandfather was. His wishes were orders...it took me a long time to accept that it's not bad to be a woman" (cited in Boudreau, 1993, p. 1). Allende says she hopes for a "world where feminine values will be validated, the same as masculine values are" (cited in "Isabel," 1994). She is the first female Latin-American author to criticize the patriarchal culture of Latin America and its politics in her writings.[10] Concerned that Hollywood would trivialize her novel (Lipman, 1994), Allende rejected several Hollywood directors before finally agreeing to allow Danish director Bille August to make the film version of *The House of the Spirits* (Eichinger & August, 1994).

ALICE WALKER AND *THE COLOR PURPLE*

The Color Purple (1985) is the story of Celie, an African-American girl growing up in the American South of the early 20th century. Walker's novel opens with the 14-year-old Celie describing her mother's death and the rapes she endures at the hands of her stepfather, which result in two children her stepfather sells. Her life does not improve when her stepfather makes a deal for Albert, a local widower with young children, to marry Celie; her husband beats and emotionally abuses Celie throughout their marriage. The little joy in Celie's life comes from her friendships with women, especially her relationships with her sister Nettie, and later, with Shug, Albert's lover. Over the decades the novel spans, Celie learns to love herself and finds the courage to leave her husband and begin a new life through the love and support she receives from the women in her life, who also help reunite Celie with her grown children.

In 1996, Alice Walker published *The Same River Twice*,[11] a book detailing her experiences with seeing *The Color Purple* translated to a film. Originally, director Steven Spielberg commissioned Walker herself to write the screenplay from her Pulitzer Prize-winning novel, which she titled, *Watch For Me In The Sunset* (Walker, p. 60). She would not give her screenplay the same title as her book because she was afraid that Spielberg's film version of *The Color Purple*[12] would not deserve the name. That was never an issue, however, as Spielberg rejected Walker's screenplay and hired Menno Meyjes to take over the film project. Not surprising, the first time Walker saw Spielberg's final product, "everything about it seemed wrong" (Walker, p. 21).[13]

Like Allende, Alice Walker based many of the characters in *The Color Purple* on her family members and her personal experiences with them, and she describes writing her novel as "a journey to the imagined and vastly rearranged lives of my mother and father and grandparents before I was born" (Walker, 1996, p. 25). In fact, when Walker's mother saw the film, she told her daughter that it reminded her of her own life. For example, Nettie, the name she gives to Celie's sister, is the name of Walker's grandmother, a woman she admired a great deal. The character of Mister/Albert is based on her grandfather, whom she described as a misogynist who "unmercifully" battered her grandmother (p. 29). Despite his abusive nature, Walker loved her grandfather, and wrote that it "broke my heart that so few people were able to really see him" in Spielberg's film (p. 34). Shug is based on one of Walker's aunts, who moved North and worked as a domestic for Whites.[14] Walker, who is bisexual, often includes bisexual and lesbian relationships as themes in her books, as they are in the characters of Celie and Shug.

Walker was the object of harsh criticism after the film's release, especially among African Americans (Walker, 1996), who accused her of hating men, particularly Black men, of degrading Blacks with the dialects she used for her characters, and of being a lesbian, "as if respecting and honoring women automatically discredited anything a woman might say" (p. 22). Walker laments that is was a "rare critic who showed any compassion for, or even noted, the suffering of the women and children explored in the book, while I was called a liar for showing that Black men sometimes perpetuate domestic violence" (pp. 38-39).[15]

TINA TURNER AND *I, TINA*

While Allende's and Walker's novels are fictionalized narratives drawn from their lives, Tina Turner's (née Anna Mae Bullock) 1986 book is autobiographical, detailing her childhood and her abusive relationship with Ike Turner.[16] Her lifestory is co-authored with Kurt Loder, whose narratives link Turner's personal stories with interviews from her friends and family members, including her former husband. Beginning with her poverty-ridden childhood in Nut Bush, Tennessee, where she was abandoned by her mother, Turner chronicles her rise to international stardom during the 1960s as a vocalist with the "Ike and Tina Turner Revue." Behind her glamorous life, however, are the details of the physical and emotional battering Turner endured during her marriage to Ike, the devastation of Ike's drug addiction and his numerous infidelities, and eventually, their fading careers. When she finally divorced Ike, Tina faced financial ruin, but she survived this desperate time in her life with the support of women who had befriended her over the years, and who now introduced her to Buddhism. Tina Turner eventually recovered both her equilibrium and her singing career, winning the 1984 Grammys for Best Female Pop Vocalist, Best Female Rock Vocal Performance and Record of the Year for "What's Love Got To Do With It?"—

the song that provides the title for the movie version of her autobiography.

Tina Turner's motivation in writing her autobiography and agreeing to a film version that would publicly reveal her as a victim of extreme domestic violence during her marriage, she explains, was to find closure: "As long as I left that under the rug, it might have held me back as well" (cited in Hamlin, 1996).[17] And although Turner was unhappy with the myriad deviations the film makes from the facts of her life (Walker, 1993), she avoids criticizing the people involved with the film's production.

It took seven years, two directors, three screenwriters and 17 drafts of Kate Lanier's screenplay for Disney to bring Turner's story to the screen in *What's Love Got To Do With It* (Chapin, Krost, & Gibson, 1993).[18] Howard Ashman, an Oscar-winning lyricist for Disney's *Beauty and the Beast* and *Little Mermaid*, was the original screenwriter, but he died in 1991. Turner's co-author Kurt Loder was then offered the job, but he declined because the producers told him they wanted the film to be "an upbeat thing. It just eluded me. I didn't see how it could possibly be" (Loder, cited in Walker, 1993, p. 5). Then Kate Lanier was hired to give an African-American woman's perspective.[19] However, the film's producers "never envisioned it as a biography.... The facts weren't adding up to anything exciting," one producer explained (Chapin, cited in Walker, p. 5). Consequently, "We leave a lot out," explains director Brian Gibson. And after complaints from Laurence Fishburne, who starred as Ike Turner, that Ike's character "wasn't fully developed," a male screenwriter was hired to "beef up Ike's part." Explained Lanier, they wanted "a man do a man's writing" (cited in Walker, p. 5).

Hegemonic Devices and Film Translations of Women's Writings

My analysis identified four ideological challenges that represent the major discourses underlying the narrative structure of each woman's text: discourse of women's empowerment; discourse of spiritualism; discourse of male violence; and discourse of discrimination. In each case, these discourses are developed by the women in ways that resist dominant ideologies and their institutional structures. However, two narrative strategies—marginalization and omission—operate as hegemonic devices that recast each discourse in forms compatible with conventional American ideologies in order to "contain" the radical aspects and challenges (Dow, 1990, p. 263) represented in the women's stories. The following discussion of these discourses articulates how the women's voices are renarrated by the directors, effectively denying the women their voices and their challenges to dominant ideologies. The result is film texts that work ideologically to produce depoliticized melodramas, moving to the margin or muting altogether pivotal elements of the women's discourses, including their complex voices and unconventional beliefs, while simultaneously seeming to support the ideological challenges found in the authors' discourses.

DISCOURSE OF WOMEN'S EMPOWERMENT

Perhaps the most powerful discourse found in the narratives of Allende, Walker and Turner's[20] stories is the empowerment that women experience through close relationships with other women. Allende writes about four generations of women who support and empower each other. The women in Walker's novel help each other grow and provide unconditional love and support. Similarly, Turner describes the important roles various women played throughout her life—during childhood, during her marriage to Ike, amid her financial and emotional struggles after her divorce and, finally, the women who introduce her to Buddhism.

In fact, Allende dedicates her novel to women: "My mother, my grandmother, and all the extraordinary women of this story."[21] *The House of the Spirits* is the story of women who strengthen and empower each other. Throughout the novel, Clara is the uniting force of the del Valle and Truba families, even after her death. Indeed, it is Clara's spirit that provides the book's title. Allende's narratives skillfully explore the interconnectiveness and complexities of female support systems. For instance, the relationships

between Clara, her daughter Blanca and granddaughter Alba, and her sister-in-law Férula, are so close that her husband Esteban is peripheral to their daily lives. Despite Esteban's attempts to become the center of Clara's life, it is her relationships with other women she most values. In fact, Esteban becomes so jealous of Clara's close relationship with his sister Férula that he banishes his sister from his house and all of their lives.

As another example, it is through the support and love of the women imprisoned in the concentration camp (as well as Clara's spirit), that Alba is able to survive torture and imprisonment. Allende carefully constructs the prison narratives in such a way as to focus on the strength of the women in enduring the violent abuse they receive from their male guards. The concentration camp is less a source of pain for Alba than one of love, support and strength from other women prisoners. Indeed, the camp is depicted by Allende as another celebration of women and their female communities, as Alba explains: "The last thing I heard when I left was the chorus of my friends singing to give me courage, just as they did with all the women when they arrived or left the camp. I wept as I walked. I had been happy here" (p. 427). Significantly, it is the "solidarity among the women" characters in Allende's novel that provides their "protection against patriarchal aggression" (Shea, 1990, p. 225).

On the surface, August's film version seems to celebrate the triumphs and strength of women. But Allende's story is recast, and we see the women through the perspectives of the primary male character, Esteban Truba, not through Allende's voice in the characters of her novel's women. Indeed, Esteban Truba and his triumphs and strength are foregrounded, and important women characters in Allende's story are missing from the film. The Mora sisters are omitted, as are Alba and the women imprisoned with her. August also represents Férula's love for Clara as perversely sexual in nature, and all of the women are depicted as relying primarily on men for their support and love rather than on women. Such portrayals deny the strength of women that is so integral to Allende's novel, thus containing her challenges to traditional patriarchal ideals. And although Esteban is a primary character in Allende's book, her narratives highlight the strength and empowerment of the women who must cope with his abusive nature in their lives. Strength and empowerment are also discourses of August's film, but it is the trials, tribulations and triumphs of Esteban that are the primary focus of the film's narrative structure.

In Walker's *The Color Purple*, the empowerment and support women derive from their friendships (McMullen & Solomon, 1994) continues to be an important discourse; Celie offers herself to her stepfather in order to protect Nettie from being raped; Nettie teaches Celie to read; Mary Agnes raises Sofia's children while she is jailed and, later, Mary Agnes has sex with her uncle (the warden) in order to get Sofia released from prison; and Sofia cares for Mary Agnes' ill daughter while she pursues a singing career. Celie learns about herself, her African heritage, an alternative spiritualism that challenges White Christianity, and eventually finds the strength to deal with her traumatic past through her friendships with women. Celie's most important relationship in the book is with Shug. Celie admires Shug's womanly strength, and it is through Shug that Celie learns to love and respect herself and discovers her own sexual identity. And after Celie receives a telegram notifying her that Nettie's ship has been sunk by German mines, it is Shug who goes to government offices for more details. Importantly, the friendship Celie finds with Shug frees her from the constraints of the males in her life. As Shug explains to Celie, "You have to git man off your eyeball, before you can see anything a'tall. Man corrupt everything" (p. 204).

Spielberg's film, however, marginalizes the role of women in Celie's life, focusing instead on developing a melodrama that highlights Mister's role in Celie's life and her eventual financial success within capitalism (McMullen & Solomon, 1994). Like *The House of the Spirits*, this movie also appears to honor women, but many important aspects of the women's supportive friendships depicted in Walker's novel are omitted from the film. Consider that spectators do not learn about Mary Agnes raising Sofia's children while she was in prison or about her role

in getting Sofia released. Both Nettie and Shug's roles in teaching the alternative spiritualism to Celie are omitted. Further, Spielberg gives Mister/Albert credit for Nettie's safe return, ignoring Shug's efforts. Significantly, viewers do not learn that Celie truly discovers her lesbian sexuality through Shug, and the prominent role Shug plays in Celie's growth and empowerment is reduced to a few scenes, including the one where spectators see Shug "seducing" Celie (McMullen & Solomon, 1994), a representation of their relationship that trivializes the loving, sexually fulfilling relationship the two women shared in Walker's novel.

Throughout her autobiography, Turner also gives credit for her eventual empowerment to many women who befriended her, from her cousin Margaret who supported her as a child, to the women who introduced her to Buddhism, and even to women who had affairs with Ike but bonded with Tina in their mutual fear of the man: "All we had was each other" (p. 141). In fact, on her autobiography's acknowledgment page, she thanks her women friends for their "loving friendship, financial support, and providing a haven for me and my family...for always being there."[22] In director Gibson's version of Turner's life, however, these women are relegated to the sidelines, and replaced with a narrative that emphasizes Ike's relationship with Turner and her financial triumph within a capitalist economic structure. In fact, all of Turner's women friends are combined into the character of one woman, Jackie, in the film, who appears in a few minor scenes. Omitting the women who formed Turner's support system over the years silences not just Tina Turner's voice and life story, but also the voices of all the women Turner included in her autobiography. As bell hooks (1996) observes, the film becomes a "narrative of Ike, more so than the narrative of Tina Turner" (p. 111).

In each film translation, women and their friendships are marginalized or omitted, while males and their perspectives are privileged. As hegemonic devices, these strategies recast the women's discourses in ways that function to reinforce male dominance and heterosexuality and minimize the power women find in their relationships with each other. As the next section demonstrates, similar hegemonic strategies are used to trivialize the value of alternative spiritualism and simultaneously reinforce patriarchal Christian ideals.

DISCOURSE OF SPIRITUALISM

Unconventional spiritualism is an important discourse in each of the women's narratives. Throughout each book, the development of the principal female characters' growth and inner strength is linked to their adoption of alternative spiritual beliefs that challenge the beliefs of Christainity. For example, in Allende's *The House of the Spirits*, Clara's father is an atheist, her mother shuns conventional Catholicism for the spirit world, and the opening pages of the book describe how Clara's early supernatural powers result in a local priest accusing her of being possessed. In the novel, Clara's paranormal spiritual powers define her character: she foresees future events; she levitates objects and herself; after her death, her spirit roams her house; and she returns in spirit form to provide Alba with the inner strength she needs to survive imprisonment. And after having curbed her spiritual activities for years to appease Esteban, Clara renews her spiritualism and clairvoyance through her relationship with the Mora sisters (who later bring Alba a warning from Clara's spirit).

Spirituality defines Clara in Allende's novel, but this aspect of her personality is rarely shown in Bille August's film, and further, the few scenes August includes trivialize her spiritual power. August recasts Clara's spirituality as an aloofness and secular stubbornness that result in representing her as somewhat frivolous and silly, especially in the scenes in which she demonstrates her supernatural abilities. On her wedding night, for instance, Clara moves a table for no apparent reason, only to be reprimanded by Esteban. The Mora sisters, who figure prominently in Clara's spiritual life, are missing in the film. With scenes that construct her abilities as frivolous, and omissions of her paranormal power as well as Clara's clairvoyant friends, August marginalizes the mystical power of women who adopt alternative spiritualism.

Walker, who describes herself as a "born-again pagan" (1996, p. 25), dedicates *The Color Purple*, "To the Spirit: Without whose assistance Neither this book Nor I Would have been Written."[23] So it is not surprising that, like Allende, unconventional views of religion and God as adopted by her women characters represent a primary discourse in Walker's *The Color Purple*. For example, when Celie tells Shug that she stopped praying because God is a man who never listens to "poor colored women" (pp. 199-200) and is "just like all the other mens I know. Trifling, forgitful and lowdown" (p. 199), Shug explains that it is Celie's perception of God as a distant, old White man that makes her feel God does not listen to her. All the colored people in the White man's Bible are always "gitting cursed" (p. 202), Shug explains, and Celie needs to stop thinking of God as the "one that's in the White folks' White bible" (p. 201). Shug's alternate concept of God rejects the fundamentalist views of the vengeful God of her minister father's faith, and she tells Celie that traditional notions of Christianity have operated to suppress women and Blacks (pp. 176-178).

Similarly, Nettie's letters to Celie from Africa frequently describe the superiority of the Olinka religion, detailing the contradictory views these African people have of God and spirituality. Nettie also explains that since coming to Africa, she has learned that the pyramids were built by "colored" Egyptians, and that, "All the Ethiopians in the bible were colored" (pp. 138, 140). Nettie's alternative views of Christianity continue:

It is the pictures in the bible that fool you.... All of the people are White and so you just think all the people from the bible were White. But really White people lived somewhere else during those times. That's why the bible says that Jesus Christ had hair like lamb's wool. Lamb's wool is not straight, Celie. (pp. 140-141)

Discussions such as these not only provide insight into the women's alternate religious views, but also into their individual characters and Celie's spiritual progression and awakening are integral to the narrative structure in

Walker's novel. Indeed, it is not until Celie denies a patriarchal White, male God that she regains her spiritual faith and believes God is hearing her prayers.

When we examine the way the film marginalizes the alternative spirituality of the women who dominate Walker's novel,[24] Spielberg's hegemonic interpretation of the women's spirituality seems obvious. Spielberg omitted most of the aforementioned women's conversations and replaced the characters' alternative religious views with a sub-plot showing Shug throughout the film trying to reconcile with her minister father and his patriarchal faith. In the book, Shug remains unapologetic for her flamboyant sexuality and lifestyle, but Spielberg invents Shug's desperate attempt to gain her father's approval as the movie's climactic scene, with a "repentant" Shug reconciling with her father (McMullen and Solomon, 1994). Thus, this subplot of reconciliation with her father functions to contain the character's patriarchal challenges, by representing religious beliefs, values and morality from a White, Christian perspective, effectively denying the alternative spiritualism so integral to Walker's characters.

Spiritualism also is an important discourse in Tina Turner's autobiography, *I, Tina*. After years of being battered by Ike, Turner credits her introduction to the Buddhist faith and her adoption of the religion's principles into her daily life with providing her with the strength to leave the abusive marriage. Her first acknowledgment in her autobiography is to the "liturgy Nichiren Shoshu for an introduction to spiritual knowledge."[25] Buddhism, Turner explains later in her book, helped "rearrange her place in the universe" (p. 173) in such a way that it provided her with the inner strength to become "less and less afraid" of Ike, thus setting her "free" (p. 174).

Brian Gibson's film, however, glosses over the significance of Buddhism in Turner's life, including only a couple of scenes dealing with Turner's dedication to Buddhist practices. For instance, although the movie shows her chanting in a couple of scenes, it fails to acknowledge that it is through Buddhism that Turner finds the courage to leave Ike and begin her life anew. The film downplays Turner's spiritual awakening and the role it plays in her emotional and financial recovery in favor of highlighting Turner's comeback career and financial success.

Just as the films recast women and their friendships, the women's rejection of patriarchal notions of Christianity also are renarrated by the directors. The unconventional spiritual views the women embrace are shown briefly, enough to give the appearance that the filmmakers are honoring the women authors' ideological challenges, but ultimately, the films' representations of their spirituality—through the hegemonic devices of marginalization or omission—support dominant ideologies and traditional religious values. Next, we'll discuss how these same hegemonic strategies deny challenges Allende, Walker and Turner make in the area of male violence against women.

DISCOURSE OF MALE VIOLENCE

An integral part of Allende's, Walker's and Turner's narratives is a discourse of male violence against women.[26] Allende develops this discourse through Esteban and, later, through his illegitimate grandson conceived from a rape, as well as via the actions of the South American political dictators she details. Walker constructs abusive males in Celie's stepfather, Mister, Harpo, and through Sofia's beatings while imprisoned; Turner describes in detail the abuse she endured from Ike.

In *The House of the Spirits*, Allende devotes much time to detailing Esteban's violent nature and his cruelty to others, especially his peasant workers. Esteban rapes dozens of peasant women and young girls, siring numerous illegitimate children, and killing the native peasants who dare to confront him about his actions. He goes on rampages of anger, beating peasants and burning their huts. He beats his daughter Blanca "mercilessly, lash after lash, until the girl fell flat and rigid to the ground" (p. 199) when he discovers her relationship with Pedro, a peasant worker on his estate, and strikes Clara so hard he knocks out her front teeth when she tries to intervene. He forces Blanca into an arranged marriage when her pregnancy by Pedro is revealed and remains emotionally distant from Blanca for most of the reminder of his life. Allende also provides vivid descriptions of the violence perpetrated on women by the ruling politicians and military personnel.

The film, however, omits virtually all of Esteban's rage and violent acts; one rape is mentioned, one beating is included, and the scene in which Esteban confronts Blanca about her affair with Pedro is toned down significantly. For example, he does not beat Blanca, and the blows Esteban inflicts on Clara that result in her losing her front teeth are reduced to mild slaps. Blanca is not forced into a loveless marriage, nor does she remain estranged from her father. Rather, they are represented as sharing a close, loving relationship. And with the exception of the depictions of the abuse Blanca receives in prison,[27] most of the violence of the dictatorship is omitted from the film. By significantly downplaying male violence, particularly in the character of Esteban, not only is Allende's voice and those of her women characters diminished, but so are the accomplishments of the women who survive despite male abuse.

Men's violence toward women also forms a major discourse of Walker's *The Color Purple*, established on the first pages with Celie's graphic descriptions of her rapes and pregnancies by her stepfather, who takes her babies while she sleeps and tells her he killed them (pp. 1-4). A few pages later, Celie tries to protect Nettie from their stepfather's sexual assaults, asking him "to take me instead" (p. 8). And early in Walker's novel, Celie writes about the beatings she suffers from her Pa: "He beat her today cause he say I winked at a boy in church" (p. 6). As Sofia explains, "A girl child ain't safe in a family of men" (p. 42). Walker continues to write about the abuse Celie endures for years after being married off to Mister—"He beat me like he beat the children.... He say, Celie, git the belt" (p. 23)—and Harpo's attempts to beat Sofia in order to "put her in her place" are included, as well as the assault and rape Squeak endures at the hands of her uncle.

These harsh accounts of male violence toward women are severely minimized or ignored in Spielberg's film. Further, Spielberg invents scenes that function to downplay the significance of male violence. For instance, Spielberg's film does not open with Celie's rape, but instead shows Celie and Nettie playing children's games in a field of flowers, with upbeat music in the background, thus diluting "the hopelessness of the novel's beginning" (McMullen & Solomon, 1994, p. 119) and minimizing the trauma of Celie's experience of incestuous rape. In a later scene, viewers see a love-sick Mister struggling unsuccessfully to cook breakfast for Shug. And as McMullen and Solomon (1994) point out, Spielberg credits Mister with bringing Nettie back to Celie. Scenes such as these are invented for the purposes of the film and direct spectators' attention from the severity of Mister's cruelty, a strategy Gibson also uses in *What's Love Got to Do With It*.

Although she carefully avoids vilifying Ike in *I, Tina*, Turner does detail the abuse she endured before and during their marriage, including beatings when she was pregnant, repeated assaults with wire hangers, hot coffee thrown in her face, lighted cigarettes rammed up her nose, and cracked ribs and broken jaws. A critical part of Turner's life story is Ike's abuse and her inability to leave the marriage until she embraced Buddhism. Turner also details Ike's numerous affairs with other women, which often involved bringing women to their home and sleeping with them in their bed. Like August's depiction of Esteban and Spielberg's portrayal of Mister, however, Gibson's film adaptation significantly downplays Ike Turner's violent nature. Ike is shown battering Turner only three times in the film, and never with the severity described in the book. His infidelity is virtually ignored, as are the children from these affairs, and is replaced with a couple of scenes where Ike merely flirts with other women. Indeed, bell hooks (1996) described *What's Love Got To Do With It* as "a very tragic film, because you sit in the theater and you see people really identify with the character of Ike, not with the character of Tina Turner" (p. 111).

Gibson's movie further marginalizes Ike's abusive behavior by constructing scenes that show him in favorable terms, while they distort historical facts. For example, Ike is shown playing the role of the devoted, proud father after Turner has given birth to their son. In a following scene, Ike "rescues" her from the hospital, then reveals his romantic plans to drive to Mexico immediately for their wedding. Subsequent scenes show the happy newlyweds in Tijuana. In reality, however, Ike was absent from his son's birth: "Ike was nowhere around, of course" (p. 85). And Turner was "rescued" from her hospital bed several weeks before the birth of their son, but not by Ike and not for marriage. Despite being hospitalized with severe jaundice and ordered by her physician to remain in bed for six weeks, Ike demanded Turner leave the hospital so she could continue performing on tours: "Ike sent somebody to pick me up...and I walked out the exit he'd told me about and out into the car and went back to the house I was renting" (p. 82). As for their later wedding, Turner describes it as an unplanned, unromantic event that she didn't really want, but didn't know how to avoid. The beatings had begun months before: "I didn't want to be a part of his life, didn't want to be another one of the five hundred women he had around him by then. But I was...well, scared. And by now, this was my life—where else could I go?" (p. 97).

Although a discourse of male violence is an integral part of each woman's story, directors August, Spielberg and Gibson marginalize or omit the severity of this issue in their respective films. By including a few scenes depicting the abusive actions of the male characters, the films seem to reflect the authors' voices and growing societal concern around domestic violence. But, the directors recast male violence into narrative forms less threatening to American culture and mythologies, narratives that actually encourage spectators to identify with the abusive males, once again demonstrating the power of marginalization and omission as hegemonic devices. A discussion of the final discourse of discrimination explores how these hegemonic devices again contain the ideological challenges made by the women authors.

DISCOURSE OF DISCRIMINATION

The insights into prejudice and discrimination expressed by Allende, Turner and Walker in their books are virtually ignored in the film versions. For example, Allende recounts examples of the prejudice against indigenous peasants and the bigotry of the wealthy families and ruling politicians toward the working classes.

Indeed, the hatred Esteban initially feels for Pedro stems from Pedro's peasant status, and although Esteban acknowledges that he sired many illegitimate children during the years he raped the peasant women working on his plantation and the neighboring plantations of his peers, he believes that none deserves his name, since they were the result of his union with lower class women. On the other hand, each of the main women characters in the book, beginning with Clara's mother, works to improve the lives of the disadvantaged and disenfranchised. For example, Clara learns compassion for others from the trips she makes as a child with her mother to take food and clothes to people living in the slums and develops a concern for women's rights while accompanying her mother to factories to speak in favor of suffrage. She continues this tradition by opening her home to the less fortunate, providing them with food and shelter. Blanca works with Down's Syndrome children. Férula devotes her life to caring for the poor after being banished from the family by Esteban. Alba takes food from her home's pantry to feed the poor after the military coup restores power to the wealthy, and she helps political dissidents escape the country.

These accounts of bigotry and oppression, and the women's attempts to fight them are, however, minimized in the film, and Allende's descriptions of the women's philanthropic work are missing. We never see the women working to improve the lives of the poor, nor do viewers witness the level of disdain Esteban feels for people "beneath his class." Further, a predominately White cast portrays Allende's South American characters, a decision by August that denies the indigenous South American experience. All of the main characters—the rich and the powerful—are played by White actors: Meryl Streep, Glenn Close, Winona Ryder and Jeremy Irons, while Antonio Banderas, a Spaniard, stars as the peasant Pedro. Indeed, even Allende was "surprised that (August) chose such an Anglo-looking cast. Everybody is so blond" (Simpson, 1994, p. 7)

The Color Purple addresses a range of issues related to racial discrimination. Walker tells about Celie's biological father's being lynched by White men. Nettie explains that on her train ride to New York City, "Only White people can ride in the beds and use the restaurant. And they have different toilets from colored" (p. 141). Later, Nettie writes lengthy letters to Celie in which she describes the bigotry of the White men who are colonizing Africa. In one letter, Nettie explains how the White settlers became angry when a Black man's store was taking their business, and in retaliation, the White settlers burned down the store and hanged the Black man and his two brothers (pp. 180-181). In another instance, Nettie writes about her concerns for Celie's children when they return to America because of the country's "hatred of Black people" (p. 265).

Walker also describes the abuse Sofia endured during her imprisonment simply because she is Black:

When I see Sofia I don't know why she still alive. They crack her skull, they crack her ribs. They tear her nose loose on one side. They blind her in one eye. She swole from head to foot. Her tongue the size of my arm, it stick out tween her teef like a piece of rubber. She can't talk. And she just about the color of a eggplant. (pp. 91-92)

As other examples, the conditions of Sofia's eventual release include working as a maid for Miz Millie, a woman whose blatant bigotry is representative of the White South. And later Sofia explains that, "Some colored people so scared of Whitefolks they claim to love the cotton gin" (p. 272).

Through omission and marginalization, Spielberg's film downplays the very racial issues Walker foregrounds in her novel (McMullen & Solomon, 1994). The details of Celie's father's lynching are missing, as are most of the details about White racism in America and Nettie's experiences with White colonialism in Africa. Spielberg's depiction of Miz Millie is more frivolous—she's a comical character—and far less bigoted than Walker's, thus diluting the impact of the White South's bigotry. And similar to August's selection of a predominately White cast to portray Allende's South American characters, the actors Spielberg chose for his film often do not match how Walker envisioned

her characters. For example, in her notes to her screenplay Walker (1996) writes that although she was pleased with Margaret Avery's portrayal of Shug in the film, she had envisioned this character's physical appearance very differently from the thin, lighter-skinned Avery. Walker saw Shug as resembling Pearl Bailey, a very dark-skinned, stout woman who reminded her of her aunt, and thus matched her descriptions of Shug in her book: skin as "Black as my shoe" and with "lips look like Black plum" (Walker, 1982, p. 21; p. 48). Walker explains that she purposely depicts Shug as very dark-skinned, because until the "stage shows and early movies produced by Whites...began to use 'high yellow' women exclusively in their cabaret and stage dance scenes," dark-skinned women were valued as much as lighter-skinned women by African-American men (Walker, 1996, p. 41).

Although racial discrimination is not a major discourse in her book, Turner nonetheless does talk about the racism she experienced, not only growing up, but in the clubs where she and Ike performed. Recalling her childhood in Tennessee, Turner writes: "There was also the segregation, of course...the Blacks 'knew their place,' right?... And you always went to the back. That was the way it was. And yes, always a tinge of fear" (p. 9). When she began touring with Ike, racism continued to be a problem, particularly in the South, a fact that led her to prefer European tours. In the film version, however, there is a complete absence of racial strife, discrimination or prejudice. The film even ignores the fact that Tina Turner preferred performing in Europe, where she lives today, because the European audiences were more receptive to Black performers than audiences in the United States.

Just as each film marginalizes women and their friendships, alternative spiritualism, and male violence, the movies minimize issues of racism and classism as well. Throughout *The House of the Spirits* and *The Color Purple*, racial and class strife are present, but in ways that contain rather than resist dominant ideals and institutions; they're missing entirely in *What's Love Got To Do With It*. Through the use of omission and marginalization, each director's film presents spectators with "tranquilizing American mythologies" (McMullen & Solomon, 1994, p. 172) that negate the challenges to dominant racial and classist ideologies embedded in the women's discourses.

Implications

The discourses that form the narrative structures of the stories by Isabel Allende (1982/1986), Alice Walker (1982) and Tina Turner (1986) not only celebrate the strengths and triumphs of women of color and the power of friendships among these women, but also resist dominant ideologies concerning gender, race, class and spirituality, with the women in each book depicted as positive forces for social and political change. Indeed, the authors' narratives celebrate women's triumphs over patriarchy, exemplified in this quote from Allende's Alba as she reflects on her fellow prisoners at the concentration camp: "I understood that the days of Colonel Garcia and all those like him are numbered, because they have not been able to destroy the spirit of these women" (p. 429).

These kinds of struggles and triumphs over racism, classism and sexism, and the spiritual discoveries of the women characters through their mutual friendships that are so prominent in each book, are either minimized or absent altogether in the film versions. Through marginalization and omission, the women's discourses are recast in ways that absorb them "into forms compatible to the core ideological structure" (Gitlin, 1982, p. 450) of American society, thus diluting their impact at the same time as the films seem to confront these issues and their consequences. One reason these challenges to dominant ideologies are lost in the film translations surely has to do, as Carolyn Anderson (1988) remarked, with "the problems of adapting an alternative literary voice to the conventionality of mainstream moviemaking" (p. 116). However, Michael Real (1996) asserts that: "Few cultural institutions have been as powerful and as exclusively male-dominated as classic Hollywood.... The world of film, owned and directed by men, has undervalued and marginalized women. The male gaze of old

Hollywood, from behind the camera and in the audience, objectifies and fetishizes women, leaving them mute and voiceless" (pp. 181, 201). Similarly, scholars such as Mary Ann Doane, Patricia Mellencamp and Linda Williams (1984) argue that films operate ideologically to accomplish "the repression of women in patriarchal culture" (p. 8), especially strong, independent women who imperil the stability of the patriarchal order. These tendencies clearly are at work in the cases of these three films.

This comparison of the original narratives and their respective film adaptations illustrates how directors Bille August, Steven Spielberg and Brian Gibson effect the patriarchal containment of Isabel Allende, Alice Walker and Tina Turner, respectively. The directors violate the stories and the unconventional discourses of the women's narratives, diminishing the significance of the women's empowerment, as well as their accounts of racism, classism and alternative spiritualism. Likewise, they replace the women's discourses with ones more acceptable to the traditional characteristics of women, race, class and religion in mainstream Hollywood films, and thus, "the narrative of the female prove[s] to be the narrative of the male" (Dittmar, 1986, p. 80). Central to this argument is that, in each instance, the directors' choices work ideologically to contain the complex voices of the women authors. In other words, these film translations of the women's stories reflect hegemonic interpretations to the extent that the ideological ideals organizing the films' texts direct spectators' attention away from the women's discourses of gender, racial and class inequities, and unconventional religious beliefs and, in turn, actually legitimize for spectators the very ideals the authors themselves reject.

Just as significant is that, as translators, August, Spielberg and Gibson present spectators with scenes that redefine and falsify the female characters—an ideological "make-over" of both characters and their ideas in their transition from the original to the Hollywood. Like Dinesen's stories in *Out of Africa* (Cooper & Descutner, 1996), Allende, Walker, and Turner's original discourses resist and subvert the constraints of dominant ideologies (see also, McMullen & Solomon, 1994). But the three directors' translations, like Sydney Pollack's translation of Dinesen's autobiography (Cooper & Descutner), reaffirm existing power structures, and thus represent the co-optation of the women's stories. Admittedly guided by commercial considerations, the directors insured that audience expectations would not be challenged by privileging in their films only dominant cultural ideologies and traditional notions of Christianity, which would not threaten Hollywood's conception of the hegemonic idealized image of American society in terms of gender, race, class and religion. Further, these translations demonstrate the semiotic power of film as cultural texts to construct meanings for significant societal issues (Fiske, 1987; Dow, 1990, Gitlin, 1982) and, accordingly, the potential of film narratives and images to become the "text and subtext of...how we view the world" (Redding & Brownworth, 1997, pp. 4-5). As Hall (1981) observed, "[T]he media are not only a powerful source of ideas about race [and gender, class and religion].... They are also one place where these ideas are articulated, worked on, transformed and elaborated" (p. 35).

My conclusions are not meant to suggest that August, Spielberg or Gibson intended to marginalize the voices of Allende, Walker and Turner, nor is it likely that they purposely imposed a "patriarchal interpretation" (McMullen & Solomon, 1994, p. 171) on the women's texts. And certainly I am not suggesting that some vast conspiracy to silence women's voices controls Hollywood. Rather, in their representations of these women's stories, August, Spielberg and Gibson chose the tried and "safe" path—to honor cinematic conventions and affirm familiar cultural myths rather than to confront the more emotionally charged and unconventional depictions that structure the discourses in these women's writings. Unfortunately, this practice is not limited to film directors, as researchers have demonstrated how journalists' reliance on "common sense" myths to report news events dealing with race, for example, "impose cultural understandings that feed a hegemonic consensus about American society," (Campbell, 1995, pp. 12-13), thus contributing to the dominant "social order that dictates who participates and who doesn't" (Campbell, p. 15). Further,

Campbell argued that the "most dangerous (and the most common) myths may be those that reflect White, middle and upper-class notions of society and impede multicultural understanding and interpretation" (p. 12). It is precisely the type of "common sense" myths these directors used that resulted in their appropriation of the women's unconventional stories. Despite the best intentions these directors surely had when they adapted the women's novels to films, their reliance on "comforting familiar narrative" and "tranquilizing American mythologies" (McMullen & Solomon, 1994, p. 172) to appeal to spectators' desires and to attract the largest audiences, has profound implications that reach far beyond the box-office: each film perpetuates myths that "preclude the kind of understanding that is necessary to attain the tolerance and compassion that must precede the elimination" of discrimination and prejudice in America (Campbell, p. 132). As Gorham (1999) argues in his reference the Barthes' articulation of myths and their power, "Those who are in a dominant social position have the power to define the dominant understandings and thus have tremendous ability to make their definitions appear natural and unarguable" (p. 232).

It is important to note that in Alice Walker's own screenplay adaptation of *The Color Purple* (1996), which Spielberg rejected, the women's empowering friendships and their triumphs over racism, sexism and male violence are not marginalized or omitted. The very discourses of Walker's novel that Spielberg negated from the film text of her adaptation: Celie and Shug's lesbian relationship remains intact,[28] as does the women's support for each other; Shug remains unapologetic for her chosen lifestyle. The discourses of violence and racism are foregrounded in Walker's version, and alternative spiritualism is celebrated, not ignored. In other words, when women authors translate their own stories to film, women and their value systems are more likely to remain the focus. As Caryl Rivers said, "It is only when women fashion their own stories, set their own agendas and tell truths about their own lives that women will be seen clearly" (1993, p. 17). Of course, there is no guarantee that a woman director or screenwriter would translate women's discourses of patriarchal resistance any differently from the prevailing Hollywood standard. Film director Martha Coolidge asserts, however, that, "Until women are in significant numbers in the industry, we won't see a difference in the kind of films being made or a lot of understanding of women's plight" (cited in Infusino, 1991, p. E4).

This case study has focused on both the strategic choices directors made in translating these women's texts into film versions and the ways in which those choices can be read critically as strategies that work to contain any challenges to dominant ideologies and norms. The three directors fundamentally misrepresent the views, emphases, and personal visions that animate the women's writings. Few films show women—of any color—succeeding on their own, focusing on their strengths or the strength of women's community, a point Walker (1996) lamented when she wrote:

> It was painful to realize that many men rarely consider reading what women write, or bother to listen to what women are saying about how we feel. How we perceive life. How we think things should be. That they cannot honor our struggles or our pain. That they see our stories as meaningless to them, or assume they are absent from them, distorted. Or think they must have control over our expressions. And us. (p. 39)

Acknowledgements

An earlier version of this chapter was published previously in the *American Communication Journal* 2(2) (1999). Reprinted by permission of the author and the *American Communication Journal* editors and is available on-line: http://acjournal.org/holdings/vol2/Iss2/articles/brendacooper/index.html

Endnotes

1. Rivers (1993, p. 17).

2. I selected these three books and films for my study because each woman's book is autobiographical in nature and challenges dominant cultural ideologies. Additionally, although voices and images of people of color are marginalized in Hollywood films, *The Color Purple* and *What's Love Got To Do With It* were box-office hits, thus widely perpetuating specific images of the women authors and their political, moral and personal beliefs. And although *The House of the Spirits* did not experience similar box-office profits as the other two movies, the well-known celebrity stars—Meryl Streep, Jeremy Irons, Glenn Close, Wynona Ryder, and Antonio Banderas—enhanced the film's potential resonance for spectators.

3. For example, see: Anderson, 1988; Aycock & Schoenecke, 1988; Cooper & Descutner, 1996; Fried, 1987; Giddings, Selby, & Wensley, 1990; MacKay, 1985; Mayne, 1988; McMullen & Solomon, 1994; Orr, 1985; Richardson, 1969; Sinyard, 1986.

4. For example, see: Barthes (1973); Fiske, (1986; 1987); Gitlin (1982); Gramsci (1971); Hanke, (1990); and, Storey (1993).

5. Although screenwriters play important roles in translating books to film versions, ultimately, directors have control of the films and the final cut, and it is their visions that dictate what is included or omitted in the scripts (Redding & Brownworth, 1997).

6. Neither Cooper and Descutner's (1996) analysis of the film translation of Dinesen's *Out of Africa* nor McMullen & Solomon's (1994) analysis of Spielberg's translation of Walker's *The Color Purple* specifically addresses the use of hegemonic devices as strategies to contain resistance to dominant ideologies embedded in women's discourses.

7. Loder's contribution to the book primarily involves interviews with people who knew Turner, and providing historical context to the events of Turner's life as she describes them in her own words.

8. For a synopsis of Allende's *The House of the Spirits*, the influence of feminism in her writings, and links to her other novels, check: http://www.emory.edu/ENGLISH/Bahri/Allende.html

9. A short biography of Allende include links to other sites discussing her assassinated uncle, Salvador Allende, and Chilean politics: http://www.emory.edu/ENGLISH/Bahri/Allende.html. Allende's personal web site that also includes background information about her as well as some additional interesting links: http://www.isabelallende.com

10. For more information about Latin-American women's writing and feminism, see for example: Berta Broncano (1998) reviews *Latin American Women's Writing: Feminist Readings in Theory and Crisis* by Jones & Davies (1996) for the *Journal of Gender Studies*. Janet Gold (1997) reviews three relevant books for *NWSA Journal*: *An Annotated Bibliography of Hispanic Feminist Criticism* (Charon-Deutsch, 1994); *Latin American Women Writers: Class, Race, and Gender* (Jehenson, 1995); and, *Lesbian Voices from Latin American: Breaking Ground* (Martinez, 1996). The reviewers discuss Allende's works in the context of a canon of Latin-American women writers articulated by marginalized women who challenge and resist the patriarchal structures that defined their lives and their cultures.

11. For a review of *The Same River Twice*, see: http://www.metroactive.com/papers/sonoma/02.15.96/walker-9607.html

12. For a synopsis of *The Color Purple*, see: http://www.educeth.ch/english/readinglist/walkera/index.html

13. Discussions of Walker's reactions to Spielberg's film adaptation of *The Color Purple* are found in the following location: http://www.salon.com/09/departments/litchat1.html. An article in the *Detroit News* by Deb Price (1996) includes numerous quotations from Walker in which she discusses her reactions to the film adaptation.

14. The following site includes biographical information about Alice Walker: "Writing & Resistance:" http://www.writingandresistance.com/walker/link.jsp (includes links to several other sites with information about Alice Walker).

15. A short interview in which Walker discusses her reactions to criticism from the African-American community is found at: http://www.salon.com/09/departments/litchat2.html

16. For an extended biography of Tina Turner, see Sherman's 1998 article in the *Philadelphia Tribune*.

17. Turner discusses her marriage to Ike, her career and her current life in Europe in an interview with Lynn Norment (1996) in *Ebony* magazine.

18. For a review of *What's Love Got To Do With It* in the *Journal of Criminal Justice and Popular Culture*, see: http://www.albany.edu/scj/jcjpc/vol3is3/love.html

19. Although an African-American woman, Kate Lanier, is the primary screenwriter for *What's Love Got To Do With It,* as stated earlier, women screenwriters may feel pressure from producers and directors to fit their narratives to prevailing dominant ideologies and traditional Hollywood conventions (Seger, 1996). Based on the comments cited earlier from this film's producers and director (Walker, 1993), it seems reasonable to assume that Lanier may have experienced such pressures.

20. In this section, no years or names will be cited after references to citations from Allende, Walker or Turner's books, nor after references to the films.

21. The acknowledgment pages in the three books are not numbered.

22. See note 21.

23. See note 21.

24. Walker (1997) discusses her alternative spirituality in an article published in *On The Issues*.

25. See note 21.

26. For a discussion of how women use writing to recover from adolescent trauma, see Sapphire's (1996) review of *A Hunger for Language* by Pemberton (1996).

27. Alba is omitted from the film and the events of Blanca and Alba's lives are combined into the character of Blanca, who is imprisoned when the dictatorship is restored.

28. An article in *Harvard Gay & Lesbian Review* (Forrest, 1996) discusses the development of lesbian themes and fiction.

Name: _____

Date: _____

1. Explain the concept of hegemonic devices and how such devices in media narratives may work to marginalize the voices of women of color, as well as other groups of disenfranchised populations in American society.

2. Explain Gledhill's concept of "women's discourse" discussed in the chapter. How does a woman's discourse contradict and make challenges to dominant hegemonic ideologies such as patriarchy? Discuss the reason why women's discourses are often discourses of resistance.

3. Cooper identified the same four discourses that represent resistance to dominant ideologies in each of the women's books, yet the women came from different backgrounds and wrote very different books. Discuss how the interaction of race and gender in their personal lives influenced the narratives of Isabel Allende, Alice Walker and Tina Turner.

4. None of the four discourses that challenged dominant ideologies in each woman's book—women's empowerment, spiritualism, male violence, and discrimination— is prominent in the film translations. Discuss possible reasons why the male directors chose to ignore or minimize these discourses of resistance underlying the women's stories.

5. The vast majority of Hollywood film directors and screenwriters are White men. How might these three films have been different if they had been written and directed by women of color?

6. Discuss whether filmmakers have a responsibility to eliminate sexist, racist and heterosexist stereotypes in their products and to reflect the reality and the diversity of our society. In other words, why should we care—or should we—about media stereotypes or lack of images of people who are not part of the dominant power groups of society (i.e., White, male, hetero-sexuals)?

1. Select one of the three movies critiqued in this chapter. After critically viewing the film, write a short reaction paper (2-3 pp.) discussing where you agree and/or disagree with Cooper's interpretation of the film. Be specific, explaining why you agree or disagree, providing support for your responses.

2. Select a film written or directed by a woman of color (e.g., *Eve's Bayou*), and compare this film's depiction of race, gender, sexuality and spiritualism to the conclusions Cooper reaches in this chapter. How are the women and men depicted in the film you select? How are racial issues represented? Sexuality? Spiritualism? Then discuss whether having women of color behind the camera makes a difference in how their stories are told in film.

3. **Team Project:** Select another book by a woman of color that has been translated to a film version. After each student finishes the selected book, view the film together as a team. Using the four women's discourses identified by Cooper in this chapter, compare the discourses in the narratives of the book with those in the film narratives. How do the women's discourses in the books compare to the discourses found in the film? What do the women's discourses "teach" us about gender and race? What do the discourses in the film's narratives "teach" us about gender and race? Who is privileged in the women's discourses? In the film's narratives? How do your results compare to those Cooper presented in this chapter? Based on your team's analysis, prepare a presentation for the class.

4. **Team Project:** For this assignment, you and your team members will be scriptwriters. After reading one of the women's books, your job is to rewrite the screenplay of the film version: *The House of the Spirits, The Color Purple,* or *What's Love Got to Do With It?* Using the four categories of women's discourses Cooper identified—women's empowerment, spiritualism, male violence, and racial discrimination—rewrite the film's script to more closely reflect the author's voice. Based on your rewrites, what suggestions do you have for filmmakers to represent gender, race, sexuality and alternative spiritualism more responsibly?

REFERENCES

Allende, I. (1986). *The house of the spirits* (M. Bogin, Trans.). New York: Bantam Books. (Original work published 1982).

Anderson, C. (1988). Film and literature. In G. R. Edgerton (Ed.), *Film and the arts in symbiosis: A resource guide* (pp. 97-134). Westport, CT: Greenwood Press.

Aycock, W., & Schoenecke, M. (1988). *Film and literature: A comparative approach to adaptation.* Lubbock, TX: Texas Tech University Press.

Barthes, R. (1973). *Mythologies.* London: Paladin.

Boudreau, J. (1993, May 31). Ever the outsider.... Novelist Isabel Allende has been an exile, a stranger, and a woman in a man's world. *The Los Angeles Times*, View, p. 1.

Broncano, B. (1998). Book reviews: Latin American women's writing: Feminist readings in theory and crisis. *Journal of Gender Studies, 7* (1), 115-116.

Campbell, C. P. (1995). *Race, myth and the news.* Thousand Oaks, CA: Sage.

Cartwright, L., & Fonoroff, N. (1994). Narrative is *narrative:* So what is new? In D. Carson, L. Dittmar, & J. R. Carson (Eds.), *Multiple voices in feminist film criticism* (pp. 124-139). Minneapolis, MN: University of Minnesota Press.

Chapin, D., & Krost, B. (Producers), & Gibson, B. (Director). (1993). *What's love got to do with it?* [Film]. (Videotape available from Buena Vista Home Video, Burbank, CA).

Charnon-Deutsch, L. (1994). *An annotated bibliography of Hispanic feminist criticism.* Stoney Brook, NY: Feministas Unidas.

Chatman, S. (1978). *Story and discourse: Narrative structure in fiction and film.* Ithaca, NY: Cornell University Press.

Cheyfitz, E. (1991). *The poetics of imperialism: Translation and colonization from The Tempest to Tarzan.* New York: Oxford University Press.

Cooper, B., & Descutner, D. (1996). "It had no voice to it": Sydney Pollack's film translation of Isak Dinesen's *Out of Africa. Quarterly Journal of Speech, 82,* 228-250.

Dittmar, L. (1986). Beyond gender, and within it: The social construction of female desire. *Wide Angle, 8*(3-4), 79-88.

Doane, M. A., Mellencamp, P., & Williams, L. (1984). Feminist film criticism: An introduction. In M. A. Doane, P. Mellencamp, and L. Williams (Eds.), *Re-Vision: Essays in feminist film criticism* (pp. 1-17). Frederick, MD: University Publications of America.

Dow, B. J. (1990). Hegemony, feminist criticism and *The Mary Tyler Moore Show. Critical Studies in Mass Communication, 7,* 261-274.

Eichinger, B. (Producer), & August, B. (Director). (1994). *The house of the spirits* [Film]. (Videotape available from Live Home Video, Van Nuys, CA.).

Fiske, J. (1986). Television: Polysemy and popularity. *Critical Studies in Mass Communication, 3,* 391-408.

Fiske, J. (1987). *Television culture:* New York: Methuen.

Forrest, K. V. (1996). Evolution of a revolution in lesbian literature. *Harvard Gay & Lesbian Review, 3*(2), 6+.

Fried, D. (1987). Hollywood's convention and film adaptation. *Theatre Journal, 39*(3), 294-306.

Fussell, B. H. (1993, May). Isabel Allende's fantasy life. *Lear's, 6,* 50-53, 80-81.

Giddings, R., Selby, K., & Wensley, C. (1990). *Screening the novel: The theory and practice of literary dramatization.* New York: St. Martin's Press.

Gitlin, T. (1982). Prime time ideology: The hegemonic process in television entertainment. In H. Newcomb (Ed.), *Television: The critical view* (3rd ed.) (pp. 426-454). New York: Oxford University Press.

Gledhill, C. (1994). Image and voice: Approaches to Marxist-feminist film criticism. In D. Carson, L. Dittmar, & J. R. Carson (Eds.), *Multiple voices in feminist film criticism* (pp. 109-123). Minneapolis, MN: University of Minnesota Press.

Gold, J. N. (1997). An annotated bibliography of Hispanic feminist criticism; Latin American women writers: Class, race and gender; Lesbian voices from Latin America: Breaking ground. *NWSA Journal, 9*(1), 126+.

Gorham, B. (1999). Stereotypes in the media: So what? *The Howard Journal of Communications, 10,* 229-247.

Gramsci, A. (1971). *Selections from prison notebooks* (Q. Hoare & G. Nowell-Smith, editors and translators). London: Lawerence and Wishart.

Griggs, B. (1996, April 14). Allende's 'Paula' brings an outpouring of empathy. *The Salt Lake Tribune,* p. E5.

Hall, S. (1981). The Whites of their eyes. In G. Bridges & R. Brunt (Eds.), *Silver linings: Some strategies for the eighties* (pp. 28-52). London: Lawrence & Wishart.

Hamlin, J. (Producer). (1996, November 10). "Tina Turner." *60 Minutes.* New York: CBS.

Hanke, R. (1990). Hegemonic masculinity in *thirtysomething. Critical Studies in Mass Communication, 7,* 231-248.

Henderson, B. (1973/1974). Critique of cine-structuralism. *Film Quarterly, 27*(2), 25-34.

Hernández, C. D. (1996, April 23). The many lives of Isabel Allende [On-line]. Available: http://www.crown.edu/grad/CLASSES/int525/crn36.htm

hooks, b. (1996). *Reel to real: Race, sex and class at the movies.* New York: Routledge.

Infusino, D. (1991, May 5). Screened out: Women in film. *San Diego Union,* pp. E1, E4.

Isabel Allende. (1994. September/October). Mother Jones [On-line]. Available: http://www.motherjones.com/mother_jones/SO94/allende.html

Jehenson, M. Y. (1995). *Latin American women writers: Class, race and gender.* Albany, NY: State University of New York Press.

Jones, A. B., & Davies, C. (Eds.) (1996). *Latin American women's writings: Feminist readings in theory and crisis.* Oxford: Oxford University Press.

Lipman, A. (1994, April). The house of the spirits [Review of the film *The House of the Spirits*]. *Sight & Sound, 4,* 43-44.

Luedtke, K., & Pollack, S. (1987). *Out of Africa: The shooting script.* New York: Newmarket Press.

MacKay, C. H. (1985). A novel's journey into film: The case of *Great Expectations. Literature/Film Quarterly, 13*(2), 127-134.

Martinez, E. M. (1996). *Lesbian voices from Latin America: Breaking ground.* New York: Garland Publishing.

Mayne, J. (1988). *Private novels, public films.* Athens, GA: The University of Georgia Press.

McMullen, W. J., & Solomon, M. (1994). The politics of adaptation: Steven Spielberg's appropriation of *The Color Purple. Text and Performance Quarterly, 14*(2), 158-174.

Mouffe, C. (1979). Hegemony and ideology in Gramsci. In C. Mouffe (Ed.), *Gramsci and Marxist theory* (pp. 168-204). London: Routledge and Kegan Paul.

Norment, L. (1996, September). Tina Turner (interview). *Ebony, 51,* 38+.

Orr, C. (1985). *Written on the Wind* and the ideology of adaptation. *Film Criticism, 10*(3), 1-8.

Parkes, C. (1995, December 15). Clancy enters cyberspace. *National Business Review, 25,* 40, 42.

Pemberton, G. (1996). A hunger for language. [review of the book *Push*] *Women's Review of Books, 14*(2), 1+.

Price, D. (1996, March 1). Alice through the looking glass. *The Detroit News.*

Real, M. R. (1996). *Exploring media culture: A guide.* Thousand Oaks, CA: Sage.

Redding, J. M., & Brownworth, V. A. (1997). *Film fatales: Independent women directors*. Seattle, WA: Seal Press.

Reynolds, P. (1993). Introduction. In P. Reynolds (Ed.), *Novel images: Literature in performance* (pp. 1-16). London: Routledge.

Richardson, R. (1969). *Literature and film*. Bloomington, IN: Indiana University Press.

Rivers, C. (1993). Bandwagons, women and cultural mythology. *Media Studies Journal, 7*(1-2), 1-17.

Sapphire (1996). *Push*. New York: Alfred A. Knopf.

Seger, L. (1996). *When women call the shots: The developing power and influence of women in television and film*. New York: Henry Holt & Company.

Shea, M. E. (1990). Love, eroticism, and pornography in the works of Isabel Allende. *Women's Studies, 18*, 223-231.

Sherman, S. (1998, May 29). Rock diva Tina Turner celebrates 40 years in music. *Philadelphia Tribune*, Magazine, p. 12.

Simpson, B. (1994, March 27). The mystical Isabel Allende. *The Los Angeles Times*, Calendar, p. 7.

Sinyard, N. (1986). *Filming literature: The art of screen adaptation*. London: Croom Helm Ltd.

Spielberg, S. (Producer & Director). (1985). *The color purple* [Film]. (Videotape available from Warner Home Video, Burbank, CA).

Storey, J. (1993). *An introductory guide to cultural theory and popular culture*. Athens, GA: University Press of Georgia.

Svetkey, B. (1998, May 22). Widowmaker. *Entertainment Weekly, 433*, 32-33.

Turner, T., with Loder, K. (1986). *I, Tina: My life story*. New York: Avon Books.

Walker, A. (1997). The only reason you want to go to Heaven is that you have been driven out of your mind (off your land and out of your lover's arms)—Clear seeing, inherited religion and reclaiming the pagan self. *On the issues, 6*(2), 16+.

Walker, A. (1982). *The color purple*. New York: Pocket Books.

Walker, A. (1996). *The same river twice: Honoring the difficult*. New York: Washington Square Press.

Walker, M. (1993, May 16). Tina Turner's story through a Disney prism. *The Los Angeles Times*, Calendar, p. 5.

The Personal Is the Political: Cinematic Representations of African-American Women in *The Color Purple* and *Waiting to Exhale*

Rebecca Brasfield

Androcentric, or male-centered approaches in film analysis, have been historically dominant in American culture. When *The Color Purple* (film version) was released in December 1985, syndicated columnist Tony Brown described the movie as "the most racist depiction of Black men since *The Birth of a Nation* and the most anti-Black family film of the modern film era" (Bobo, 1992, p. 90). Reviewer Charles Brown stated that *Waiting to Exhale* was "a tough love letter to black males everywhere" (Hutchinson, 1994). Although the films are primarily about the lives of African-American women, the discussion and controversy following the release of these films largely focused on the cinematic portrayal of African-American men. The representation of African-American women in contemporary American film is often overlooked in favor of commentary about African-American male imagery. In studying the films it is important to promote awareness regarding the sexism present when deconstructing the relationship between mass media contents and mass media effects.

The Color Purple and *Waiting to Exhale* are films based on novels written by African-American women. *The Color Purple* captures a Black woman's struggle toward autonomy and wholeness in the early 20th century southern United

States. Celie, the protagonist, comes to realize that she has her own voice during her battle against sexist oppression. Her stepfather repeatedly rapes her. Her children are taken away from her. She is given away as a wife to a man she calls "Mister." In this relationship, she is abused and exploited. Throughout the story, Celie bonds with the women in her life, who assist her in learning to love herself. The film portrays her efforts to self-actualize in a world that degrades and oppresses her.

Waiting to Exhale takes place in a modern era. The film adaptation details four African-American women's desperate search for African-American male love. All of the women are successful in their professional lives. The film characterizes the women as victims of African-American men who lack morality. The film also portrays the women as victims of their own poor choices in relationships. The heroines are projected as successful because of their ability to expel contemptible African-American men from their lives. Only one character develops a loving and intimate relationship with a Black man. However, her story is obscured by the tribulations of the other three women.

The Color Purple and *Waiting to Exhale* have been heavily criticized for their portrayal of African-American male characters. When asked how she felt about the negative representation of Black men in *The Color Purple*, Walker responded:

> I felt thoroughly trashed for many years because the attacks didn't just happen around the showing of the film; they continued for a long time. The only way I could keep going was to stay in my work. Black men—not all black men, but the ones who were violently opposed to my work—I think were dealing out of ego and were unable to even see the male characters that I had created (Zinn, 1996, p. 2).

While it is important to discuss the characterization of the African-American men in the films, it is crucial to develop a discourse on the representation of the narrative of the African-American female voices imparting their stories. The women's points of view must not be overlooked or forgotten.

Hollywood cinema is an institution which has historically promoted homogenization in its representation of African-American images. In *Framing Blackness* (1993, p. 2), Ed Guerrero explains:

> The representation of Black people on the commercial screen has amounted to one grand, multifaceted illusion. For Blacks have been subordinated, marginalized, positioned, and devalued in every possible manner to glorify and relentlessly hold in place the white-dominated symbolic order and racial hierarchy of American society.

The actual realities of life for African Americans are repeatedly portrayed inaccurately. Films such as *Glory* (1989), *Driving Miss Daisy* (1990) and *Monster's Ball* (2001) are examples of movies that confront African-American experiences and were also blockbuster hits in the United States. However, apology and sympathy for bigoted White characters veil the racism and sexual exploitation in the films. The images depicted in the films are presented in a manner that fails to address the collective systems of racial, sexual and class exploitation facing African Americans in the United States.

Although African-American women produced the novels *The Color Purple* and *Waiting to Exhale*, the novels are not armed with politi-cal resistance. The female characters seem to identify the sources of their oppression with individuals rather than with *systems of exploitation*. The films based on these novels do the same. The stories these women tell are crucial in developing a dialogue on race, gender and sexuality within Black communities. *The novels do not dictate radical political objectives which challenge the social ills on a community level rather than an individual level.* That failure by both African American novelists was critical in the decision to market these films to a broad audience.

Personal vs. Political Resistance

The women in *The Color Purple* and *Waiting to Exhale* undergo incomplete transformations. Personal resistance is opposition on an individual level and on an individual basis. Political resistance incorporates the consciousness attained from the personal struggle for independence with the progressive effort to assign social and political accountability to the fundamental and institutional causes of the oppression. Personal resistance and political resistance are two ways of confronting victimization. However, there are political limitations when African-American women are viewed as countering their oppression on an individual level rather than regarding their exploitation as systemic and institutionally based.

Racism and sexism can influence both White and non-White controlled cinematic productions of Blackness. It is unfair to assume that non-White productions of media images of people of color are always more progressive and radical than their White counterparts. Spike Lee, a critically acclaimed African-American director, wrote and directed the movie *School Daze* (1988). The film addressed the prevalence of internalized racism and overt sexism and homophobia within the Black college community. While it was clear that *School Daze* was critical in its view of the color caste and internalized racism, the sexism and homophobia were not critically examined. Their presence in the film was merely an accessory to the real problem of racism. In this instance, an African-American male director confronted one social problem, with little regard to its influence and relationship to others. In this way, this film also lacks radical political objectives.

When literary works are reproduced as cinematic works, cultural representations reach larger audiences. Thus, the messages must then appeal to larger ticket buying audiences. This occurs in order to feed the capitalism on which our country thrives. While discussing the politics involving the films' production, one must keep in mind that these films were made by large Hollywood production companies. 20th Century Fox produced *Waiting to Exhale*. *The Color Purple* was made by Warner Brothers Studios. Forest Whitaker, an African-American man, directed *Waiting to Exhale*. *The Color Purple* was directed by a White man, Steven Spielberg. Alice Walker sold the screenplay rights of *The Color Purple* because she valued the importance of having the messages in her text reach audiences who would not read her book (Bobo, 1988). Hollywood is composed of Eurocentrically owned corporations and businesses. They have little concern with developing progressive subject matter in films that address people of color.

A major weakness of both the novels and the films is that they fail to show how African-American female characters can transform their personal resistance into political resistance. The women rise to individual self-awareness, but not to a level of political awareness and action. These characters fail to ascertain the politic dimensions of their struggles.

Producers of film media encounter obstacles transforming characters to political resistance. *The Color Purple* and *Waiting to Exhale* showcase social problems packaged as individual struggles. Within this framework, the films feature obligatory happy endings, highlighting individual triumphs. The African-American women are therefore cast into socially constructed, marginal roles. The women are empowered by developing self-esteem and removing the destructive presence of African-American men. The producers, in fact, advocate the societal problem of patriarchy, which they initially set out to condemn.

Miss Evers Boys (1997) portrays an African-American female nurse's effort to wage both personal and political resistance to the unethical and murderous medical research study officially titled, "Tuskegee Study of Untreated Syphilis in the Negro Male." The film is a docudrama that focuses on Eunice Stone. She is the nurse who participated in the "healthcare" of the Black men in the study. She is portrayed as genuinely caring for the men and their plight during this injustice. However, her testimony to the United States Senate (political resistance) forces the audience to question her complicity in this horrendous act. In this instance, an African-American female character is represented as transforming her personal resistance to a mild form of political resistance. However, the film focuses on her guilt in the process with little criticism of racism or the White individuals who were responsible for orchestrating the murder of African-American men in the experiment. The film does not portray her act of testifying about the case as political resistance. The film fails to confront racism as an important component in these atrocities by focusing on the Black nurse's role in the study. It chooses to focus on her individual efforts to help the men and question her role in their disabling and deadly fate.

Political resistance requires political consciousness. The characters from *The Color Purple* and *Waiting to Exhale* fail to recognize that women, as a gender, face similar struggles. However, because the women approach their battles on an individual level and are successful rejecting their own oppression, individual triumph is represented as the logical end of their resistance. A similar problem is conveyed in *Roots* (1977). Enslaved Africans, as individuals, were depicted as attempting to flee slavery. It is crucial to understand that instances in which enslaved Africans escaped slavery or were occasionally "awarded" freedom by their masters serve as examples of individual triumph. Slavery as an institution remained intact in spite of these individual efforts. The women in the films may free themselves from their personal turmoil. However, the women are unable to understand that overcoming that struggle does not free them from the institutions of sexism and racism.

Media Politics and Consciousness Transformation

In order to understand the role of film in contemporary American culture, one must understand that American society is racist, sexist, ageist, capitalist and homophobic. These cultural phenomenons can be traced back to 17th century Britain's obsession with imperialism and its colonization of the Americas. The political and social agenda of these colonizers is present four hundred years later. Those ideologies that justified White supremacy are still present, in large part, because of the perpetuation of discriminatory stereotypes and the collective psychological, physical and emotional destruction of colonized people (the subaltern) and their culture.

Today, the misappropriation of social, political and cultural dominance is evident in many aspects of American society. Film production is one area within the media domain. Film is a powerful mechanism used to shape social consciousness. The domination that takes place in film, radio, television and advertising is called media imperialism (Tomlimson, 1991). It is not feasible to engage in a discussion about media imperialism without understanding how cultural domination factors into this process. Cultural supremacy and domination occur in the filmmaking industry. Social discourse is controlled, produced and regulated through film media.

Popular culture has immense power in mediating culture to the public. Much of what the general public is ignorant of, it "learns" about from television and film. Television and film have the tendency to project very distinct representations of Americans and American life. Media have the ability to inhabit ambiguous spaces in our minds. These representations perpetuate ignorance and promote the validation of stereotype formation and bigotry. Stereotypes about minorities thrive because they are socially tolerated and are continually reintroduced by the media.

The problems the women confront in *The Color Purple* and *Waiting to Exhale* are portrayed as their own. Individual resistance struggles cannot ensure successful resolutions of the is-sues involved, if individuals are expected to fight institutional battles. According to bell hooks, Toni Morrison reminds us that:

> Popular culture, shaped by film, theater, advertising, the press, television and literature is heavily engaged in race talk...She calls race talk the explicit insertion into everyday life of racial signs and symbols that have no meaning other than pressing African-Americans to the lowest level of the racial hierarchy" (hooks, 1995, 23).

The messages expressed in these films propagate cultural colonialism through cinematic representation. African-American women's subjugation is a problem for which the American public is responsible. All marginalized groups in this society who suffer grave injustices, who are victimized by institutionalized systems of domination (race, class, gender, etc.), are faced with the difficult task of developing strategies that draw attention to their predicament without re-inscribing a paradigm of victimization (hooks, 1995, p. 58).

Media shape and control our cultural perceptions and understandings. For example, news broadcasters select which types of stories are covered each night. Sitcoms portray certain types of people, families, lifestyles, predicaments, etc. Other media outlets follow suit.

African-American female authors have creative and political power. They should not ignore the value of literary work as political and as potential propaganda. Authors Alice Walker and Terry McMillan are capable of using their creative and political influence to eradicate representations of African-American women that promote cultural colonialism and media imperialism. "The communications media, by affirming already existing social patterns, has both perpetuated and fostered racism and sexism to new generations" (Larkin, 1988, p. 158). But both the authors have produced characterizations of African-American women that fail to embrace radical approaches that would identify the oppressive forces in their lives as part of a system of domination in the context in which it exists. While the African-American women in *The Color Purple* and *Waiting to Exhale* are fictional, they are presented to the public as very real. In that respect, the discussion on the representation of

African-American women in literature is substantive and relevant.

Characterizations of African-American Women

The African-American women in *The Color Purple* are successful in resisting sexist opression. Celie, Nettie, Sophia and Shug Avery are all able to resist the sexist brutality they face at the hands of African-American men. Celie is the main character in this film. At the age of fourteen, her stepfather rapes her. She gives birth to two children, both fathered by him. He steals those children from her, leaving her unsure whether they are alive or dead. Her stepfather makes her marry a man (Mister) she does not love or know, for that matter. Both her stepfather and Mister sexually, physically and psychologically abuse her. She is in a situation of forced servitude and abuse with no apparent means of escape.

Celie finds love, which helps her find herself. Shug Avery and Celie love each other. Celie transcends abject circumstances through her friendship with other women (Moritz, 1984). In that respect, Celie's lesbian relationship is a way for her to resist male domination. All of her relationships with women are in some sense acts of resistance to life in a male-dominated world. "Western heterosexuality, which advances male supremacy, continues to be upheld by many Black people, especially Black men, as the most desired state of affairs between men and women" (Clark, 1995, 245). Celie's relationship with Shug Avery eventually denies Mister the opportunity to tyrannize or manipulate her.

As she grows, Celie confronts Mister and even begins to call him Albert towards the end of the movie. Celie stops using the title because she feels she is no longer subordinate to him. Finally she walks out on him. Leaving Albert is just one step in her journey to self-discovery. When her stepfather dies, she realizes that she and her sister are the inheritors of his estate. She is left with his home and his business. She moves in to his home and opens a pants shop. She uses her domestic skills to earn economic freedom. To add to her empowerment, Celie is reunited with her sister and the children that were stolen from her

at their birth. She is able to self-actualize with the people who love her.

Celie's sister Nettie understands the patriarchal culture she is confronted with. She learns to live in a world where male domination prevails. After Celie is married to Mister, Nettie is forced to deal with the advances of her stepfather. She fights him off and eventually runs away in search of Celie. However, when she finds Celie, the sexual advances of Mister lead her again to run away from this sexually violent culture. In fact, her escape takes her all the way to the Olinka tribe in Africa, where she works as a missionary teaching the children and assisting the tribe in their medical needs. But the Olinka hold sexist attitudes toward women. They do not believe it is important to educate the women. Nettie rebels against all such oppressors, refusing to remain where sexual exploitation can defeat her. She tells Celie, "You gotta fight back." So, Nettie represents female independence. Yet she does not become politically empowered.

The heroines' personal empowerment manifests itself in different ways. Celie leaves her husband, Mister, and learns to love Shug Avery. (The film grossly minimizes the importance of Celie's love for the woman Shug.) Nettie runs away from Mister, another brutal Black male presence in her life. She discovers both her cultural and familial roots in Africa. Sophia stands up to every man who tries to oppress her. Finally, despite rejection from her religious father, Shug lives her life by her own rules without apologizing to anyone. These four women are survivors of their once victimized state.

Empowerment means transformation from a state of victimization to a state of raised consciousness. The characters embrace personal empowerment and reject oppressive forces in their lives, but they do not take on political resistance. The women in *The Color Purple* no longer face the brutal violence and exploitation of the African-American male characters. They reject sexist domination as it affects their individual lives. In that respect, they empower themselves on an individual or personal level.

Likewise, the women in *Waiting to Exhale* stop making choices that lead to unhappiness and become conscious of their own needs, independent of other's expectations.

"Bernadine was married to John." This is an ironic way to begin describing her. Actually, she went to school for an MBA, but never uses the degree. She was a secretary for her husband in order to help further his career. She never followed her own dream to start a catering business because he advised against it. All of "their" assets were in John's name. She allowed him to handle all of their finances. And then John left her for a White woman! Bernadine had signed over her life to John for the span of their marriage. She had lost her identity by making very poor choices. However, she regains her independence and self-confidence over the course of the divorce proceedings. Her awards from the divorce settlement are symbolic of her gains in personal development.

Bernadine's growth is exemplified in one scene toward the end of the movie. She and her daughter look through the window at the rain. The daughter says, "Mommy, God stopped crying." Bernadine replies, "I don't think those are God's tears at all. That's just his way of making sure things keep growing." She is able to redefine the traumatic and devastating divorce into an experience that promotes her growth as an individual. This is an example of consciousness transformation.

The African-American women in *Waiting to Exhale* succeed in making "better" choices for themselves. Bernadine, Gloria, Robin and Savannah grow during the film, i.e., break free of their patterns of victimization and come to new understandings.

Personal consciousness is presented as if it were the final step in the women's transformations. The message from both the authors and filmmakers is that personal consciousness is the goal of self-actualization. It simply is not. Unfortunately, none of the women moves beyond to embrace political consciousness or social activism toward the destructive forces they have faced.

In an essay titled "Radical Black Female Subjects," bell hooks defines a radical subject as an individual who promotes feminist consciousness and opposes sexism and racism at all times. A radical subject is someone who combines personal empowerment with political activism (hooks, 1992, 47-60). According to this definition, the women in these films are not radical Black female subjects because they do not try to change society. Radical feminists would understand their oppression in the context in which it continues to exist, a patriarchal culture which devalues women. That is, radical subjects understand the framework of their individual circumstances.

These films narrate stories of African-American women struggling for independence. But they simply lack radical political objectives. Revolutionary feminists not only oppose exploitation and marginalization, but also strive to change existing norms as a result of that resistance, a journey from victimization to political consciousness. The African-American women characterized in these books and their films do not succeed, therefore, in transforming their personal empowerment into political resistance. The unfortunate implication is that those individual, poor choices (self-blame) and the sexist oppression of African-American men *alone* exploit African-American women. In effect, the rest of society can ignore its responsibility and role in the subjugation of African-American women and, by extension, all other oppressed groups.

Conclusion

Feminism's goal is to create a society void of patriarchy and all forms of oppression. The feminist movement has produced many authors, women and men, who have created works which promote this cause. Terry McMillan and Alice Walker have written novels that give voice to African-American women. The women in their novels are oppressed because of their gender, their race, their class and their sexuality. But the novels and their cinematic adaptations fail to communicate the systemic and institutional sources of that oppression.

A White man and a Black man direct the cinematic adaptions of *The Color Purple* and *Waiting to Exhale*. The films are directed with similar objectives in spite of this difference. These two blockbuster hits lack an examination of the systemic and institutional impediments facing the women.

The films' African-American women emerge as true survivors. How are they able to reject male domination and male dependence? In *The Color Purple*, Celie, Nettie, Sophia and Shug Avery shine as independent African-American women. They confront the sexist brutality of their existence and prevail as heroes. In *Waiting to Exhale*, Savannah, Bernadine, Gloria and Robin live their lives according to mainstream social mores. Their relationships with Black men seem to result from a desperate attempt to fill a void in their lives. Eventually these women re-alize the void within can only be filled from within.

These fictional characters do not view their problems from a political standpoint. While they eradicate their victimization and seize control over their lives, there is no acknowledgement—in either novel or film—that they comprehend the social and political framework that continues to shape their oppression. Instead, they fight their individual battles on an individual level; their personal resistance never transforms itself into political self-determination. But without political resistance, cultural oppression will never be eradicated.

1. Do you believe the gender, race or sexuality of an author should be referenced and discussed when analyzing the text? How often do you attend to the demographics of the authors you read?

2. Watch a film which portrays African-American female characters. Describe their roles and discuss whether or not you believe the characters depict racial or gender stereotypes.

3. If you were cast as an actor or an actress in a mainstream movie, what types of roles might you receive? What leads you to believe this?

4. Discuss the impact of film media on your understanding of the world. Do you feel that you have developed stereotypes about groups based on their representations in film?

Name: _____

Date: _____

1. Collect two newspaper or magazine articles about two different films. One article should discuss a film which features a largely White cast. The other article should discuss a film with African-American cast members. Write about the similarities and differences in the ways the films are described.

2. Research films which have won an Academy Award for Best Picture over the last ten years. Do these films feature persons of color? What are their roles in the films?

REFERENCES

Blake, G. (Producer), & Lee, S. (Director). (1988). *School daze* [Film]. (Available from Columbia Pictures Corporation)

Bobo, J. (1988). *The color purple*: Black women as cultural readers. In D. Pribram (Ed.), *Female spectators: Looking at film and television* (pp. 90-109). London: Verso.

Brown, D. (Producer), & Beresford, B. (Director). (1989). *Driving Miss Daisy* [Film]. (Available from Warner Brothers)

Burns, M. (Director), & Forster, M. (Producer). (2001). *Monster's ball* [Film]. (Available from Lions Gate Films Inc.)

Field, F. (Producer), & Awick, E. (Director). (1989). *Glory* [Film]. (Available from Warner Brothers)

Fishbourne, L. (Producer), & Sargen, J. (Director). (1997). *Miss Evers boys* [Film]. (Available from Home Box Office)

Guber, P. (Producer), & Spielberg, S. (Director). (1985). *The color purple* [Film]. (Available from Warner Brothers)

Guerrero, E. (1993). *Framing blackness*. Philadelphia: Temple University Press.

hooks, b. (1992). *Black looks: Race and representation*. Boston: South End Press.

hooks, b. (1995). *Killing rage: Ending racism*. New York: Henry Holt and Company, Inc.

hooks, b. (1989). *Talking back: Thinking feminist, thinking black*. Boston: South End Press.

hooks, bell. (1990). *Yearning: Race, gender, and cultural politics*. Boston: South End Press.

Hutchinson, E.O. (1994). *Assassination of the black male image*. Los Angeles: Middle Passage Press.

Larkin, A.S. (1992). Black women filmmakers defining ourselves: Feminism in our own voice. In D. Pribram (Ed.), *Female spectators: Looking at film and television* (pp. 157-173). London: Verso.

McMillan, T. (1992). *Waiting to exhale*. New York: Pocket Star Books.

McMillan, T. (Producer), & Whitaker, F. (Director). (1995). *Waiting to exhale*. [Film]. (Available from the 20th Century Fox Film Corporation)

Mortz, C. (1984). The Search for identity in the works of Alice Walker. In C. Moritz (Ed.) *Current biography yearbook 1984* (pp. 1-6). New York: Wilson.

Tomlinson, A. (1991). *Cultural imperialism*. London: Piner Publishers.

Walker, A. (1982). *The color purple*. New York: Pocket Star Books.

Wolper, D. (Producer), & Moses, G. (Director). (1977). *Roots* [Film]. (Available from Warner Brothers)

Zinn, H. (1996). Lit chat with Alice Walker. *Salon.com* [Online]. Available: http://www.salon.com/09/departments/litchat2.html

Our Message is Not on the Media

Alice A. Tait

Introduction

The goal of this chapter is to provide the reader with a model for the portrayal of African Americans in the mass media. The model is needed because of the media habits of society, especially children's perceptions of race based on their exposure to mass media and mass media's influence. Afrocentric theory is utilized to interpret how African Americans are portrayed and should be portrayed in the influential mass media.

Why Should Our Message/ Images Be On the Media?

MEDIA HABITS OF SOCIETY

America is a highly mediated society. Approximately 99 percent of Americans own televisions, 70 percent of whom subscribe to cable; 100 percent own radios; and 77 percent subscribe to newspapers. In most homes, the television set is on at least seven hours per day, though studies find children watch from three to eight hours a day. While Americans receive most of their news from television, they also spend, on average, 2.5 hours listening to the radio and 45 minutes reading their daily newspapers. These statistics constitute a potentially large and diverse audience base, yet an overwhelming Eurocentric slant continues to dominate what is heard and viewed in the media.

MEDIA HABITS OF CHILDREN

Children watch a vast amount of television, including a variety of programs, and agree it is important for young people to see individuals of their own race in the media, although African-, Latino/Hispanic-, Asian- and Native-American (ALANA) children have stronger feelings about this than White children. Children across all races associate positive characteristics more with the White characters they see in the media and negative characteristics more with the ALANA characters. Although children believe that all races are shown doing both good and bad things on the news, they agree that the news media tend to portray both African-American and Latino-American people more negatively than White or Asian-American individuals. African-American children feel that entertainment media represent their race more fairly than the news, while White and Latino-American children are split between the two. ALANA children primarily choose African Americans as those they like on television, and White children usually choose White figures as their favorites. When asked why, most children first answer, "Because they are funny." Then, ALANA children are more likely to say, "Because I look up to them," and White children often say, "Because they act the way I want to act." Both White and African-American children say they see people of their race on television, while Latino-American and Asian-American children are much less likely to see their races represented. ALANA children think families on television have more money than their own families, while White children are equally likely to say that families on TV have the same amount of money as their families. All ages and races express faith that the media could help bring people together by showing individuals of varying races interacting together (Lake et al., 1998).

MEDIA'S INFLUENCE

"Because the media set an agenda, confer status, and interpret meaning, one effect of television is that it legitimizes deviant, threatening and unintelligent behavior," particularly that of ALANA, and a self-fulfilling prophecy emerges. The media create the problem and, because of their power and appeal, perpetuate the problem by socializing ALANA into believing that deviant behavior is acceptable and rewarding (Tait & Perry, 1994, p. 196). Furthermore, Caucasian Americans interpret the ALANA behaviors that appear in the media—and, subsequently, the ones that do not—to be indicative of all ALANA, thereby fostering stereotypes and misconceptions.

What is the Eurocentric Media Message?

In an attempt to organize the way Eurocentric media have portrayed ALANA over time, Clark and Wilson & Gutiérrez have developed the following typologies. The longer an ALANA group has been treated by mainstream media, the more likely it is to have progressed through one or more of these stages or phases. But since television and movies, for example, are constantly recycling their products, one may see images of, say, African Americans that represent earlier stages or phases out of their natural progression. For instance, current television and movie portrayals of African Americans are generally considered Stage Four entertainment, Egalitarian or Respectable. But, in the same evening one may see an episode of *Amos & Andy*, a Stage Two Ridicule program. The same is true for the other ALANA groups.

CLARK'S STAGES

Clark chronicles four stages in the representation of ALANA in the **entertainment media**. The *Non-recognition* or *Invisible Stage* occurs when there is zero ALANA representation in the media. The *Ridicule Stage* includes ALANA representation, but characters of color are objects of ridicule like buffoons, fall guys or other derogatory figures created to cater to and boost the dominant culture's self-esteem. The *Regulatory Stage* portrays ALANA as "good guys," who are connected with an organization or establishment devoted to maintaining social norms, and occurs as a reaction to previous stereotyping and as a result of pressure groups' protest. This stage serves as a means for reducing criticism of stereotypes while neutralizing the fears of the dominant culture. The *Egalitarian* or *Respectable Stage* exhibits ALANA in roles that are more representative of society and encompass a wide variety of occupations and responsibilities. These roles demonstrate a strong degree of assimilation as well as contrast, and ALANA often lose their ethnic identity (Clark, 1969).

WILSON AND GUTIÉRREZ EVOLUTIONARY PHASES

On the other hand, Wilson and Gutiérrez chronicle five Evolutionary Phases in the representation of ALANA in the **news media**. In the *Exclusionary Phase* there is no presence of ALANA in media. "The inference to be drawn was that ALANA are not important to the well-being of society" (Wilson & Gutiérrez, 1995, pp. 152-153). Excluding ALANA from coverage signified a lack of status that is continually affirmed, because the function of news is to reflect social reality" (Wilson & Gutiérrez, 1995, p. 153). In the *Threatening-Issue Phase*, ALANA make their presence in news reports "because they were at the time perceived as a threat to the existing social order" (Wilson & Gutiérrez, 1995, p. 153). The news media endorsed the displacement of Native Americans from their lands and called them savages to further the cause of the European settlers. Blacks were portrayed as the "object of fear," Chinese as people who threatened the labor market of the White population, and Mexicans were depicted as "illegals" and "aliens," thus polarizing the races even further. In the *Confrontation Phase,* the media elicit fear in the dominant population, which results in social confrontation from lynchings to the Mexican War to legislative moves created to legally keep ALANA powerless. The *Stereotypical Phase* enables Whites to neutralize their apprehension of ALANA including "[i]nformation items that conform to existing White attitudes toward other groups, [which] are then selected for inclusion in news media and given repeated emphasis until they reach thematic proportions" (Wilson & Gutiérrez, 1995, p. 157). This practice only further enflames the "us versus them syndrome" by affirming the stereotypical beliefs that ALANA are a burden to society. The *Multiracial Coverage Phase* is the direct opposite of the Exclusionary Phase and has not yet been achieved by any ALANA group. Ideally, in this phase "ALANA will be reflected in all types of news" (Wilson & Gutiérrez, 1995, p. 158).

Are Eurocentric Images Improving?

Although television appeared to have made notable gains in the 70s, 80s and mid-90s with a handful of dramatic series and situation comedies that featured African Americans, television seemed to usher in the millennium in retrogressive style. All-White casts dominated show after show on what is highly regarded as the most powerful, most persuasive medium in today's society.

In 1999-2000, NAACP Chairman Kweisi Mfume echoed the frustrations and sentiments of African Americans and other ALANA when he blasted the media for allowing a "virtual whitewash in programming" to flourish in an industry where ALANA have been historically under-represented and exploited. African Americans were appalled at the dearth of Black characters on television. At the start of the 1999-2000 season, the NAACP launched a headline-grabbing protest targeting the four major television networks for near exclusion of ALANA actors from the networks' fall lineups.

None of the 26 series premiering in the fall had an ALANA in a lead role. The NAACP threatened to boycott the networks in the event they would be unable to reach an agreement that would promote diversity in front of and behind the cameras. The well-publicized controversy prompted network executives to add ALANA characters at the last minute to existing shows and to new shows that had premiered.

Syndicated columnist Clarence Page described the lack of full ALANA representation as a "sin of omission" on the part of the media in a January 2000 *TV Guide* article. "I do not believe the networks set out to discriminate against Blacks or Hispanics or Asians or Native Americans. They just kind of forgot about us. And that's a form of racism in the broad cosmic sense." Page went on to explain how the NAACP campaign put the networks on notice: "I think the criticism of this season's shows put the fear of God into the networks. I just want them to think about diversity.... I just want them to view us as equals. If there's anything that makes people angry, it's invisibility."

In the same article, *Time* magazine columnist Jack E. White related the frustration and alienation he felt as an African American in observing television's lapse with reality. "The disconnect between reality as shown on network television and reality as I live it as a Black American is so vast that it's alienating." White stated, "...I was appalled to learn that when they created *The West Wing,* it didn't have major ALANA characters.... When television is less representative than the cabinets of right-wing Republicans like Bush and Reagan, it shows how retrogressive the industry is."

The institutionalized, pervasive discrimination is reflected by networks' overall under-representation of African Americans, Latino Americans, Asian Americans and Native Americans behind the camera as well. Yvette Lee Bowser, creator and executive producer of *For Your Love* and *Living Single* indicated in the January 2000 *TV Guide* article that the television industry is not doing all it could to reflect the face of America. "I think there has to be a raising of consciousness among all executives. I don't think diversity training would hurt...Executives have to realize there's a browning of America going on and that, like everyone else, we want our stories told on television and in films."

ALANA fare no better in representation or inclusiveness with the news media. The television news industry has systematically excluded Blacks from key positions of power. The top spots, both in front of and behind the camera, have historically been reserved for Whites. According to findings released in the study "Best Practices in Television Journalism," closet racism is alive and well in television news. And in news coverage, the proverbial crime or poverty story will invariably show footage of ALANA, while given a choice for profiling a Black or White family, producers will opt for the White family because they believe Whites appeal to more viewers.

Both print and electronic media often bow to pressure from advertisers, who will often go as far as to encourage the killing of viable stories. Some media executives have not been hesitant to admit that racial division exists and have attempted to explain away the polarization with the argument that they are not social reformers; they are simply running a business—a business that only needs to measure its success by high ratings and the approval of advertisers with deep pockets. Besides advertisers, majority viewers (White viewers), the people advertisers perceive as their preferred customers, are one other driving force behind the programming networks choose to offer.

Historically, ALANA have endured decade after decade of stereotypical images, misrepresentation and under-representation. But African Americans, like other ALANA groups, have begun to establish their own media organizations, while continuing to push Eurocentric media organizations to improve their treatment of ethnic groups. As a result, Afrocentric media play a pivotal role, evolving as arbiter, as well as messenger, in setting the pace for positive portrayals and the depiction of accurate images.

Afrocentric Media Message

The first African-American newspaper, *Freedom's Journal,* was founded in 1827 by John B. Russwurm and Samuel E. Cornish. "Origi-

nally, *Freedom's Journal,* a weekly, was issued in New York City as means of answering attacks on African Americans" (Tait, 1997, p. 36) by the pro-slavery newspaper the *Enquirer.* "Between 1827-1896, the common theme of the Black Press was the quest for a national identity and a response to White racism and assertion of self-determination." "During World War I, a sizable number of newspapers advocated retaliation, blood for blood, life for life.... During World War II, the Black press was the single most important information source for African Americans." (Tait, 1997, p. 36). In the late 1940s, the Black press focused coverage on NAACP lawsuits, integration and voting rights for African Americans. During the 1950s and '60s, the Black press further focused on integration, demonstrations, sit-ins and Africa. "In the 1970s and '80s, the crusade against racism was the most successful of any campaigns by the press... The Black press in America includes nearly 300 newspapers and a weekly readership of more than 12 million" (Tait, 1997, p.37). Three-fourths of these individuals subscribe to White newspapers, with an equal number of African Americans subscribing to one or more African-American magazines. However, as the population of Black Americans increases, circulation is decreasing. Aside from the newspapers, as of 1996, the African-American news media consisted of:

> A national Black press wire service (NNPA); a national television cable news show (BET); a national radio network (African American Urban Networks); at least ten national magazines; at least ten televised public affairs shows, with at least one in every major city with a significant African American population; and a growing African American Internet Universe with at least three Black newspapers on-line, the most prominent being the *Afro-American* (www.afroam.org) (Tait, 1997, p.39).

African-American media exist primarily as a voice of the African-American community. As long as the community exists, so shall the African-American media (Tait, 1997).

In Afrocentric terms, television programming that depicts accurate images of African Americans is a form of Nommo (Asante, 1989). In entertainment, *The Cosby Show,* although not explicating every avenue of African-American life, represents the prototype Afrocentric television program, as the images consistently reflect African-American culture. The direction of the programming was African American influenced. Conversely, the *Amos and Andy* show was the antithesis of Afrocentrism (Tait & Perry, 1994, p.196).

In news and information, *Black Journal* is an early example of an Afrocentric program. *Black Journal,* the first national African-American public affairs series, premiered in June 1969 after Alvin Perlmutter, staff producer at National Education Television (now PBS) conceived of the idea. "Aired one hour each month, *Black Journal's* mission was to (1) define the African American reality of any potential film situation, (2) identify the causes of any problems in that situation, and (3) document attempts to resolve those problems, whether successful or not." (Bourne, 1988, p. 10). As production funds diminished, it was difficult to sustain the original high standard. The program first changed to a talk show format under the direction of Tony Brown and was called *Tony Brown's Journal,* and was later called *Detroit Black Journal,* with guests including Rosa Parks, Ruby Dee, Nikki Giovanni, and Alex Haley Jr. *DBJ* is now called *American Black Journal* (Bourne, 1988).

From November 1969 through December 1979, WWJ-TV (Detroit) produced "and broadcast *Profiles...,* a half-hour weekly television community service series." (Tait, 1998, p. 151). Host and producer Gilbert Maddox "portrayed the African-American community's hopes and frustrations and highlighted their accomplishments and achievements." (Tait, 1998, p. 152). *For My People* began in 1970 under the direction of executive producer/director and interviewer David Rambeau. The program was "planned as a continuation of the Black Power movement." (Tait, 1998, p. 152). It currently airs on WKBD Channel 50 on Saturday mornings and also appears seven days a week on a Detroit-based independent cable station. "Topics for discussion focus primarily on economics/finance, politics, education, and social struggle." (Tait, 1998, p. 153).

The first Black owned-and-operated TV station in the United States, WGPR-TV, debuted September 1974. "WGPR's philosophy was that African Americans living in Detroit deserve a television station attuned to their community the same way that the 'mainstream' media are attuned to the White community. WGPR's stated purpose was to provide African Americans the opportunity to have experiences with the broadcast industry, so they stress training and community access, emphasizing a Black perspective to the largest degree possible" (Tait, 1998, p.154). All programs were products of the African-American movement, as a response to an admitted deficiency: to serve an audience that had never been adequately addressed directly before. These pioneering programs performed a necessary function quite effectively by documenting, exploring and articulating African-American political, economic and cultural issues (Tait, 1998, p.155).

The African-American media have traditionally provided African Americans with a voice when mainstream outlets refuse to tell their success stories. But a disturbing trend has emerged over the years: the black-owned outlets have struggled, and many succumbed, to the pressures inherent in takeovers by media conglomerates. Insuring ALANA voices are heard is largely contingent on the success of ALANA-owned media. But the takeovers are an unfortunate trend that no one seems to be able to control.

Emerge, heralded as America's best Black newsmagazine, is an example of a publication whose voice was silenced. Acquired and then immediately killed by Keith Clinkscales, the up and coming African-American magazine mogul and founder of Vanguarde Media Inc., *Emerge* explored social implications and political issues surrounding White institutions and was often critical of some Black leaders.

Clinkscales launched *Savoy,* described as a "Black *Vanity Fair,*" to replace *Emerge.* Advertisers had already proven how hesitant they can be when it comes to spending with Black media, and Clinkscales attempted to explain his actions in a March, 2001 story in *The Washington Post:* "Making a magazine property work, you've got to think about a lot of things—the audience, the newsstand, the advertising...I've taken some knocks because I want to have an elite publication, but I think what I want is to have a business" (Carlson, 2001, p. C8).

Most troubling of all the acquisitions was Viacom's $3 billion purchase of BET (Black Entertainment Television) in 2000 from founder Robert Johnson. Acquiring successful Black-owned companies is driven by a desire to get a piece of a prosperous sector of the market that had historically been ignored by White firms.

Byron Lewis, the founder of Uniworld, the only remaining 100 percent Black-owned advertising agency, in a June 2000 article in *Black Enterprise*, stated: "It was a long time coming, but companies are finally recognizing African Americans' culture" (Hayes, 2000, p. 190).

The resounding success of hip-hop artists and writers who are using comics as a viable form of socio/political expression is indicative of the fact that some media are finally waking up and smelling the coffee. Aaron McGruder, the African-American creator of the controversial "The Boondocks" comic strip, has met with great success though the strip does not hesitate to take on anything or anyone. McGruder's characters examine a variety of social and political issues, from biracial identity to White supremacy, with a hip-hop flavor. It is continuing to make waves since its debut in 1999 in nearly 160 newspapers. "The Boondocks" features witty banter, biting satire and a tough edge; but, most importantly, it provides an ever-present voice in the media at a time when so many ALANA voices have been silenced.

What Exactly is Afrocentricity in Media Messages?

"Afrocentricity involves a systematic exploration of relationships, social codes, cultural and commercial customs, mythoforms, oral traditions and proverbs of the peoples of Africa… and is the belief in the centrality of Africans in postmodern history" (Asante, 1998, p. 6). Building on their identification with all things African, African Americans have attempted to replicate the central role of village meetings in African history. The African word Njia, translated "The Way," refers to the collective expression of the African world view toward issues

that were discussed in such village meetings. Afrocentric media are the vehicles for creating an electronic/print Njia meeting in America. True Afrocentric content approaches all issues from a collective perspective, unlike Eurocentric media's individualism. This recognizes that power rests in group solidarity and shows how that is pertinent to the African-American experience. Afrocentrism also stresses a liberationist perspective on social and cultural issues. There are six parts to the traditional African Njia meeting:

1. Libation to Ancestors (honor ancestors)
2. Poetry and Music Creativity (free expression of creativity)
3. Nommo: Generative Word Power (Afrocentric discussion of all world problems)
4. Affirmation (reinforce victorious beliefs)
5. Teachings from Njia (Afrocentric ideology)
6. Libation to Posterity.

Nommo is essentially the modality of Afrocentric media (Barber, 2000, p.114) and is especially relevant to any analysis of Afrocentric media. It provides a place where facts are disseminated and offers an opportunity for the discussion of historical, cultural, social and political issues and concerns (Tait & Perry, 1994, p. 196). In the process, Afrocentric media may use all or some of these six meeting concepts in various forms.

Three major categories are played out in Afrocentric news, public affairs and entertainment programming. These are: *the oral tradition; subjective analytical base;* and *collectivistic political, social and geographical orientations.*

Application of Afrocentricity

The following Afrocentricity evaluation form can be used as a guide to analyzing any mass medium to determine whether or not it is Afrocentric and, therefore, provides a realistic image of African Americans. One may use the form to analyze content by checking the appropriate blank when that particular concept is discussed as one watches the program and reviewing the results to determine if the program is Afrocentric and to what degree it represents African Americans realistically. At this time, there is no quantitative scale for interpreting the results. If fifty percent of the categories are represented, one might say, however, that the content is Afrocentric.

Acknowledgements

I would like to acknowledge the work of Sharon Campbell in the early stages of revising this chapter.

Category I: Oral Tradition

The oral tradition is a strong African-American tradition. It is a primary platform for the transmission of culture and was used as a tool during slavery. Because the oral tradition is so critical, it must serve several purposes or contain information that will enlighten African Americans and society about African Americans. Six concepts that explicate the category of oral tradition are discussed below.

DISCUSSION OF ACTIVISM

One purpose of the oral tradition is to include discussions about social activism designed to change or improve conditions of African Americans. One of the goals of *Profiles* was to determine to what extent guests used their occupational skills to upgrade or provide community service to the African-American community. For example, if the host interviewed an outstanding teacher, he would want to know if that teacher volunteered to tutor children in their community. Another example of activism can be found in Spike Lee's film *Do the Right Thing* as discussed by Brenda Cooper in Part IV of this text. Neighborhood Blacks organize a boycott of a pizzeria because the pictures on the pizzeria's "Wall of Fame" include only Italian Americans, while most customers are African Americans and there are no pictures of African Americans (Cooper, 2003, p.1).

1 _____ Community level

2 _____ City Municipality level

3 _____ National level

4 _____ International level

DISCUSSION OF LIBERATION

A second purpose of oral tradition is to liberate African Americans from systematic and cultural oppression by encouraging African Americans to accept their culture. For example, Haile Gerima directed the film *Sankofa,* an Akan word meaning a return to home by returning to one's culture. In the film, an African-American model who lacks knowledge of her history is magically returned to slavery and its origins (Williams, 2003, p.32).

1 _____ Depressed economic conditions

2 _____ Racism and/or racist policies and institutions

3 _____ Socio-cultural oppression

DISCUSSION OF UNIFICATION

Unifying African Americans is a third purpose of the oral tradition. Unification is achieved through educating African Americans on the advantages of standing as one, as a group, and how that translates into collective empowerment. African-American newspapers' coverage of Africa during the 1950s and 60s represented an attempt to reconnect African Americans to their roots and educate them on the notion that they are stronger as a people when connected to their roots.

1 _____ Promotes cohesiveness among socioeconomic classes

2 _____ Emphasizes removal of obstacles such as tribal, religious and ethnic affiliations

3 _____ Renounces non-Afrocentric divisive moral and social codes

ENGAGING AND RELATIONAL

The oral tradition must involve a process that engages the listener.

1 _____ Emphasizes responsibility to the community of people of African descent

2 _____ Acknowledges contributions or derogations to the community of people of African descent by the guest/guest's organization

3 _____ Poses follow-up questions to address the discussion to any issues which were not discussed Afrocentrically

LANGUAGE INVERSION AND EBONICS

Inversion involves eliminating or redefining words that minimize the status of African Americans due to their inherent racist and derogatory nature, denial of individual ethnic identity based on a Eurocentric basis for identification and disregard of a worldview in which persons of European descent (i.e., White) are actually a "minority." The use of the term "minority" to refer to African Americans is considered inappropriate because it denies the ethnic identity of African Americans. Therefore, one would not expect an Afrocentric program to use this term or, if used, it should not be the only term used to refer to African Americans. An example of inversion and Ebonics (the incorporation of the African influence into the English language that African Americans speak) can be found in the film *Daughters of the Dust,* the story of an African-American family's move from a mythical South Carolina island to the mainland. The characters in the movie speak in a Gullah-accented English. Gullah is an African derived language developed in the Sea Islands of Georgia and South Carolina (Williams, 2003, p.29).

1 _____ Uses inappropriate terminology or language

2 _____ Uses Ebonics

3 _____ Uses inversion

1 _____ Call and response pattern

2 _____ Voice and speech inflections (especially when making an important point)

3 _____ Communicates personal feelings and beliefs

Category II: Subjective Analytical Base

The subjective analytical base refers to the discussion of methods for self-determination, self-definition and specific or special needs of people of African descent. Self-determination is the desire of African Americans to control institutions that affect their lives. African-American newspapers during the 40s focusing on voting rights for African Americans is an example of providing coverage of political strategies that will allow African Americans to influence institutions. Self-definition is the desire of African Americans to construct symbols and identities that represent their culture as viewed through their own eyes and their experiences. *Cleopatra Jones, a* 1970s African-American action film contributed a new definition of African-American femininity by redefining beauty (natural hairstyle), sexuality (beauty and liberation) and womanhood (versatility) (Sims, 2003, p.17). The following three concepts explore how content might incorporate the subjective analytical base:

AFROCENTRIC WORLD VIEW

1 _____ Discusses methods for self-determination and self-definition

2 _____ Discusses goal-directed activities within any field (i.e., business, education, psychology, etc.) from a perspective that places Africans in the center

3 _____ Discusses issues in terms of the "special" needs of people of African descent (i.e., needs regarded as separate from what is considered status quo)

BASED ON PEOPLE OF AFRICAN DESCENT AND CONTINENTAL AFRICANS

1 _____ Focuses on the impact of political processes on people of African descent

2 _____ Emphasizes the turning inward and explicit rejection of the legitimacy of Eurocentric institutions to address the needs of people of African descent

3 _____ Displays African motifs through customs of language, dress, behavior, and/or games

RESIST OBJECTIFYING METHODS

1 _____ Discusses issues and topics with particular basis in the African world

2 _____ Discusses issues in terms of integration, or impacts on cultural orientation

3 _____ Provides qualitative and interpretive analysis of current news and issues based on the interests of people of African descent

Category III: Collectivistic Socio-political Orientation

The collectivistic social, political and geographical orientation includes recognition of the common heritage of people of African descent. It seeks to diminish the artificial distinctions such as class and geography. *Profiles* interviewed African-American guests who represented a variety of occupations in an attempt to show that all African Americans make a contribution and all African Americans regardless of income, education or skin color are influenced by racism. Yousman (2003) describes Spike Lee's film *Jungle Fever* as "conveying images, language and narrative that reinforces rather than diminishes distinctions between African Americans based on economic class" (p.12). The following three concepts explore how content might provide collectivistic socio-political orientation:

BASED ON RECOGNITION OF COMMON HERITAGE

1 _____ Defines in-group in terms of any and all individuals who recognize themselves as sharing a heritage based on African-oriented cultural customs

2 _____ Defines in-group in terms of the specific area in a locality in which people of African descent are concentrated

3 _____ Focuses on activities that are practiced by people of African descent

DOWNPLAY INDIVIDUALISTIC GOALS WHILE ADVOCATING COLLECTIVE ACTION

1 _____ Advocates collective local, state, etc. action

2 _____ Discusses issues in terms of intracultural responsibility

3 _____ Discusses issues in terms of the "common fate" concept, (e.g. in terms of how the situation of Africans in South Africa affects the quality of life for African Americans)

CULTURAL CONSTRAINTS (those Eurocentric cultural characteristics African Americans acquired that do not allow them to embrace Afrocentricity)

1 _____ Discusses the difficulty people of African descent may have in subordinating mainstream individualistic ideologies

2 _____ Acknowledges the overall individualistic socio-cultural orientation evident in the United States

3 _____ Focuses on the destructive nature of individualism on the quality of life for people of African descent

1. Explain the differences between Clark's Stages and those of Wilson and Gutiérrez.

2. Create a model for describing how ALANA (African, Latino, Asian and Native Americans) are portrayed in Eurocentric media.

3. Create a model for describing how ALANA (African, Latino, Asian and Native Americans) are portrayed in ALANA owned, operated or influenced media.

1. Analyze a medium (e.g., a television program) using the Afrocentricity evaluation form to determine whether or not the medium is an accurate portrayal of African Americans.

2. Analyze a medium (e.g., a newspaper edition) using Clark's Stages to determine what "stage" any one ALANA (African, Latino, Asian and Native Americans) group is being portrayed as.

3. Analyze a medium (e.g., a movie) using Wilson and Gutiérrez Evolutionary Phases to determine how any ALANA group is being portrayed according to the model.

REFERENCES

A question of color. (2000, January 15). *TV Guide, 37*, 40-52.

Asante, M.K. (1998). *Afrocentricity*. Trenton, NJ: Africa World Press.

Barber, J.T. & Tait, A.A. (2001). The new model of Black media entrepreneurship: BET holdings, inc. In J.T. Barber , A.A. Tait (Eds.), *The information society and the Black community* (pp.111-126). Westport, CT: Praeger Publishers.

Bourne, S. (1998, May). Bright moments. *The Independent*, 10-11.

Carlson, P. Inc. in his veins. (2001, March 6). *The Washington Post*, pp. C5, C8.

Clark, C. (1969). Television and social controls: Some observations on the portrayal of ethnic minorities. *Television Quarterly*, 181-222.

Cooper, B. (2004). The White-Black fault line: Relevancy of race and racism in spectators' experiences of Spike Lee's *Do The Right Thing*. In G.T Meiss & AA. Tait (Eds.), *Ethnic Media in America: Vol 3. Images, Audiences and Transforming Forces*. Dubuque, IA: Kendall/Hunt.

Decode profile, Comic Relief. (2000, September) *Code, 28*.

Hayes, C. (2000 June). B.E. Advertising Agency of the Year, Changing culture. *Black Enterprise*, 188-196.

Jackson, J. (2000, January/February). Anything but racism. *Extra!*, 6-8.

Lake Sosin Snell Perry & Assoc. (1998). *A different world: Children's perceptions of race and class in the media*. Oakland, CA: Children Now.

Morse, S. (2001, March 22). Technology and the Black press in the 21st century. *Daily Challenge*, 4-5.

O'Neal-Parker, L. Funnies man: Aaron McGruder's The Boondocks has a point, and it's not afraid to poke fun. (1999, April 26). *The Washington Post*, pp. C1-C4.

Sims, Yvonne. (2003). *From headscarves to afros: Redefining African-American femininity and empowerment in selected 1970s Black action films*. Manuscript in preparation.

Tait, A.A. (1998). Ethnic voices: Afrocentric public affairs television programming. In Y.R. Kamalipour, T. Carilli (Eds.), *Cultural diversity and the U.S. media* (pp.149-156). Albany, NY: State University of New York Press.

Tait, A.A. (1997). The African-American (Black) press. In C.B. Chan, K. Fearn-Banks (Eds.), *People to people: An introduction to communications* (pp. 36-39). New York: American Heritage Custom Publishing.

Tait, A.A. & Perry, R.L. (1994). African Americans in television: An Afrocentric analysis. *The Western Journal of Black Studies, 18(4)*, 195-200.

Williams, D.A. (2003). *Owning the image: The cultural politics of Black independent cinema*. Manuscript in preparation, Florida A&M University.

Wilson, C.C., II & Gutiérrez, F. (1995). *Race, multiculturalism, and the media; From mass to class communication* (2nd ed.). Thousand Oaks, CA: Sage Publications, Inc.

Yousman, W. (2003). *Jungle Fever and beyond: An intertextual analysis of gender, race, and class ideologies in Spike Lee's filmography*. Manuscript in preparation.

The Ethnic Audiences

IV

Beyond the Textual Paradigm: Latina/o Film and the Presence of Audiences

Fernando Delgado

Before *Resurrection Boulevard, Greetings from Tucson* or *The George Lopez Show;* before the popular music phenomena of Jennifer Lopez, Shakira, Ricky Martin and Marc Anthony; before the arrival of *Frida, Tortilla Soup* and the success of the *Spy Kids* movies; before each of these exemplars of contemporary Latina/o crossover success and marketability, there was another burst, perhaps a decade too early, which produced a Latina/o boom in Hollywood, anticipated the crossover viability of Latina/o media products and producers and demonstrated the presence of a robust Latina/o media market. While we might now take for granted the visibility of Latina/os in the media and the efforts of both Hollywood and Madison Avenue to reach out to Latina/o audiences and consumers, this integrative turn has arrived at the end of several decades of fits and starts (Dávila, 2001).

Shifting U.S. demographics and the vitality and youthfulness of the Latina/o community have created a synergy between mass media producers and consumers since the late 1990s, a relationship that has been embraced by mainstream outlets, advertisers and audiences. For contemporary audiences and media consumers, the presence of Latina/os may be unremarkable. Indeed, many young people of all races and ethnicities may not question the contemporary role of Latina/os in popular culture. Of course, while that youthful demographic is vital to the

economically driven popular culture, it also unfortunately lacks cultural memory.

Racial and ethnic minorities have long had a problematic relationship with U.S. media industries. While contemporary U.S. popular culture is unthinkable without minority performers and audiences, minorities have struggled to gain artistic and creative acceptance within the mainstream media. In the instance of Latina/os and the film industry, Noriega (1998) has observed how the American Film Institute's list of the 100 greatest U.S. films reinforces that historical exclusion. Succinctly put, "Hollywood is not an equal opportunity employer and each year the employment numbers get worse" (Noriega, p. 65). Current events, however, suggest a trend toward greater opportunity for Latina/os in the media.

Clearly, Latina/os are enjoying a period of heightened presence and success. But it has yet to be demonstrated if the acceptance of Latina/os will persist. In some respects the attention directed at Latina/os is similar to the late 1980s and early 1990s African-American popular culture boom, when mainstream America simultaneously took note of Bill Cosby, rap music and Spike Lee (among others), and generated new Black aesthetic practices (Boyd, 1997). For Latina/os to gain mainstream acceptance, efforts must continue on multiple fronts: creative talent has to strive for access and (almost immediate) success; key industry decision-makers supportive of minority creative talent have to act affirmatively; and audiences and consumers have to be supportive of Latina/o cultural products. Latina/o creative talent must continue to challenge assumptions of what is marketable and mainstream. They must also pursue access to mainstream film and television productions (see Noriega, 1996 for a useful overview of these strategies) by creating, or participating in the creation of, alternative and mainstream narratives.

The history of Latina/os in Hollywood suggests a muted but long-standing presence, albeit often in narrow and stereotyped roles (Cortés, 1983; Petit, 1980; Woll, 1974a; 1974b) and limited, but growing, opportunities within film and television (Keller, 1994; Noriega, 1992). The frustration over limited media opportunities has led to eruptions like *Cine-Aztlan*'s manifesto, which claimed that Hollywood is an integral component of "yankee imperialism" (Noriega, 1992), a sentiment echoed by Ramírez Berg (1993) nearly a decade ago after the Hispanic Hollywood boom appeared to leave little in its wake. While creating an alternative cinema, Latina/o cultural workers have also pursued their crossover dreams linked to Hollywood's economic might and instant commercial legitimacy (Noriega, 2000; Noriega & López, 1996).

The future of Latina/os in Hollywood is unclear, but developments in film, television and music provide hopeful indications. Indeed, the current trend toward legitimation and integration within the structures of media corporations may finally realize the hopes of the "Hispanic Hollywood" boom as Latina/o artists, celebrities and creative talent enter "the discourse of general interest, business, and industry magazines" (Keller, 1994, p. 163) and capture the attention of larger and broader audiences.

While Latina/o creators were honing their production skills, Latina/o scholars were developing their investigative and critical methods (Fregoso, 1993; Keller, 1985; List, 1996). Not surprisingly, the result of these efforts is an impressive body of work that highlights Latina/o contributions to popular culture and an emer-

gent understanding of Latina/o media preferences (Dávila, 2000; Greenberg et al, 1983). How mass-media content impacts audiences needs greater study, particularly in the area of films. While scholars have presented institutional histories (Keller, 1994; Noriega, 2000), critiqued stereotypical representations (Ramírez Berg, 1990; Noriega, 1992; Fregoso, 1993) and explored self-representations in film and television (List, 1996; Noriega & López, 1996), they have often missed the crucial point that, once in the mainstream, Latina/o media products circulate and appeal to diverse audiences. Also, these audiences are variously situated and bring divergent cultural and personal resources to their interactions with mediated texts.

Building on the arguments advanced by Delgado (1995; 1998a), this essay intends to provoke conversation and further exploration into what the evolving presence of Latina/os in the mainstream media actually means to producers and consumers of mass media. Using Cheech Marin's 1988 hit film *Born in East L.A.* as an exemplar, I posit that an interactive, rather than textual, approach—attuned to the means of production, the constituents of the message and the message's circulation to the "wider world of meaning, significance and interpretation" (Carey, 1977, p. 425)—to Latina/o cinema products and audiences provides a more complex understanding of how cinematic meanings circulate than does a text-based analysis, a point suggested by Bordwell (1989, pp. 1-18). From this perspective film products are seen as "a means of communication, a set of languages, a system of signification" (Turner, 1988, p. 40) that interact with audiences who also bring with them systems of culture, language and meaning. Such a communicative understanding of the circulation and reception of Latina/o films addresses the complexities of self-representation through popular culture products aimed at mass (and inherently diverse) audiences, a posture that has gained currency through the deployment of Stuart Hall's encoding/decoding model (Hall, 1980), and through the subsequent work of scholars who explore the interpretive habits of audiences (Nightingale, 1996).

Text-Centricity: The Biases of Latina/o Film Scholars

The biases of Latina/o film scholars, many of whom have been formally trained in departments of language, literature or cinema, have produced one-sided interpretations of the intentions of the artists and the meanings in the texts. Barrera (1997) argues that a great deal of "Latino film analysis is now being done by scholars whose graduate training was in literature programs, and while there has been a growing orientation toward popular culture, there are still considerable holdovers from the biases of literary analysis" (p. 171). While Barrera's critique centers on the ideological focus of Latina/o film scholars, his presentation of the limitations of text-centric analyses also underscores their failure to understand the economic imperative that drives the media to be mainstream: the creation of media products for consumption by the largest audience possible, thereby maximizing profits.

Surprisingly, despite the number of textual and institutional analyses, Latina/o audiences, indeed all audiences of Latina/o films, are largely absent from Latina/o scholarship. So, while Fregoso (1993) has acknowledged that Latina/o films have been made for and about Latina/os, she fails to engage the issues of circulation, reception and audience decoding. Fregoso's (1993) analysis of *American Me* does affirm the need to understand those who view the screen, and she does call for a "return to the aesthetics of reception" and the "politics of spectatorship" (p. 128); still, Fregoso does not actually engage in such a project.

The imagined or actual role of audiences in the making, marketing and meaning of Latina/o films is left largely untouched by Latina/os scholars. Though Noriega (1988-1990) has analyzed critics' receptions of several films produced during the Hispanic Hollywood period, the established community of scholars who work on Latina/o cinematic and media representations has traditionally focused on the limited possibilities for Latina/o artists (and characters) and, more recently, the characteristics of Latina/o-themed films and Chicana/o cinema (Fregoso, 1993; List, 1995). Ramírez Berg

(1990), for example, suggests the motivation of these scholars, noting,

> there are few—very, very, few—non-stereotypical portrayals of Hispanics in Hollywood cinema. Before *Zoot Suit* (1981), *La Bamba* (1987), and *Stand and Deliver* (1988)—all films with Hispanics in key creative positions—it is difficult to find examples of Hispanic characters in mainstream Hollywood cinema who are complex and self-determining (p. 286).

This concern with how Hollywood has treated and represented Latina/os has yielded two predominant and valuable lines of research: (1) the historical characterization of mainstream representations of the Latina/o other and (2) self-representation in Latina/o-produced films on both sides of the 1980s Hispanic Hollywood boom period.

In the first approach, scholars have focused on the systematic misrepresentation and stereotyping of Latina/os (Lamb, 1975; Noriega, 1991; and Woll, 1974a; 1974b). They provide specificity to the forms of Latina/o stereotyping and, as Ramírez Berg (1990) argues, vividly demonstrate how scholarship on "Hispanic stereotypes have focused on this historical fact" (p. 286). The textual record of U.S. mass-media representations of Latina/os is thus presented as a lamentable series of distorted expressions of Latina/o identities and communities, though scholars such as Keller (1994) have suggested that a more nuanced view of this history is needed.

In the aftermath of this history of textual distortion, Chicana/o cinema significantly arose as "a revolutionary cinema of opposition" (Ramírez Berg, 1990, p. 96). Chicana/o scholars then began to center on the act of self-representation and, in this second approach, test the text for fidelity to the ideological thrust of one or another Latina/o intellectual or cultural praxis. Thus, such a critique often "explores a film culture by, for, and about Chicanas and Chicanos" (Fregoso, 1993, p. xv). List (1996) explains that "Chicano feature films are situated in a social/artistic matrix that foregrounds important questions about the relationship between ethnicity and activist cinema" (p. 17). Arguably then, like-minded critics fulfill a similar role, examining ethnicity and probing the dimensions of self and other representations as constructed by a media text.

Working from literary, aesthetic or historical traditions, many Latina/o scholars have thus articulated their text-centric approaches through the framework of ideological analyses, often rooted in the Chicana/o paradigm that arose in universities and academic disciplines in the aftermath of the Chicana/o student movement. Barrera (1997) has noted that the ideological tendencies of Latina/o scholarship are founded on the critical and cultural nationalist politics of the Chicana/o movement (see Contreras, 1997 for a parallel and more elaborate discussion of Chicana/o nationalist politics in the social sciences). In addition, intellectual biases lead to a focus on the text, and privilege the scholar's voice, to the exclusion of both the audience and the *communicative moment* between media text and media consumer.

The tendency to privilege the text is logical, given Latina/o scholars' academic training. Film scholarship has focused on the aesthetic and political meanings of the cinematic or video text, a possible result of film studies' connection to literature departments and literary theory (Bordwell, 1989); mass communication and media studies perspectives, however, offer a more dynamic, inherently communicative, approach to the production *and* reception of media products. As Bordwell argues,

> When film study broke from journalism on the one side and fandom on the other—when, that is, it became academic—it could have become a subdivision of sociology or mass communication studies. It was instead ushered into the academy by humanists, chiefly teachers of literature, drama, and art. As a result, cinema was naturally subsumed within the interpretive frames of reference that rule those disciplines. (p. 17)

As a consequence of these intellectual and ideological dynamics, the text-centered analyses dominant among Latina/o film scholars limited their scholarship. As Bordwell (1989) has stated in his own argument for a move away from "a passive receiver to an active mobilizer of [cognitive and cultural] structures and processes" (p. 3):

> to assume that sense is "in" the text is to reify what can only be the result of a process.... The text is inert until a reader or listener or spectator does something to it and with it. (pp. 2-3)

Bordwell thus suggests that media texts' meanings lie both in the text and elsewhere, presumably in the audience, a sentiment echoed by Turner (1988) in his exploration of film as a social practice. Many film scholars remain mired in their focus on the aesthetic and ideological elements of the cinematic text, and ignore calls to recognize the relevance and meaning-making role of audiences and spectators. But, as Judith Mayne (1994) has written, the basic premise of cinema, and presumably other forms of mass media, is "to seduce, entertain, and otherwise appeal to its audiences" (p. 155).

Latina/o film scholarship thus appears to have been blunted by the text-based paradigm and the absence of audience analysis. This limitation is lamentable, given the populist leanings of many Latina/o scholars, particularly those influenced by Chicana/o nationalist ideology. Moreover, the centrality of identity politics (Delgado, 1998b; Saldívar, 1997) in Latina/o scholarship across various academic fields (Contreras, 1997; Fregoso, 1993; Gutiérrez-Jones, 1995) suggests some continuities and parallels to media studies that emphasize the salience of cultural identity in audience interpretations of media products (Ang & Hermes, 1996; Cohen, 1991; Fiske, 1991a; Moores, 1993).

While there is much to commend such text-based approaches, they fail at the moment of interaction between text and audience, a crucial moment, particularly when one is arguing the effects of social phenomena such as stereotypes. Barrera (1997) argues:

> Until film scholars resolve to understand films from the perspective of filmmakers, and to take into account real world constraints, they will continue to engage in misinterpretations and in unrealistic, unbalanced prescriptions of the types of Latino films they would like to see. (p. 172)

Noriega's (2000) recent examination of Chicana/o cinema also notes an active audience engaging in interpretive and resistant practices (pp. 31-32). But these are still exceptions to the Latina/o cinematic text bias.

Complicating the Text and Attending to the Audience

Readers of academic journals in the areas of communication studies and mass communication research are well aware that the move from cinema studies to communication (or cultural and media) studies implies the presence and relevance of audiences and their interpretive and meaning-making behaviors (see Moores, 1993). In contrast to Latina/o cinematic scholarship, mass communication scholars, many working out of a uses-and-gratifications paradigm, have explored the relationships between mass media content and Latina/o audiences (Aguirre, 1988; Escalante, 1992; Faber, O' Guinn, & Meyer, 1987; Schement, 1976; Subervi-Velez, 1986; Subervi-Velez, Herrera, & Begay, 1987; Subervi-Velez & Necochea, 1990; Tan, 1978). Such research has suggested that Latina/os do decode mass-mediated messages—television, advertising, newspaper coverage and film—differently from other audiences, particularly when the content represents, or is perceived to represent, them.

One recent development, firmly rooted in a uses-and-gratifications framework of audience analysis, suggests a dichotomous relationship between media product and audience (Ríos, 1996; n.d.). Ríos (1996) concludes that Latina/o audiences can be active and purposeful in their interpretations and mediations of media texts, often leading to "resistance and conditional acceptance of mainstream culture elements" (p. 128). Ríos argues that scholars should attend to, among other things, Latina/o audiences and their complicated relations with various media texts, including Spanish-language and foreign-produced films and television programming. Ríos' position is buttressed by past research (Faber, O'Guinn, & Meyer, 1987) and more recent findings that highlight language use and ethnic identity as factors in the use and interpretation of the mass media and its content (Ríos & Gaines, 1997).

The tendency within mass communication and media studies has been to engage the text and audience more fully. Thus, from the uses-and-gratifications paradigm to perspectives even more attuned to active audiences, the locus switches from the text, pure and monological, to texts that are dialogical and fuzzy. Media scholars analyze film and television, in part, by examining "how (specific) audiences make meanings and pleasures in their engagement with television programs [and films] in the context of everyday life" (Seiter et al., 1991, p. 3). This approach is nicely summarized by Fiske (1991b), who observes: "Watching television is a process of making meanings and pleasures, and this process is determined by two parallel and interlocking sets of forces" (p. 57); these are (1) the social, which relates to "the subjectivity of the viewer," and (2)"the textuality of television" (p. 57).

Moores (1993) observes that "what finally determines meaning is a 'dialogic' encounter between the two [text and audience]—and it is this continual conversation between texts and readers that qualitative audience research initially set out to explore" (p. 6). Nightingale's (1996) explanation offers a clear distinction, and suggests the tension between film studies' text-centered biases and the more flexible cultural and communication studies perspectives:

> [T]he projects challenged the separation which had divided audience research from the study of texts—films, television, programmes, books—and promised to consolidate a new era of "balanced" cultural criticism, in which equal weight was to be accorded to text and audience (p. viii).

I make no claim to divining what an audience may think or do. I suggest that any film scholar might have an inadequate or false reading of a film per se. I do claim that the audience and the film scholar can and often do interpret a film in disparate and equally legitimate ways. The point is that meaning is not fixed in the text, and any discussion of media stereotyping, self-directed or otherwise, is subject to the perceptions and interpretations of audiences. To suggest, as some have, that Cheech Marin's *Born in East L.A.* is *simply* an emancipatory and progressive critique of Whiteness and the hypocrisy of American ideals of citizenship and identity is insufficient from a communicative approach that holds that realities are socially constructed and perceived by individuals or audiences. The following comparison between Latina/o scholars' reacting to *Born in East L.A.* and Latino and Anglo audiences reacting to the text reinforces the notion that media meanings float and are framed by the particular cultural and ideological constructs held by individual consumers.

Latina/o Critics and the Meaning of *Born in East L.A.*

Born in East L.A. is especially useful because, though created from Marin's Mexican-American perspective, it so clearly reproduces—for comedic effect—common Mexican, Mexican-American, and Euro-American stereotypes. Writer, director and star Cheech Marin plays off the received stereotypes of each group, parodying them and reflecting them back on the screen. Thus, one *possible* read of *Born in East L.A.* is that it attempts to subvert cultural stereotypes through parody and self-directed satire (List, 1996, pp. 27-58; Fregoso, 1990). An expansion of a music video parody of Bruce Springsteen's hit song, "Born in the U. S. A.," *Born in East L.A.* presents the story of Rudy Robles and his efforts to return home to Los Angeles after being mistakenly identified as an illegal alien and deported to Tijuana. As a virtually monolingual Chicano, Rudy must confront a liminal reality where he is naturally situated in neither Mexico nor the United States. Differentiated by language and culture, Rudy discovers he does not easily fit into Mexico despite the INS officials' classification of him as a non-U.S. citizen and as a Mexican—a judgment based upon context (Robles was in the wrong place at the wrong time), phenotype and appearance.

His deportation experience provokes a journey wherein Rudy tries to find his way back home, in both symbolic and corporeal terms. His experience leads to a crisis caused by his apparent inability to fit in on either side of the border, and his sudden shifts in national and cultural identity. Noriega (1995) explains that through his misadventures "Rudy comes to realize that (1) American society views him as more Mexi-

can than American, (2) Mexicans see him as American or *pocho*, and (3) his attitudes toward women and immigrants have been callous" (p. 110). By interrogating his split consciousness and endeavoring to overcome the dualistic elements of his cultural and national identities, Rudy Robles becomes a citizen of both sides of the border.

Not surprisingly, given the timing of its production, *Born in East L.A.* received a good deal of attention among film scholars intrigued by its narrative, its focus on identity and Cheech Marin as the creative impulse of the film. Scholarly examinations of *Born in East L.A.* (Fregoso, 1990; List, 1995; Noriega, 1995; Tafoya, 1993; Fuentes, 1992) have typically been appreciative of Marin's effort and his articulation of identity politics. As Fregoso (1993) argues, Marin's film does "provide a powerful indictment of dominant [Anglo] society [in the U. S.]" (p. 267).

Scholarly treatments of *Born in East L.A.* have tended to focus on its use of ethnic humor as a subversive or transgressive act. Fregoso (1993) notes that the humorous plot explores and challenges the construction of (ethnic) appearances and their relationship to space, in this case of nations and borders. Building on the issues of appearance and expectations, List (1995) argues that "the film shows how heavily dependent perceptions of nativeness are based on stereotypes of Chicanos and Mexicans" (p. 114). These scholars applaud Marin's humorous subversion of ethnic and national identity, arguing that "*Born in East L.A.* becomes an alternative way of saying America for Americans" (Fregoso, 1993, p. 270).

Noriega (1995) argues that Marin's film is a critique of the English-only movement and its correlation to conceptions of nation and race/ethnicity. For Noriega the film explores "the relationship between race and citizenship within a spatial logic more than a narrative one" (p. 110). Nonetheless, the film tells a story that "challenges Hollywood conventions of the barrio" (p. 111), offers competing reactions to the "traditional" Mexican-American home, and complicates the barrio-based manifestations of machismo and assimilation. Moreover, in moving from the barrio to the border, Marin's film continues to challenge accepted notions of regions, people and activities. Noriega concludes,

> These cracks in the image of a monolithic Chicano/Mexican-descent culture may, in fact, explain the film's progressive appeal for Chicana and Chicano critics: it is seen to destabilize the essentialist underpinnings of Chicano nationalism while still offering a critique of dominant culture (p. 121).

In contrast, Tafoya (1993) asserts that the film was directly a critique of immigration policy and values: "Taking the Simpson-Rodino Immigration Reform Act of 1986 as its central target, the film also addressed the wars in Latin America and discrimination against the Chicano within the U.S. borders" (p. 123). For Tafoya, the politics of the border and identity are subsumed under a grander narrative of oppression and subjugation. Tafoya argues that this grander narrative has direct connections to the Jews' flight from Egypt described in the Book of Exodus, and that Rudy Robles is a modern-day, Mexican-American Moses. The parallels between the biblical Moses and Robles are clear to Tafoya, who argues that both are Messianic figures, leading their respective peoples to the Promised Land. Tafoya is then drawn to the inevitable conclusion:

> *Born in East L.A.* is a political statement as it suggests that the border Rudy is really trying to cross is not a fence running across a mesa, a line on a map, or a check station, but rather the way people look, act, talk, and the customs they practice. (p. 126)

In these analyses each scholar attempts to say something meaningful about the cinematic text. Taken together they make implicit that: (1) they know what the film is about because they have examined it; (2) they know what Marin was intending to do, without necessarily talking to Marin; and (3) by accomplishing the first two items they have nailed down the meaning of the film for everyone else.

However, despite their clear and vehement assertions that *Born in East L.A.* is an avowedly political film based on its construction and narrative structure, some evidence points to the contrary. According to Marin, there was a degree of reflexivity and intentionality in what he was trying to do: "[U]nder the guise of comedy, I'll be exposing, not condemning issues. I'm just throwing some light over it and letting the audience make their own decisions" (Guevara, 1987, p. 18). So, while Marin does state that the Simpson-Rodino Act is "a sham" that reflects the absence of an "enlightened policy towards Mexico," (p. 19) he also avows "these are not black-and-white issues. Some of the I.N.S. are good guys, some are not so good, and some are caught in the middle, as are some of the lead characters" (p. 18). In short, Marin may not be as political or as strident as some scholars would want him to be. And, perhaps, that is a telling feature of text-centric scholarship: the text becomes imprinted with the aspirations and impressions of the scholar.

Audiences and Difference and *Born in East L.A.*

Still, even if Marin were explicitly politicizing his comedy in the way that critics attribute to him, we still must confront that space that divides good intentions from concurrent reception. What Marin, or any scholar (or critic), believes is articulated through the film may not be what is received by audiences. Audience analysis "largely directs attention away from such questions as what's on the screen" and "offers the advantage of avoiding possibly idiosyncratic explanations of screen images by individuals with highly specialized knowledge in favor of a more popular or broad-based and audience centered response" (Austin, 1983, p. 34).

In this turn toward audiences, I sought out individuals who might represent parallel class, geographic, educational and gender demographics but who would clearly diverge in their cultural experiences and ethnic identity. Moreover, I sought participants who would fit the demographic for a Cheech Marin movie, males between the ages of 16 and 25. Having selected six students from the undergraduate population of a large Midwestern university—three Euro-American males (identified as EA1, EA2, and

EA3) and three self-identified Mexican-American males (identified as MA1, MA2, MA3)—I set out to examine the resources they brought to interpreting *Born in East L.A.* and their understanding of the actions, motives and meanings observed in the film. These participants were open in sharing their reactions and the underlying structures that encouraged their reads of the text. Over the course of three hours the participants revealed their relative insights into and perspectives on the movie, the characters' identities and actions and the movie's message.

In almost stereotypical fashion one Euro-American participant offered that he was "just a typical (Midwesterner), nothing special, you know?" (EA3). And yet he and the others are remarkable because they constitute viewers—people who might watch some or all of the film as it replayed on cable or broadcast television or perhaps rent it at the local video outlet—and interact with the film irrespective, even ignorant, of the complex renderings offered by media scholars. In short, they are reflective of the film-going masses who possess little or none of the "specialized knowledge" that Latina/o scholars brought to bear in their reactions to *Born in East L.A.*

For the Euro-American participants it would seem that one person's subversion of stereotypes is another's consistent patterning of stereotypes. As one participant (EA1) noted, those Mexicans in the Tijuana jail scene seemed "more like the types of Mexicans I expected. It's not that I think all Mexicans are criminals or anything, but I just thought that there would be more of those scenes and characters…. They were familiar." That familiarity resonated with at least one Mexican-American participant, who assented "it was funny but I've seen that thing before. Wasn't that like a scene in Phil Collins' video?" (MA1). The reference is to Phil Collins' video for "Illegal Alien," conjuring further debates about what or who constitutes parodic subversions of stereotypes or merely re-presents denigrative images.

In reaction to the conclusion of the film, when several illegals attempt to blend into their East L.A. environs by donning Ben Davis work pants, Pendleton flannel shirts and bandanas and chanting "Go, Raiders" to inquisitive police of-ficers, the Euro-American participants laughed at the broad comedy of the scene while explaining that it was funny how the illegals "got one over on the cop" (EA1). One Mexican-American participant, however, went deeper. Although he thought the scene was funny, he noted how the humor was akin to "an inside joke…you know, all Mexicans are Raiders fans, silver and black and Los Angeles…not me, I'm a Bears fan but I've got cousins who clue me in [on] this stuff" (MA2).

Unlike the highly politicized and allegorical readings of *Born in East L.A.* by the Latina/o scholars, these naïve readers bring with them only their personal experiences and cultural understanding, however limited that might be. Thus, the plot is simple enough to follow and the humor grows from the episodic situations that Rudy Robles encounters. For one Mexican-American participant, Rudy is like a lot of celluloid characters, "pretty much like people I know but not really what I would call true Mexicans" (MA1). While a fellow participant (MA3) noted that "Rudy was probably the most realistic but I can't say that he is like all or most of the guys I know."

Thus, the issue of identity is not one of character development and the motivations of the plot. Rather, these audience members are interested in whether or not Marin is funny because they may remember when he was "that stoner guy in those *Up In Smoke* movies…that is what I was expecting" (EA3). Indeed, the Cheech and Chong movies appear to have been an important reference point because "that's what I remember him in, that scene with the van with all the smoke coming out of it…funny" (MA2). Perhaps far from being Moses, Marin's character elicits a more straightforward response: "Rudy seems cool" (EA1).

Each student recognized *Born in East L. A.* as simply a comic film with little impact on or rhetoric about immigration policies. Asked what they thought about the movie's story and what it was trying to convey, the participants' responses were unsurprisingly direct and broad. For one Euro-American participant the movie was "about this poor guy who gets shafted and tries to get back home" (EA3). For another it was something more familiar, "I heard about people back home in Texas where that happens" (MA1). The issues of satire and critique were only slightly understood: "That cop who busted the illegals was like a John Wayne thing, you know, big bad White guy...but he seemed stupid" (EA3).

For most of the participants the movie was simply "pretty funny" (MA1) though disappointing: "I thought it was going to be like those Cheech and Chong movies, too. I don't know, maybe he was going to sell some dope or sneak back" (EA1). The scholar's stance that Marin had somehow wrested control of Mexican stereotypes from the dominant culture is also not so easily sustained with either group of participants. For Mexican-American participants there was concern that this "is the same old stuff, I mean its funny, but Mexicans aren't really like that" (MA3) and that it was removed from their own experiences since they "never lived in a barrio, (I) wouldn't want to go to East L.A" (MA1). Euro-Americans noted, "I've seen characters like that Paul Rodriguez guy before...you know, slow and kinda stupid" (EA3). For such audiences the film might serve as a window: "We see when we go down to the border, your homeless guys, people begging, that stuff is all over the border down south" (EA3). Indeed, it would seem that for some, *Born in East L.A.* is a reminder: "I guess Tijuana could be like that" (EA2). Such reads may be erroneous or superficial, but they do reflect what audiences bring to their interactions with media texts and what they may take away from their interactions.

Conclusion

In no way would I claim that six college-age males interviewed for three hours would exhaust the possibilities of meaning in a given film, much less be representative of audience perspectives. But, then, that is the point. Media products are distributed to entertain a target audience but can still be understood in a variety of ways.

Indeed, the reality is that the larger and broader the audience the greater the variety of interpretive frames of reference.

In this exercise I have pointed to the limitations of individual and privileged reads, and suggested the dangers when such interpretations argue that a text has altered social relations. For people of color the continuing question of stereotyping looms large. Whether self or other-directed, stereotypes can have a cumulatively negative effect on society's perceptions of others and an individual's perception of self. As an academician of color, I would like to believe that the space of comedy, satire and irony could provoke thoughtfulness and subvert the social categories that are in play. However, as the analysis above suggests, despite scholars' projections of or aspirations for films and filmmakers, the truer meaning of the circulation and reception of ethnic and racial images is left to audiences.

Spike Lee's recent film, *Bamboozled*, vividly demonstrates the dangers of parody and the use of stereotypes. In the end, Lee's film reminds us that one person's over-the-top indictment of racial stereotypes is another person's actual worldview and preferred form of entertainment. In the present case I would never presume to argue that Latina/o film scholars or critics could not read into the film what they have. Rather, the point is to be cautious about what we see and what we presume others can see in a film. Any text is a rich site to mine for meaning and consequence, from a communication perspective; however, the richer site is found in and among audiences.

Acknowldgements

Portions of this manuscript appeared as part of the author's doctoral dissertation under the direction of Michael Calvin McGee. The author would also like to thank Bruce Gronbeck and Samuel Becker for their assistance and guidance on the project.

1. What comprises an audience for a film or video? Are audiences groups of individuals, or groups in and of themselves?

2. How do multiple meanings in a film or video operate? Can there be a right meaning? Is it important to note what the author (director/producer/writer) meant in making the film?

3. What is a stereotype, and how does it affect audiences? Do people believe stereotypes? Do you take stereotypes from films or videos and use them in day-to-day life?

4. If Cheech Marin is satirizing stereotypes, how does his film treat stereotypes of Mexicans, Anglo-Americans or Mexican Americans? Do you think he is reinforcing stereotypes?

5. If you were to make a movie that challenged or questioned stereotypes, how would you construct it?

1. Discuss, within groups, what kinds of images of Latinas or Latinos you would expect to find in popular magazines, films, television or music videos. Now—having explored such impressions of images—each group member should write out a list of adjectives, labels and terms that are associated with her or his notions of Latina or Latino identity. The group as a whole will then categorize the elements of the list into positive, negative or neutral categories, discussing the values attached to each category.

2. During one week of watching television, keep track of the types of roles Latinas and Latinos play, and how they are portrayed in those roles; catalog them as hero, villain or victim. Report these back to the class and compare and contrast with students who have done the same exercise with a week of newspaper coverage, magazine coverage and film watching. Students will discuss the presence and impact of such portrayals.

3. In groups, sketch out a plot for a book, film or television program that does not have a single instance of gender, racial and sexual orientation stereotyping. The group must describe at least five characters and devise a plot that suggests an arc of action for the characters. The group must also identify at least one actress or actor for each role.

REFERENCES

Ang, I., & Hermes, J. (1996). Gender and/in media consumption. In J. Curran & M. Gurevitch (Eds.), *Mass media and society* (2nd. ed.) (pp. 325-348). London: Edward Arnold.

Austin, B. (1983). Researching the film audience: Purposes, procedures, and problems. *Journal of the Film and Video Association, 35*(3), 34-43.

Barrera, M. (1997). Missing the myth: What gets left out of Latino film analysis. *Perspectives in Mexican American Studies, 6*, 168-194.

Bordwell, D. (1989). *Making meaning: Inference and rhetoric in the interpretation of cinema.* Cambridge, MA: Harvard University Press.

Boyd, T. (1997). *Am I black enough for you? Popular culture from the 'hood and beyond.* Bloomington, IN: Indiana University Press.

Carey, J. (1977). Mass communication research and cultural studies: An American view. In J. Curran, M. Gurevitch, & J. Woollacott (Eds.), *Mass communication and society* (pp. 409-425). Beverly Hills, CA: Sage.

Cohen, J. R. (1991). The "relevance" of cultural identity in audiences' interpretations of mass media. *Critical Studies in Mass Communication, 8*, 442-454.

Contreras, R. (1997). Chicano movement Chicano studies: Social science and self-conscious ideology. *Perspectives in Mexican American Studies, 6*, 20-51.

Cortés, C. (1983). *The greaser's revenge* to *boulevard nights*: The mass media curriculum on Chicanos. In M. T. Garcia (Ed.), *History, culture, and society: Chicano studies in the 1980s* (pp. 125-140). Ypsilanti, MI: Bilingual Press.

Dávila, A. (2001). *Latinos, Inc.: The marketing and making of a people.* Berkeley and Los Angeles: University of California Press.

Delgado, F. P. (1995). Review essay: Coloring the screen bronze. *Text and Performance Quarterly, 15*, 160-167.

Delgado, F. P. (1998a). Moving beyond the screen: Hollywood and Mexican American stereotypes. In Y. R. Kamalipour & T. Carilli (Eds.), *Cultural diversity and the U.S. media* (pp. 169-182). Albany, NY: SUNY Press.

Delgado, F. P. (1998b). When the silenced speak: The textualization and complications of Latina/o identity. *Western Journal of Communication, 62*, 420-438.

Escalante, V. (1992). In pursuit of ethnic audiences: The media and Latinos. *Renato Rosaldo Lecture Series Monograph, 7*, 29-53.

Faber, R. J., O'Guinn, T. C., & Meyer, T. P. (1987). Televised portrayals of Hispanics: A comparison of ethnic perceptions. *International Journal of Intercultural Relations, 11*, 155-169.

Fiske, J. (1991a). For cultural interpretation: A study of the culture of homelessness. *Critical Studies in Mass Communication, 8*, 455-474.

Fiske, J. (1991b). Moments of television: Neither the text nor the audience. In E. Seiter, H. Borchers, G. Kreutzner, E. M. Warth (Eds.), *Remote control: Television, audiences, and cultural power* (pp. 56-78). New York: Routledge.

Fregoso, R. L. (1990). *Born in East L.A.* and the politics of representation. *Cultural Studies, 4*, 264-280.

Fregoso, R. L. (1993). *The bronze screen: Chicana and Chicano film culture.* Minneapolis: University of Minnesota Press.

Guevara, R. (2001, June/July). An interview with Richard "Cheech" Marin. *Americas 2001*, pp. 18-21.

Greenberg, B. S., Burgoon, M., Burgoon, J. K., & Korzenny, F. (1983). *Mexican Americans and the mass media*. Norwood, NJ: Ablex Publishing.

Gutiérrez-Jones, C. (1995). *Rethinking the borderlands: Between Chicano culture and legal discourse*. Berkeley: University of California Press.

Hall, S. (1980). Encoding/decoding. In S. Hall, D. Hobson. A. Lowe, & P. Willis (Eds.), *Culture, media, language* (pp. 128-139). London: Hutchinson.

Keller, G. D. (1994). *Hispanics and United States film: An overview and handbook*. Tempe, AZ: Bilingual Review/Press.

Keller, G. D. (Ed.). (1985). *Chicano cinema: Research, reviews, and resources*. Tempe, AZ: Bilingual Review/Press.

Mayne, J. (1994). Paradoxes of spectatorship. In L. Williams (Ed.), *Viewing positions: Ways of seeing things* (pp. 155-183). New Brunswick, NJ: Rutgers University Press.

Moores, S. (1993). *Interpreting audiences: The ethnography of media consumption*. Thousand Oaks, CA: Sage.

Nightingale, V. (1996). *Studying audiences: The shock of the real*. New York: Routledge.

Noriega, C. A. (1988-1990). Chicano cinema and the horizon of expectations: A discursive analysis of film reviews in the mainstream, alternative, and Hispanic press, 1987-1988. *Aztlán: Journal of Chicano Studies, 19*, 1-32.

Noriega, C. A. (Ed.). (1992). *Chicanos and film: Essays on Chicano representation and resistance*. New York: Garland Publishing.

Noriega, C. (1995). "Waas sappening?": Narrative structure and iconography in *Born in East L. A. Studies in American Popular Culture, 14*, 107-128.

Noriega, C. A. (1996). Imagined borders: Locating Chicano cinema in America/América. In C. A. Noriega & A. M. López (Eds.), *The ethnic eye: Latino media arts* (pp. 3-21). Minneapolis: University of Minnesota Press.

Noriega, C. A. (1998). The Aztlán Film Institute's top 100 films. *Jump Cut, 42*, 65-67.

Noriega, C. A. (2000). *Shot in America: Television, the state, and the rise of Chicano cinema*. Minneapolis: University of Minnesota Press.

Noriega, C. A., & López, A. M. (Eds.). (1996). *The ethnic eye: Latino media arts*. Minneapolis: University of Minnesota Press.

Ramírez Berg, C. (1990). Stereotyping in films in general and of the Hispanic in particular. *Howard Journal of Communications, 2*, 286-300.

Ramírez Berg, C. (1993). ¡Ya basta con the Hollywood paradigm! *Jump Cut, 38*, 96-104.

Ríos, D. I. (n.d.). *The contemporary Chicana/o audience's problematic relationship with media*. Unpublished manuscript, University of New Mexico.

Ríos, D. I. (1994). Chicano cultural resistance with mass media. In R. De Anda (Ed), *Chicanas and Chicanos in contemporary society* (pp. 127-141). Boston, MA: Allyn and Bacon.

Ríos, D. I.. & Gaines, S. O., Jr. (1997). Impact of gender and ethnic subgroup membership on Mexican Americans' use of mass media for cultural maintenance. *Howard Journal of Communications, 8*, 197-216.

Schement, J. (1976). Literature on the Chicano audience in review. *Aztlan, 7*, 119-124.

Seiter, E., Borchers, H., Kreutzner, G., & Warth, E. M. (Eds.). (1991). *Remote control: Television, audiences, and cultural power*. London: Routledge.

Subervi-Velez, F. A. (1986). The mass media and ethnic assimilation and pluralism: A review and research proposal with special focus on Hispanics. *Communication Research, 13*(1), 71-96.

Subervi-Velez, F. A., Herrera, R., & Begay, M. (1987). Toward an understanding of the role of the mass media in Latino political life. *Social Science Quarterly, 68*, 185-196.

Subervi-Vélez, F. A., & Necochea, J. (1990). Television viewing and self-concept among Hispanic American children—A pilot study. *Howard Journal of Communications, 2,* 315-329.

Turner, G. (1988). *Film as social practice.* New York: Routledge.

Tafoya, E. (1993). *Born in East L.A.*: Cheech as the Chicano Moses. *Journal of Popular Culture, 26*(4), 123-129.

Woll, A. L. (1974a). Hollywood's good neighbor policy: The Latin American image in American film, 1939-1946. *Journal of Popular Film, 3,* 283-285.

Woll, A. L. (1974b). Latin American images in American films. *Journal of Mexican History, 4,* 28-40.

Woll, A. L. (1993). Hollywood views the Mexican-American: From *the greaser's revenge* to *the milagro beanfield war*. In R. B. Toplin (Ed.), *Hollywood as mirror: Changing views of "outsiders" and "enemies" in American movies* (pp. 41-52). Westport, CT: Greenwood Press.

"The White-Black Fault Line": Relevancy of Race and Racism in Spectator's Experiences of Spike Lee's *Do the Right Thing*

Brenda Cooper

Racism has always been a sensitive issue for the American public, but few Hollywood films dealing with racism have generated the level of controversy of Spike Lee's *Do the Right Thing* (1989a). Set in the New York City neighborhood of Bedford-Stuyvesant on a hot summer Saturday, Lee's film chronicles the lives of the community's Black and Hispanic residents, and their tenuous relationship with Sal, the Italian-American owner and operator of the neighborhood's only pizzeria, "Sal's Famous," and his sons Pino and Vito. The main Black character in the movie is Mookie, played by Spike Lee, who earns $250 a week delivering Sal's pizzas to the neighborhood customers. When Buggin' Out, one of Mookie's friends, complains to Sal that all of the pictures on the pizzeria's "Wall of Fame" are Italian Americans, yet most of his customers are Blacks, tension mounts. Buggin' Out enlists another Black man, Radio Raheem, in his boycott of Sal's pizzeria to protest the absence of pictures of African Americans on the "Wall of Fame." The two men confront Sal, and when Radio Raheem refuses to lower the volume of his boom box, Sal smashes his radio with a baseball bat, and calls his customers "niggers"; a brawl begins. Police

arrive to control the disturbance, and while restraining Radio Raheem, a White officer kills him. As the angry residents yell at Sal and his sons, Mookie throws a garbage can through the window of the pizzeria, and a riot erupts that ends with Sal's business going up in flames.

Lee was both praised and vilified by critics and the public for his depiction of race relations in America, even among political liberals: "Not since the Black Panthers cowed Manhattan's glitterati 20 years ago has there been such a virulent outbreak of radical chic—or so many political-disease detectives ready to stanch the epidemic.... Everywhere, the film has polarized White Liberals," writes Richard Corliss of *Time* (1989, p. 62). Critical acclaim for Lee's bold, realistic representation of racism in America came from critics of all perspectives. A review in *African Commentary* reads: "Lee is fast fortifying his credentials as American's 'enfant terrible' of the cinema, igniter of controversies and the fearless prophet who forthrightly holds up the mirror-image of American's apocalypse to its frightened face" (cited in Chrisman, 1990, p. 53). Jacquie Jones, an editor from *Black Film Review*, says, "*Do the Right Thing* is a well orchestrated look at the reality, the humanity of racism.... [I]t also shows us how everyday events...can combine to explode the latent hostility bred in a society that is inherently racist, persistently unequal" (1990, p. 34). Film critic Roger Ebert calls the movie "the most honest, complex and unblinking film I have ever seen about the subject of racism" (cited in Kunen, 1989, p. 67). Writing for *The Christian Century*, James Wall praises Lee and his film: "Lee renders with considerable accuracy the Black experience from within.... [I]t will resonate with the experience of many Blacks" (1989, p. 739). Similarly, *Rolling Stone* film critic Peter Travers cheers *Do the Right Thing* for its "devastating portrait of Black America pushed to the limit" (1989, p. 29); *Newsweek's* David Ansen agrees, referring to *Do the Right Thing* as the "most informed view of racism an American filmmaker has given us" (Ansen, 1989, p. 66).

Lee wrote, directed, produced and starred in the film, and his explanation that he based his screenplay on actual incidents of police brutality and racial violence against African Americans in New York City (Blacks Michael Stewart and Eleanor Bumpurs were killed by New York City police officers, and another Black man, Michael Griffith, was struck and killed by a passing car while trying to escape a group of White Howard Beach teen-agers chasing him and his friends with baseball bats.) did little to appease his critics' charges of an anti-White film that would lead to more racial tension and outbreaks of violence across the country (Glicksman, 1989). Joe Klein's scathing review in *New York* magazine complains about the "dangerous stupidity of Spike Lee's message" that teaches viewers, especially Black teen-agers, that the police and White people "are your enemy" (1989, p. 15): "[T]here's a good chance the message they will take from the film will increase racial tensions in the city" (p. 14). A review in the *Economist* echoes Klein's criticisms, charging that, "The message of 'Do the Right Thing' is that behaviour that is plainly racist when practised by Whites is probably not racist when practised by Blacks; Blacks, after all, are an oppressed underclass" ("American cinema," 1989, p. 89). Columnist Stanley Crouch (1989), writing for *The Village Voice*, asserts the "unarguable persistence of a declining racism" (p. 74) in America, then accuses Lee of producing Black nationalism

power thinking propaganda in his film, similar to the type of propaganda produced by Nazi filmmaker Leni Rienfenstahl, and implies Lee himself is a racist and a fascist. About the film's riot scene, David Denby writes in *New York* that Lee "created the dramatic structure that primes Black people to cheer the explosion as an act of revenge.... The end of this movie is a shambles, and if some audiences go wild, he's partly responsible" (1989, p. 54). Robert Chrisman's review in *The Black Scholar* does not criticize the film's riot scene, which he says reinforces the message of "Fight the Power" heard throughout the film, but he charges that the ending, where Mookie goes back to the scene of the riot the following morning to collect his salary from Sal, trivializes Radio Raheem's death and the community's outrage that resulted: "It is like watching a slave rebellion being betrayed," and "raises the question, indeed, what is the right thing?" (1990, p. 57). Jack Kroll of *Newsweek* ends his review of Lee's film with a harsh indictment: "Lee has done the wrong thing" (1989, p. 65).

Lee responded to some of his critics' charges in a letter to the editor of *New York* magazine (1989b) and in interviews when *Do the Right Thing* was released. He defended his depiction of race relations in his film, explaining: "What I have done is to tell the story of race relations in this city from the point of view of Black New Yorkers. Certainly it's one side of the story.... but it's the side I want to tell" (p. 6). Lee dismissed his critics' charges that his film is anti-White, asserting that these kinds of comments "only feed White fears and White hysteria" (p. 6). And in response to accusations that the movie's riot scene is not justified, and could spark increased racial tensions and more violence, Lee says these are purely racist reactions to a film "about racism" from a non-White perspective (cited in Handelman, 1989, p. 174):

Are we to conclude that only Whites are intellectually and morally endowed to tackle an issue as complex as race relations in New York City?... It's hard to justify it [the film's end] only if you feel that when "some White policemen arrive and kill a Black boy" it's an event of little consequence, but the burning of Sal's pizzeria is of major consequence. (Lee, p. 6)

Lee continues: "The critics are focusing on the burning of the pizzeria, and nobody ever mentions the death of Radio Raheem, because to them Sal's property is more important than another death of a young Black kid, another Black 'hoodlum'" (cited in Kunen, 1989, p. 68). Although Lee said he was not advocating violence in his film, he understood the frustration of Black oppression that can lead to it.

The conflicting and often highly charged reactions from these reviewers, and Lee's responses to their critiques, raise a provocative question: How do average viewers of different races and demographic and cultural backgrounds interpret *Do the Right Thing*? Consider that although the race of spectators generally has been ignored in reception research (Diawara, 1990), Manthia Diawara (1988) argues we should not assume that Black and White spectators will share the same "pleasures" (p. 72) in their film experiences. Even among Black spectators, differences have been revealed; for example, African-American women spectators tend to praise *The Color Purple* and identify with its images of Black women and their experiences (Bobo, 1988), while many African-American men do not, and instead complain that it perpetuates racist stereotypes of Black men (Walker, 1996). Operating from these preliminary observations, I explicated viewers' experiences of Spike Lee's film, specifying the differences in their processes of interpretation in this case study of the relationship between relevancy and spectatorship, and *Do the Right Thing*.

Relevancy and Spectatorship

Most research examining film content has focused primarily on how a film may affect audience viewers—rather than attempting to explicate directly viewers' experiences and subsequent understandings of the film—thus failing to address adequately the processes used by viewers to make sense of their film experiences (Crow, 1981; Stadler, 1990). Reception research has articulated concepts to examine viewers' interpretation processes. For example, three different responses to media texts—dominant (reading as intended), negotiated (decoding the hegemonic position) and oppositional (placing the text into an alternative frame of reference)—have been used to explain individuals' varying interpretations of the same mediated text (Hall, 1980; Morley, 1980). Diawara (1990) asserts, however, that these kinds of approaches to spectatorship and identification research do not adequately explain the relationship between the spectator and the screen images. Jodi Cohen (1991a) agrees, arguing that research explicating the "relevant moments of meaning" (p. 443) occurring at the intersection of spectators' cultural subjectivities and mediated texts are critical to identifying and understanding the interpretation processes used by spectators, because the concept of "relevancy allows for a much more elaborated view of *how* spectators selectively draw from the text and their identities at different moments of interpretation" (p. 453), thus helping to explain *why* texts may be read as dominant, negotiated or oppositional.

This approach, as it relates to spectators' viewing experiences, offers researchers a critical tool for understanding the various and often contradictory interpretations that spectators may assign to media texts, a tool which often is lacking in other critical examinations of socially situated interpretations of media texts (Cohen, 1991a; 1991b). For example, Morley's 1980 study, *The 'Nationwide' Audience,* reports that Black students participating in his study fail to make connections with *Nationwide's* discourse because the program is not relevant to their lives, thus implicitly introducing relevancy as a factor in viewers' relationship with media texts: "The concerns of *Nationwide* are not the concerns of their world" (p. 134). In later research, Morley (1986) addresses the concept of relevancy more specifically, concluding that the individuals' family context—in this case working-class, White families—is a relevant factor in determining the family members' selection and use of television programs. As a result of his research, Morley articulated a theory of discourse to explain audience members' readings of media texts, with discourse referring to a "socially located way of making sense of an important area of social experience" (Fiske, 1992, p. 301). Thus, the meanings spectators assign to mediated texts will vary "according to the discourses (knowledges, prejudices, resistances, etc.) brought to bear by the reader, and the crucial factor in the encounter of audience/subject and text will be the range of discourses at the disposal of the audience" (Morley, 1985, p. 239).

Fiske (1988) provides further articulation of relevancy as a factor in spectatorship, emphasizing the social history that people bring to their viewing experiences, and thus defining relevancy as a social concept:

> ...[T]he person is an historical and social construct formed both by his or her material social history and by the discourses through which he or she has experienced that history.... [T]he viewer makes meanings and pleasures from television that are relevant to his or her social allegiances at the moment of viewing; the criteria for relevance *precede* the viewing moment. (p. 247)

The meanings viewers assign to a media text are, therefore, produced when their own discourses intersect with those of the media discourse "in a moment of semiosis" (p. 247). Further, Fiske (1988) argues that viewers find these meanings most pleasurable when they are "pertinent" to their social allegiances (p. 247). Consequently, mediated texts are "no longer a stable structure of signifiers" (p. 247), but an "open potential" of meaning, "produced and determined by the social allegiances" of viewers within the limitations of the discursive boundaries of the text (p. 248).

Cohen (1991a) refers to this intersection between spectators and mediated texts as "relevant moments of meaning" (p. 444). In her study of homosexual and heterosexual male spectators, Cohen finds that relevancy—or the lack of it—assigned to the gay-themed teleplay, *Tidy Endings*, by these two groups of men significantly influences how they frame the teleplay's narrative, judge the characters and events, distance themselves critically from the play's narratives and explore social and personal issues of gay identity. For example, gay oppression is relevant to how the gay spectators interpret *Tidy Endings*, but is not nearly as relevant for the interpretations of the heterosexual men. Cohen also states that the relevancy of AIDS does not function similarly for the gay and non-gay men; unlike

the gay men, heterosexual men frame the teleplay as a "story about the effects of AIDS on the heterosexual population" (p. 448), linking AIDS with homosexuality, while gay men recognize that AIDS is not solely a homosexual disease: "[T]heir knowledge of and experiences with AIDS—different from the knowledge and experiences of heterosexuals—influenced their perception and evaluation of the dramatic events" depicted in the teleplay (p. 452).

Lind (1996) also reports that relevancy is a critical factor in how White and Black viewers interpret a television news report on housing discrimination against African Americans. She articulates four relevancies of race—oppression, racism, characters and home ownership—that influence how spectators construct their meanings to the news account. Just as Cohen (1991a) reports the relevance of gay oppression for gay men, but not heterosexual men in their respective interpretations of *Tidy Endings*, Lind finds similar differences between White and Black viewers. For instance, most African-American viewers respond to the negative images of Blacks in media stories, perceiving these images as a "tool of oppression" (p. 59) that perpetuates stereotypes of their race as uneducated and inarticulate, in other words, inferior to Whites. These negative images of African Americans, however, are not mentioned by the White viewers, indicating the images' lack of relevancy in the White viewers' interpretation processes.

The major assumptions underlying inquiries of viewers' responses to media texts in terms of the texts' relevancies to their social allegiances and cultural subjectivities can be situated within the larger context of film spectatorship. For example, Christine Gledhill (1988) articulates the concept of "negotiational pleasures" (p. 84), an approach to film spectatorship that accounts for how viewers with opposing values and from divergent backgrounds can negotiate a pleasurable reading from the same film, fitting the film's text to their relevant life experiences. For instance, even texts in films with anti-racist narratives can have a "double-sidedness" (p. 87) quality that can be read from a racist stance. Thus, Gledhill characterizes the cultural exchange between film texts and spectators as a struggle among the experiences, motivations and frames of reference between the films' spectators and those involved in producing the films' texts. Similarly, Elizabeth Ellsworth (1986) explains that individuals manipulate specific features of a film's narratives to make them fit relevant aspects of their self-definitions within a specific cinematic context. Also, although certain strategies may be used in media narratives in attempts to "contain subversive readings" (Griggers, 1993, p. 132), because spectators generate their own meanings in the reception process, these types of readings cannot be completely controlled. These perspectives illustrate the shared assumptions among film spectatorship investigations and the concept of relevancy: the relationship between mediated texts and viewers is reciprocal, as media narratives merely provide frameworks for possible interpretations, and viewers individually and creatively use media texts to fit their individual life experiences and cultural subjectivities during their processes of interpretative reflection (Nelson, 1986).

Description of Study

After viewing *Do The Right Thing*, 65 university students[1] who were enrolled in upper-division undergraduate communication courses at two universities were asked to write their reactions to the film as part of in-class, ungraded assignments. The student population at one institution is racially diverse, with approximately one-third of the students members of racial minority groups, while the student population at the other university is around 90 percent White. The racially diverse institution is located in an urban city near New York City, while the predominantly White-populated university is situated in a rural Western college town. The religious background of the students from the urban university is also diverse, whereas approximately 90 percent of the students attending the Western university are members of an ultra-conservative religion.[2]

Following Eric Peterson's (1987) method of open-ended, self-report essays, I used the students' written self-reports for my analysis. My instructions were non-directive, simply asking students to write essays in which they describe

their reactions to Lee's film. I chose to use self-report essays because this approach to data collection "posits the individual as the conscious and causative agent in media interaction" (Thomas, 1981, p. 3). As a self-report technique, the essays express the "conscious experience of a communicative event," and thus allow spectators to "describe the context of their experience in terms of affective, cognitive, and intersubjective dimensions" not always apparent in observable behavior (Nelson, 1987, pp. 314-315).[3] Importantly, because self-report essays allow the spectators to contextualize their own experiences and responses, researchers have minimal influence on their responses (Nelson, 1987).[4]

The arguments and positions taken by these student spectators in discussing the film's positive and negative aspects reveal recurring themes that in turn allow the explication of the relevancies where the spectators' "cultural subjectivities" and the film "text come together in specific moments" (Cohen, 1991a, p. 443) in their processes of interpreting *Do the Right Thing*. In other words, analysis of the spectators' varying arguments to support their interpretations of the film identify the "discourses which informed" these interpretations, and thus allow the relevancies of their interpretation processes to be explicated from their personal narratives (Lind, 1996, p. 58). Hence, my analysis of the self-report essays identified the essential "relevant moments of meaning" (Cohen, 1991, p. 444) occurring during the spectators' reflections on their film experience, and provided further insights into the "decoding processes audience members routinely employ" (Lull, 1987, p. 321) to construct their meanings of film texts, particularly in terms of the "radical reality" (Studlar, 1990, p. 2) of race and racism in their lives.

Discussion of Relevancies

My analysis of the spectators' essays reveals contradictory interpretations of *Do The Right Thing* between the non-African Americans and the African Americans, based on their cultural subjectivities and corresponding discourses.[5] Overall, the majority of the non-African-American spectators do not like Spike Lee's film, nor do they think that Lee "did the right thing" in his cinematic representation of race relations in America. In contrast, the African-American spectators say they like the movie, and generally believe that Lee did "do the right thing." Significantly, the White and Hispanic spectators minimize the issues of racism and oppression underlying the film's narratives, while Blacks identify with this depiction and relate it to their life experiences. In other words, racism and its consequences are not a relevant factor for the non-African-American spectators. We can begin to understand these differences by relating the spectators' responses to five relevant moments of meaning explicated from their essays: *relevancy of characters, relevancy of riot, relevancy of racism, relevancy of realism and identification,* and *relevancy of "doing the right thing."*

RELEVANCY OF CHARACTERS

Regardless of race or background, Sal and Mookie are the characters the spectators mention most often. However, the spectators' responses indicate contradictory interpretations of these two characters and their actions: Whites and Hispanics sympathize with Sal, describing him both as a paragon of fairness and the victim of racist actions at the hands of Mookie and his African-American friends. In contrast, for African Americans, Sal represents a symbol of oppression of their race endemic in American society, and their empathy lies with Mookie and his Black friends. For example, White and Hispanic spectators describe Sal as a hard worker, and interpret his actions with the African Americans who frequent his pizzeria as evidence of his genuine sense of fairness and lack of bigotry toward an unappreciative Mookie and the other Blacks of the neighborhood. Typical statements[6] from non-African-American spectators describing Sal's relationship with Mookie are: "Sal's character was a loving, hardworking man and he treated Mookie like one of his own sons" (7); "Sal treated Mookie with a lot of respect, considering Mookie was a lazy worker" (10); "Mookie took advantage of Sal" (15); "He also continually supported Mookie even though he was a terrible worker" (24); "Sal seemed to treat Mookie like a third son.... Sal had Mookie's best interests at heart" (106); and, "I think Mookie

should have been fired at the beginning of the movie.... Mookie tried to play Sal off as someone who owed him something" (113).

The non-African-American spectators also believe Sal is fair and generous to the film's other Black characters, as these comments illustrate: "Sal tried to get along with everyone. He saw Black people not niggers" (16); "Sal was not racist and I believe he tried to do what was right" (22); "Sal, despite his hard-hitting attitude, genuinely cared for the people of the community. He showed this by giving money to 'Da Mayor' and to Smiley" (24); "Sal seemed fairly willing to help the people in the community—he didn't just want to earn a dollar, like when he gave Da Mayor money to sweep up or Smiley some money for the pictures" (118); "I liked Sal and understood him.... Sal actually loved these people and all he wanted was just to make pizza and be happy" (123); and, "Sal seems fair towards Blacks.... He treats Mookie fairly and everyone else in the neighborhood too. He even credits Blacks for making his business a success" (124).

In contrast, African-American spectators interpret Sal's actions and his relationship with Mookie and his Black customers as racist and exploitative, and importantly, as representative of the larger issues of Black oppression in American society. Further, many African Americans see Sal's actions as economically motivated, not because "He loves providing his service to the community," as one White man concludes (107). Consider these examples from Black spectators: "Sal's interactions with the different characters were strictly business. He considered himself to be king of the block and the African Americans were his servants" (1); "Mookie and Sal's relationship looked close only on the surface.... The 'love and respect' for his Black customers was based on economics" (3); "Yes, it's true that Sal seemed to take Mookie under his wings a little and give him leeway, but that's only because Mookie was doing a job neither he nor his sons wanted to do and that's going into the community.... [T]he store's four walls gave Sal all of the security he needed to continue working in Bed-Stuy" (4); "Sal always reprimanded Mookie like a kid" (101); "Sal did not interact in a positive way with Blacks in the neighborhood.... He dominated everyone. He simply gave orders and demanded what should be done.... And he and Mookie have an underlying dislike for each other" (102); and, "Sal & Mookie didn't care too much for one another.... There is no reason that they (Sal & Koreans) should come in Blacks' neighborhoods and disrespect them" (105).

Further, unlike the White spectators who write that Sal "loved the Black people because he had spent so much time with them watching them grow and change" (27) and, "He is part of the Black families that he feeds" (107), some Black men point out that Whites only spend time in neighborhoods such as Bed-Stuy to run their businesses and make money from the residents: "In my community I see exactly what Spike filmed—Whites operate their businesses in Black neighborhoods and yet they do not live in that neighborhood. He [Lee] demonstrates the racial tension that has taken a strong hold on society" (102); and, "The way Sal interacted with the people of the community was like how most White store owners in a Black community feel, like they are doing us a favor" (103).

What is relevant for these African-American spectators is that Sal's actions represent what they perceive as the underlying prejudice Whites harbor toward Blacks, even if the Whites try to hide that prejudice, as these responses from Black spectators illustrate: "He showed his true colors (prejudice and mistreatment) to the Blacks" (1); "Sal's true colors came forward with the names and racial slurs he used ... and in his confrontations with Buggin' Out and Radio Raheem" (3); and, "Sal's real feelings come out in the end" (101).

The spectators also label Mookie differently. Until he throws the garbage can through the window of Sal's pizzeria, Mookie is viewed as a peacemaker by the majority of non-African-American spectators, who often write that they admire his attempts to encourage his Black friends to co-exist with Sal: "He tries to get along with everyone. He knows his heritage yet doesn't try to force it on other people" (9); "Mookie often tried to keep the peace by telling other Black kids to 'step off'" (14); "I liked Mookie until the end because he stood up for Sal a few times—telling his 'brothers' to back off" (29); and, "He seemed to be the peacemaker of the neighborhood" (106).

Rather than viewing Mookie as a peacemaker, the African-American men interpret his interactions with his Black neighbors and friends and with Sal as those of an "Uncle Tom": "Mookie was a sellout" (101); and, "He seemed to be uninterested in the other Blacks' affairs unless it interfered with his wants" (102). Black women, however, are less harsh in their appraisal of Mookie, writing that his actions represent both the struggles of a young Black man trying to get by with "whatever little he had in life" (2), and the "everyday survival for a young Black man in the inner city" (4).

RELEVANCY OF RIOT

Similarly contradictory interpretations of the riot and its causes are found between the non-African-American and African-American spectators. While African-American spectators identify the racist attitudes underlying the riot, and express empathy for the resulting frustrations of Mookie and his Black friends, Whites and Hispanics express their sympathy for Sal, and write about their inability to understand why Mookie "started the riot" (29). Further, the police brutality is virtually ignored by non-African-Americans, and Sal's rights of ownership and loss of his pizzeria take precedence over Buggin' Out's boycott and Radio Raheem's death.

For instance, the non-African-American spectators fail to recognize the implied racism in Sal's refusal to meet Buggin' Out's demand for photos of famous African Americans on his pizzeria's "Wall of Fame," or even the significance of Buggin' Out's demand. Typical statements from the White and Hispanic spectators include: "Sal felt it was his business and he worked hard for it. He felt certain rules needed to be followed, for example, no Black people on the wall and no loud radios" (15); "Buggin' Out came along and threw a fit because there was not a picture of a Black man on the wall. Big deal, it is not your place to begin with" (40); "Sal doesn't take any trouble from anyone, especially a militant Black [Buggin' Out] complaining about his restaurant" (112); and, "I think that the whole thing about the wall of fame was ridiculous" (113).

Even the few non-African-American spectators who agree that pictures of Black people should be on the wall still sympathize with Sal's rights as owner of the pizzeria: "Buggin' Out did have a valid point, but...Sal's prerogative outweighs Buggin' Out's point" (23); and, "The Black people did have a right to want to see Black people on the wall, but it was Sal's place" (36). Further, some non-African Americans frame Buggin' Out's demand as a case of special pleading from Blacks, as this example demonstrates: "If a Black man would have owned that pizzeria, and had pictures of just Black men, none of this would have started. I also don't think that a White man would ever ask a Black person who owned something, to put up pictures of some White guy who Blacks neither like nor know what that person did" (113).

The non-African-American spectators also defend Sal's claim that Blacks are to blame for Radio Raheem's death, and issues of racism, oppression and police brutality are ignored. Consider the following statements: "I think the Blacks' attitudes of hate and tension and disrespect caused the problems, not the fact that there were no pictures of Black leaders on the wall" (14); "I have to agree with Sal when he told Mookie that his friend (with the crazy hair) was the one to blame for Raheem's death" (15); "Radio did die and that was very wrong, but they were in Sal's place" (36); "The guys who came in breaking Sal's rules incited Sal to react negatively" (39); "Even though the Black boy with the radio was killed by the White cops, I do not believe that justifies the cruel act of destroying a man's business" (41); "I think he [Sal] had every right to smash the radio. Raheem was completely out of line. He went in there with a violent attitude" (110); and, "I have to say—I think Radio Raheem and his sidekick were radicals & deserved to be recipients of consequences equaling their behaviors (which was clearly not socially acceptable), but not death certainly" (117).

Finally, the White and Hispanic spectators blame Mookie's decision to throw the garbage can through the window of Sal's pizzeria for the riot, and express their lack of understanding for his action and their sympathy for Sal. Representative statements from non-African-American

spectators are: "I felt sorry for Sal because he worked really hard to get what he had and it was all destroyed over hate and dislike for one another" (9); "Mookie turned on Sal for the sake of his race.... I don't think they [Blacks] followed their own advice to 'Always Do the Right Thing'" (14); "It really upset me when Mookie threw the garbage can through the window. I think that Sal treated him fair throughout the film...it wasn't his fault Radio Raheem got killed" (18); "I had a different opinion of him after he started the riot by throwing the can through the window. I just don't understand I guess" (29); "The whole reason for the riot was pretty stupid too, I thought, because they blamed Sal for the cops killing Radio Raheem, and Sal, and Vito and Pino had nothing to do with it" (113); "I couldn't understand why they turned on Sal. It was not Sal's fault that Radio Raheem died.... The thing that I thought was odd was that Mookie was the one who threw the first stone by tossing the garbage can...why bite the hand that feeds you?" (115); "I can't understand why he [Mookie] felt he had to start the riot" (123); and, "I was disappointed in the Black community's reaction to the killing of Raheem— IT WAS NOT Sal's fault—He reaped consequences of an action that wasn't his" (117).

African-American spectators express contradictory reactions to Buggin' Out's request, as well as the riot and its cause, which they identify as racism. And although some write that they do not necessarily condone violence, they do understand the frustration with racism that may lead to violent actions, and overall defend Mookie's decision and empathize with the film's Black characters. Some Black spectators write about the "Wall of Fame" as follows: "When Buggin' Out asked Sal why he didn't have Black people's pictures on his pizzeria wall, Sal just said to him that he should get his own pizzeria in order to put Black pictures on the wall" (1); "I saw his [Buggin' Out] point when he made the statement that if 99% of your business comes from Blacks, then why aren't there any Blacks on the wall" (5); and, "Buggin' Out wanted some pictures of Black people on the wall of 'Sal's famous.' He figured that it's the Black people in the neighborhood who are giving Sal his business" (104).

Comments from the African-American spectators about Radio Raheem's death and the subsequent riot also reflect an identification with the Black characters and the racism they face in the film: "Sal destroyed his radio—which meant that Sal destroyed a part of Raheem.... Mookie realized that racism shouldn't be tolerated anymore. That is why Mookie decided to put an end to Sal's pizzeria" (1); "We received a clear picture of brutality when one of Mookie's friends is killed by the White police. This incident showed us that a Black man was convicted before he was tried" (2); and, "Radio Raheem is a victim of an incident like one that occurred in the hood and was reported on TV. There are people who have never been right since" (105). One Black man defends Mookie's action by explaining that despite Radio Raheem's death and the racism toward Blacks leading to it, Mookie is actually trying to prevent further violence toward Sal and his sons by throwing the garbage can through the pizzeria's window:

> Mookie did the right thing by throwing the garbage can through Sal's window. Mookie shattered the window to help Sal rather than to offend. I believe he had foresight.... he knew there would be tensions and possibly assaults toward Sal, Vito, and Pino. It helped everyone to channel their anger on Sal's property rather than to allow the crowd to continue to attack Sal in revenge for Radio's death. (102)

A critic from *The Christian Century* agrees with this spectator's interpretation of Mookie's action: "Mookie did the right thing by diverting a crowd's anger away from Sal and his two sons. Better to destroy property than life" (Wall, 1989, p. 740). The non-African-American spectators, however, fail to recognize the possibility that Mookie may have acted to protect Sal, and interpret his actions solely as those of an unappreciative Black man, unfairly venting his misguided anger toward the White man who provided his livelihood.

RELEVANCY OF RACISM

For White and Hispanic students, the issue of racism is relevant only in terms of describing the film's popularity and controversy; Sal's actions and the underlying racism that led to Radio Raheem's death are ignored. African-American spectators, in contrast, identify with the racism portrayed in *Do The Right Thing*, relating it to their personal life experiences that form their cultural subjectivities. For instance, in writing about why the film was controversial, non-African-American spectators overwhelmingly cite the movie's depiction of racial strife, often linking the controversy to the discomfort viewers may experience when confronted with the harsh reality of racism with which they are basically unfamiliar, and often feel is exaggerated or imaged. Some White and Hispanic spectators write: "I didn't like how the movie made me feel.... It is a hard movie to watch" (18); "Most of us do not like to believe that discrimination does exist" (23); "People don't want to believe that things like this really happen" (26); "It is sometimes hard to realize how serious racism is when you don't see it every day" (27); "Racism is something we all try to hide and keep out of discussion. This movie brought everything out into the open and I don't think that a lot of people were comfortable with that idea" (110); "It portrayed today's society and it scares people" (119); and, "These films are hard. They make people like me remember...when a 'nigger joke' was told in the locker room, and even the coach laughed" (122).

Some non-African Americans also relate the film's controversy to what they perceive to be Lee's unfair depictions of Whites as racists, and exaggerated portrayals of the racism Blacks experience: "I also think the Whites were angry because it implied that many Whites are prejudiced" (13); "This film gives a negative view of White people. He makes them out to be all racists and not easy people to get along with. People only see racism in White people, but Black people, as well as other races, are racists. But in the film he makes the Black people victims the whole time" (40); and, "I felt angry.... I get so sick and tired of people making everything out to be a racial thing.... I understand pride in one's race, but why do people have to be so outspoken about it?" (119).

It is discouraging that many White and Hispanic spectators respond to the film's depiction of racism and its subsequent controversy by attempting to justify rather than question or challenge racist attitudes, with comments such as the following: "This may be a narrow-minded way of thinking, but I believe that everyone deep down inside is racist, and those who claim they are not are just trying to prove that they are not" (37); "It pissed me off because I feel we all have some racist or prejudicial feelings within ourselves, and this movie pushed my buttons" (106); "The film caused controversy because of the fact we all feel this way towards other races but submerge our thoughts and feelings unless we are with our peers.... The movie exemplifies the feelings of all Black men toward Whites and how Blacks stick together" (111); and, "They [Blacks] generate just as much hate as White racists" (119).

African Americans also cite the film representation of racism as the primary reason for the controversy it generated, and note that Lee's depictions of racism may be uncomfortable for many non-African-American viewers, as evidenced in these comments from Black spectators: "Some people didn't want to see the racial issues shown in the movie because they came too close to home and people don't want to believe that this racism exists, especially in New York City.... New York City had a lot of racial problems and still has them to this present day" (1); "It told the truth and people don't like to hear the truth when it's their wrongdoings that create the truth.... We tend to become upset when our acts of violence, hate, etc. are exposed" (4); "The movie demonstrates the racial tension that has taken a strong hold on society" (102); and, "When you raise an issue like racism, it stirs up people so much" (103).

Blacks, however, write that it is not simply the film's representation of racism that resulted in the controversy or the discomfort it generates for some viewers, but also the fact that the film's White characters are not the heroes: "The Whites were the evil ones in the movie and not the stars" (104). In fact, most Hollywood-produced films dealing with race have featured White actors in the roles of the heroes, such as *Mississippi Burning* and *Ghosts of Mississippi;* in both films, the "heroic" actions of the Whites overshadow the hardships of Blacks and ignore their contributions to the Civil Rights Move-

ment, a representation of African Americans that Spike Lee finds appalling (Svetkey, 1997).

In fact, it is director Spike Lee and the starring roles of people of color in his film that White and Hispanic spectators cite as the primary reason for the popularity of *Do the Right Thing,* especially with people of color: "Lee emerged as a leader in the film industry. Black people felt a sense of accomplishment" (6); "Blacks like to see movies with them as the main characters and I think that Spike Lee has a large following—people just go to see it because he directed it" (12); "I feel Spike Lee is a popular producer among minorities" (15); "It was based on a view of how Black people see the world around us" (40); "It was directed by Spike Lee and the movie came out during a time when there were not too many Black directors around" (115); "The film probably appealed to Blacks because it had many of them in it" (117); and, "It showed how life was for those people" (118).

Although many Blacks agree that Spike Lee's use of African-American actors and his depiction of racial strife contribute to the film's box office appeal for people of color (e.g., "Spike Lee was fresh on the scene and many African Americans supported him in numbers" (3); and (104), "Blacks, Hispanics, and Asians came out to support it because they finally saw their ethnic groups playing starring roles in a movie.... Lee showed more than White people can act.... He had non-Whites playing major roles"), they also relate the popularity of *Do The Right Thing* to specific racial incidents that occurred in New York City. Further, the film's controversial portrayal of racism is also the reason cited by Blacks for the film's box-office success, as the depiction of racial strife from a non-White perspective is something Blacks report they find affirming: "It realistically showed Black and White relations" (1); "It focused on the very sensitive topic of racism that exists towards Blacks in our society today" (2); "The racial controversy in NYC was on the news, and the movie came out in the middle of it...it's a real tale of inner city life" (101); and, "Lee's film was timely and racially enlightening. He did not over-exaggerate and falsify anything. All were true representations of how society is run" (102).

RELEVANCY OF REALISM AND IDENTIFICATION

Spectators from all races write about the film's realism in terms of depicting race relations in America, but their perceptions of the film's true-to-life portrayals are based on different experiences and subsequent cultural subjectivities; African Americans identify with the racist attitudes and actions expressed toward Blacks depicted in the film, but non-African-American spectators seem to identify with the racist feelings exhibited by Sal and his sons, linking the characters' biases to their personal feelings toward other races, and what they perceive as the overall racist attitudes in society. Importantly, the non-African-American spectators use their seemingly biased racial attitudes to justify the actions of the White characters in *Do the Right Thing*. Examples from White and Hispanic spectators regarding the film's realism are: "The film correctly identified the feelings that exist between different races" (14); "I really feel that the film was typical about interactions among different races. Blacks have a different language, Koreans don't speak good English and get rich off of our government" (33); "It is what really happens when you have so many races in large numbers interacting with each other.... I think that many races will interact with each other, but when it comes down to it, people of the same race will always stick together" (37); "Pino seemed to know off-hand that Mookie, or any Black man, would one day back stab them" (41); "It was realistic. It shed light on how people truly felt" (106); and, "This movie told how people really feel about other races. We, on the most part, cope with other races but in our minds we hold firm stereotypes.... The film brought attention to the anger we all store" (111).

Further, the White and Hispanic spectators seem to lack any direct identification with the film's depiction of racism and its consequences for African Americans, writing about their lack of understanding of the Black characters and their actions in *Do the Right Thing*, and in fact, discounting the film as exaggerated: "I can't imagine being involved in something like that [riot].... Is this really what it's like in those neighborhoods?" (21); "While viewing this, I felt more like an outsider than one who understands.... I

did not really identify with this movie" (23); "I was raised in a small town...I've never lived in a big city with a high percentage of all races—but I can't imagine it [racism] being that bad!" (29); "It was hard to see why they would burn down the Italian store and not the Korean store" (36); and, "I was confused because of the characters' responses to life, especially on the part of the Blacks" (119). In fact, only three non-African-American spectators, all male and from the New York City area university (107, 109, 124), relate the film's plot to the real-life racial incidents that occurred there. While it is not surprising that these incidents of White brutality against Blacks are not part of the film experiences of the spectators from the Western university, more than half of the spectators lived in the greater New York City area at the time of the racially motivated deaths of Michael Stewart, Eleanor Bumpurs and Michael Griffith, all of which were the objects of intense coverage by the local media. These omissions thus indicate an overall lack of relevance among the non-African-American spectators not only with *Do the Right Thing*, but also with the issues of racism and oppression occurring in their own communities.

In contrast, racism is relevant to the Blacks participating in my study; these spectators form their conclusions from their personal life experiences and corresponding cultural subjectivities, as well as the incidents of racial tension and discrimination in the New York City area, leading to identification with the film's plot and characters. African-American spectators write: "I could relate to the film.... Some of the things that happened in the neighborhood in the film can be compared to the racial problems or racial polarization in New York's neighborhoods today.... It realistically showed Black and White relations. There were past issues that appeared in the film.... The scene (Radio Raheem's death by police) represented the Michael Stewart killing by White police" (1); "Lee displayed the overriding issue that the world was still very much dominated by Whites" (2); "The movie couldn't have been released at a more critical time in relation to events in NYC.... In a lot of inner cities across the country, audiences could identify" (101); and, "Lee showed how White cops still come and disturb the community by killing non-Whites" (104).

RELEVANCY OF DO THE RIGHT THING

Many spectators express their feelings related to the film's title in the context of whether Spike Lee "did the right thing" with his film's depiction of racial strife. For the vast majority of non-African Americans, Spike Lee did *not* do the right thing, while for African Americans, he *did*. Consider these reactions from White and Hispanic spectators: "I think he [Spike Lee] is racist & portrays every White person in his movies as evil.... It sends viewers a very scary message: 'Fight the Power'" (7); "The movie makes me very angry.... It really offended me, and actually makes me *sick*" (9); "It did nothing to help racial problems in our society, it probably damaged them even more—what was the point?" (11); "This film portrayed very mixed and twisted messages—WARPED is the only word I can think of to describe this film" (22); "My main reaction to the film was disgust" (27); "[T]he film is racist. It expressed ethnocentric views—favoring the Black community" (41); "By using violence as a form of retaliation, Lee only exhibited the Blacks as animals, unable to divert their feelings in a healthy fashion and as dumb, leaving them in a worse predicament than before the burning of Sal's (the loss of the street's favorite and only pizzeria). And because he is a role model to many Black grown-ups and Black youths, it's inevitable that with Spike's [Mookie's] actions, an idea was implanted in their minds to use violence as a solution, whenever they feel victimized" (111); and, "I believe it promotes aggression. Spike Lee makes it seem like their lives are so hard" (115).

In contrast, the African-American spectators agree that Spike Lee did the right thing with his depiction of race relations. Some examples from the Black spectators are: "The film focused upon the life of a young Black man struggling to make it in the inner city's rough neighborhoods, and these kind of movies are needed.... I think that Spike Lee (Mookie) did a good job of showing racial issues" (2); "In this movie I do think that Spike Lee did the right thing because he brought out some of the problems that underlie racial tension in this world.... That was an excellent

topic to cover" (4); "Director/producer/actor Spike Lee has done phenomenal work on positive and realistic images of African Americans" (5); "Spike Lee did 'Do The Right Thing'.... He used real-life events for the foundation of his script. For example, the Howard Beach incident" (101); "I think Spike Lee did the right thing. His movie exhibited a racial tension that exists in society.... White and Korean men in power running businesses and owning property in Black neighborhoods" (102); and, "I think he created a more conscious awareness toward the seemingly increasing racial tension between Blacks and Whites.... He [Lee] captured the feelings of many Blacks" (103).

Overall, the Black spectators overwhelmingly interpret the events in the movie as evidence of their continued oppression in American society, while non-Blacks fail to make this connection. Accordingly, two events that the Black spectators describe frequently as evidence of their marginalization—Buggin' Out's demand for pictures of Black leaders on Sal's "Wall of Fame," and the murder of Radio Raheem—are virtually ignored by the Whites and Hispanics. Buggin' Out's demand is minimized, ignored or ridiculed by non-African Americans, while the murder is mentioned primarily in terms of describing the plot of the movie, not as symbolic of any more significant theme. In other words, the non-African-American spectators trivialize the very issues Black spectators see as central to their film experience, thus paralleling Spike Lee's accusations leveled toward critics of his film: "The White critics identify with Sal, but the movie's not about him. You cannot equate a human life with the destruction of a pizzeria. Why does no one ask me if the cops are going to be tried for the murder?" (cited in Handelman, 1989, p. 174).

Implications

The differences between how these African-American and non-African-American spectators experience Spike Lee's film are dramatic. African-American spectators' cultural subjectivities seem to allow them to identify far more easily with the symbolism underlying the narrative structure of *Do the Right Thing* and the societal biases represented in it than do the cultural subjectivities of the non-African-American spectators. A few dissenting voices emerge, however, from the responses of the non-African-American spectators. For instance, not all of the non-African-American spectators sympathize with Sal, and in fact, a few agree with the Black spectators' assessment of his character, as these comments indicate: "Sal really didn't treat Mookie with respect...he thought he was his slave" (8); "Mookie was the slave, he walked around town all day delivering pizzas. Neither Sal nor his sons had respect for Mookie" (31); "I think he [Sal] had a bit of racism to him...he may have felt a little above them" (106); and, "With the exception of Jade, he [Sal] treated the Blacks in the neighborhood as just pain in the ass customers" (110).

Similarly, a few non-African Americans do not blame Mookie for inciting the riot, nor do they express sympathy for Sal or condone his actions. For example, one White woman feels that, "Sal started the violence with the bat" (36). Another White woman points out that, "When the violence broke out the police went directly to the Black people and did not even question Sal" (31), while one White man places the blame for the riot on the police: "The cause of the tension was the police. By killing Raheem, they brought out a lot of anger.... They stirred up everybody and then left" (110). And some White spectators acknowledge that Lee's film "dealt with a lot of issues that are often ignored, or looked at as unimportant because a minority experienced it, not a White man" (15).

The overwhelming similarity of responses by race, however, is an indication not only of the conflicting cultural subjectivities of the African-American and non-African-American spectators, but also of the level of racial division in America. Regardless of their geographic or cultural environments, their religious backgrounds or their ethnicities—Hispanic, Italian American, White[7]—the non-African Americans are virtually universal in their denunciation of Spike Lee and his film, reflecting similar attitudes as those voiced by Lee's critics cited earlier (e.g., "American cinema," 1989; Denby, 1989; Klein, 1989; and Kroll, 1989). While the cultural subjectivities of the non-African Americans deny the relevance

of racism, this is precisely the major relevant issue for African Americans' viewing experiences. Just as the news story of housing discrimination against Blacks in Lind's study (1996) does not resonate with Whites' cultural subjectivities (and so they render the story irrelevant), Spike Lee's story of the oppression, discrimination and brutality against African Americans in American society fails to resonate with the non-African-American spectators participating in my study. Recall that only three of the non-Black spectators (107, 109, 124) link the film's plot to the Stewart, Bumpurs and Griffith deaths. The lack of identification with the film for the non-African Americans is exemplified in this comment from one Hispanic woman: "Without a doubt, this film was very pro-Black. I was not pleased. I would have regretted spending money to see this movie and I would never consider renting it" (41).

Even more striking than the similarity of views among non-Blacks toward race relations as depicted in the film is that these attitudes hold for White and Hispanic spectators—women and men—regardless of religious background, or whether they live in the urban New York City area or in the predominately White rural Western college town. This implies that cultural subjectivities in terms of race may be more significant than other factors in framing perceptions of race, ethnicity and racism, and thus supports Lind's (1996) argument that "identification with a cultural sub-group" is perhaps the most important aspect in spectators' interpretations of mediated texts (p. 54). Consider that the responses of the non-Black spectators reflect a discourse of *race*, while the Black spectators' reactions reflect a discourse of *racism*.[8] In other words, for non-African Americans, their *race* and their defense of it are relevant factors of their discourse, but for African Americans, the *racism* they personally experience is the most crucial relevancy in their film experience. For these Black spectators, racism is a primary factor in their identification with the film, perhaps tapping into their cultural subjectivities concerning issues of their overall subordination and marginalization as African Americans in our society, and relating this "radical reality"

(Studlar, 1990, p. 72) of their lives to the film's protagonist and text.

It is important to keep in mind that the Black spectators participating in this study lived primarily in urban areas not far from New York City. These communities have all of the problems associated with urban life in America, but this is perhaps even more pronounced for the Black spectators participating in my study. For African Americans who truly live the daily lives of the marginalized and disadvantaged, the racism portrayed in *Do The Right Thing* is of primary relevancy to their film experience, influencing how they interpret the characters and events Lee presents in his movie.

For their part, the White and Hispanic spectators do not interpret the racism depicted in the movie as representative of Blacks' subordinate position in society, which supports Lind's (1996) results showing that White viewers do not link news reports of housing discrimination against Blacks to overall issues of Black subordination. Perhaps the non-African-American spectators in my study may have interpreted the film from cultural subjectivities that expect Blacks and other racial and ethnic groups not to have the same power and respect in American society as Whites, and, thus, they did not recognize or could not relate to Spike Lee's emphasis on the oppression of African Americans and their continuing marginalized status. This phenomenon—of not recognizing the marginalized status of other races because one's own race is not marginalized—is evidenced in the following statement from one White spectator: "I can't imagine it [racism] being that bad" (29).

Perhaps the interpretations of the non-African-American spectators can also be understood by considering that, as one film critic observes, "Hollywood films are based on the premise that a Black man or woman can't lead you anywhere. Which is to say that Whites' moral/psychological identification can't be with a Black person" (Glicksman, 1989, p. 18). Another critic agrees: "[F]ilmmakers have been reluctant to make films that were honest about those aspects of the Black experience that are 'other than' the White experience" (Wall, 1989, p. 739). The responses from the White spectators support these arguments: *Do the Right Thing* features a Black man leading the audience through Black experiences that are "other than" typical White experiences, and it is only the Black members of the audience whose "moral/psychological identification" is with Mookie or the experiences of the other African-American characters. Referring to van Dijk's critical theory of racism (1993), Lind argues: "To the degree that a particular segment of society (e.g., a given race) is perceived as Other People, that race and the social realities in which that race exists probably will not be relevant" (1996, p. 56). And as Wall laments, Whites tend to see Blacks as the "Other": "What exactly does it feel like to be one of 29 million Black people in this country? White observers don't really know the answer to that question" (1989, p. 739). Apparently, the non-African Americans participating in my study not only do not know that answer, but many do not *want* to know the answer to the question, confirming one critic's observation that non-African-American viewers are, "more comfortable with Raheem being a nuisance than Sal being a bigot, because *we know* Sal" (Jones, 1990, p. 34).

Race in Hollywood films, if confronted at all, is in fact generally from "the perspective of White filmmakers" (Sanoff, 1989, p. 51), with Black characters situated "primarily for the pleasure of White spectators (male or female)" and "punished if they humiliate the White characters" (Diawara, 1988, pp. 70-71). But *Do the Right Thing* turns the tables. Although Buggin' Out is arrested and Radio Raheem is killed after challenging Sal, Lee uses this scene not to "punish" Blacks, but to illustrate the consequences of racism for the African-American community (Lee, 1989c). Similarly, Mookie is not "punished" for throwing the garbage can through Sal's pizzeria window, hence Lee's film violates the "narrative patterns of Blacks playing by hegemonic rules" (Diawara, p. 72). This violation may negate the possibility of direct identification with the film and its characters for non-African Americans, as it presents these spectators with a social reality that may be unsettling: "[T]he film depicts White bigotry with all due contempt.... The melanin-impaired will therefore feel uncomfortable with this film, and with good reason" (Klawans, 1989, p. 99). Richard Edson, the actor who portrays Vito, agrees with this critic, recalling how, even for the actors starring in *Do the Right Thing*, it was difficult to discuss the film's theme: "It's an indication of how divided the races are that you can't even talk about racism.... There's too much distrust, too historical a thing.... To even bring it up is a threat, to both Blacks and Whites" (cited in Handelman, 1989, p. 109). Indeed, many of the responses from the non-African-American spectators cited earlier indicate their frustrations with seeing Lee's depiction of White racism and its consequences: "Many people do not agree with Spike Lee's view.... This film gives a negative view of White people. He makes them out to all be racists" (40); and, "Racism is something we all try to hide" (110).

What insights can we gain from these contradictory responses of the African-American and non-African-American spectators to *Do the Right Thing*? My study claims no generalizability; although the racial composition of the women and men spectators is fairly diverse, they are all undergraduate students who were enrolled in mass communication courses, most 20 to 25 years old. The purpose of my study is not to predict how *all* people will respond to Lee's film, however, but to explicate viewers' film experiences in a particular situation. Nonetheless, these spectators' responses can be related specifically to many commonly held cultural myths in American society, which may be indications of the spectators' cultural subjectivities and the discourses that inform them. One could argue that the conflicting film experiences of the spectators are simply a consequence of the fact that African-American and non-African-American spectators tend to prefer different types of film and television programs (Diawara, 1988; Farhi, 1997). But as Staiger (1992) suggests, we cannot fully comprehend how spectators resist, negotiate or accept media texts without considering the influence of cultural and structural contributions: "[R]eaders are complex historical individuals capable of acting within the contradictions of their own construction as selves and as reading selves.... The interpretative event occurs at the intersection of multiple determinations" (p. 48). Thus, perhaps we can start to understand some larger implications by

considering these viewers' reactions within broader societal and cultural perspectives.

For example, consider that 84 percent of Blacks polled in a national survey blame discrimination for their social and economic problems, compared to only 30 percent of Whites (Zucker, 1995). Similarly, 80 percent of the African Americans in another survey believed Whites have too much power, compared to 2 percent of Whites who believe the same about their own race (Henry, 1994). Perhaps these conflicting perceptions should not be surprising if we acknowledge that, as a result of their different life experiences, Blacks are more likely than Whites to question testimony from law enforcement officers, and, overall, "distrust the criminal justice system far more than do Whites" (Pertman, 1994, p. A7), a claim Spike Lee also makes when he says his film "is very accurate in its portrayal of the attitude that Black and Hispanic New Yorkers have toward the police" (1989b, p. 6).

Many of the statements of the non-African-American spectators in my case study reflect the belief reported in the national poll (Zucker, 1995) that impoverished and marginalized groups of people—not discrimination—are responsible for their own oppressed state. This attitude is reflected in the following statement from a White spectator: "I would hope that those people (Blacks specifically) that believe that just being Black is the source of all their problems—didn't have that particular opinion strengthened" (35). By accepting the ideal that hard work is all it takes to achieve the American dream, Whites can deny responsibility, personally and societally, for the negative life experiences and lack of opportunities of marginalized peoples. Perhaps this attitude is not surprising in an era when then-House Speaker Newt Gingrich blames the "bad habits" of African Americans for most of their problems (White, 1995, p. 36); when a columnist writing for a New York City newspaper places the blame for Blacks' problems on their "[i]ntellectual cowardice, opportunism, and the itch for riches by almost any means necessary" (Crouch, 1989, p. 74); when White New York City police continue to be charged with other brutal beatings of Black men (Lacayo, 1997); and in which images of race are "mangled" in the mass media: "In the year that saw a Black man elected president of South Africa, there is irony in the fact that apartheid still rules the information age in America" (Dates & Pease, 1994, p. 90).

These different cultural subjectivities are a consequence of each person's life experiences and, in turn, result in different understandings and subsequent interpretations of *Do the Right Thing* for many African-American and non-African-American spectators. African Americans who have experienced discrimination and obstacles to succeed in a White world may understand discrimination and racism in such a way that they endorse Lee's representation of racial strife, even if they may disagree with parts of his film, such as the violence, as the African-American woman who writes: "Although I feel that Spike Lee was trying to show exactly what does happen in Bed-Stuy and other urban areas, I was extremely disappointed with the unnecessary violence Lee advocated with his ending scenes" (5). Accordingly, it is logical to assume that the reason African-American spectators respond favorably to Lee's film is that its message of society's continued oppression of Blacks is relevant to their experiences with racism. For instance, I recall the day when one of the African-American spectators from the urban university arrived late for our class and was obviously upset. When I approached him after class, he explained that he had missed his bus and decided to wave down a cab (a luxury he could not afford). And while he was standing in the winter cold and snow, empty cabs repeatedly passed him by, but stopped to pick up White pedestrians. My student's experience is, unfortunately, a common experience for African Americans from all walks of life (Enda, 1997, p. A5).

Non-African Americans who have not had similar experiences, on the other hand, would likely interpret discrimination and racism differently and thus have different understandings of these concepts, resulting in their denouncing Lee. For example, some of the non-African-American spectators define racism differently, understanding it to mean reverse discrimination, often in the form of what they perceive as special pleadings from "militant" Blacks (113) who take advantage of Whites and the govern-

ment (15). Such cultural subjectivities would necessarily pre-empt the likelihood of finding Lee's message of White oppression of Blacks relevant to their lives, thus supporting Fiske's (1992) position that spectators' discourses represent a "socially produced way of talking or thinking about a topic," defined by their social experiences (p. 301). As Pease argues, "[W]hites still have no idea what it means to be not White in this society" (1995, p. 10). In other words, we do not respond directly to words such as racism and discrimination, but to our experiences with the words that subsequently form our cultural subjectivities. For Blacks and non-Blacks, these cultural subjectivities are often contradictory, confirming that, "[I]t is the meanings a person attaches to and generates from the situation that are most relevant" (Nelson, 1987, p. 313).

Despite the fact that Hispanics are also a marginalized group in American society, the Hispanic spectators' cultural subjectivities are aligned with those of the Whites in my study. In fact, some of the most critical comments to Lee's film come from Hispanic spectators. Despite living in the metropolitan New York City area, however, the Hispanic spectators nonetheless lived primarily in racially segregated communities, and were far more likely to have experienced interactions with Whites than with Blacks in their daily lives; as one Hispanic woman explained to me, "I'd never had any Blacks in my class until I started college. I just saw how much crime they committed on the news." Thus, perhaps for the Hispanics participating in my study, their interpretations of Lee's film are one consequence of "[T]he White-Black fault line, deep and ever tremulous" that "still deforms our national life and the lives of our communities as no other matter does" (Teepen, 1997, p. 6A). This is not to imply, however, that this would be the film experiences of all Hispanic spectators with *Do the Right Thing*.

The responses of non-African-American viewers, particularly in terms of their failure to denounce Radio Raheem's murder or to link his murder to societal prejudice toward Blacks, seem to suggest their adoption of subtle forms of racism. For example, the spectators who write that they cannot believe racism is "that bad," reflect a form of modern (Entman, 1990) or enlightened racism (Jhally & Lewis, 1992), in which individuals assume that people of color now have equal opportunity with Whites and discrimination and racism no longer exist. Aversive racism (Dovidio, 1997) offers another explanation for the responses of the White and Hispanic spectators. Aversive racists respond to people of color not with open expressions of hostility or dislike, but rather with expressions of anxiety, discomfort or avoidance of interracial interactions and racial issues, an attitude reflected in the many comments from Whites and Hispanics expressing how difficult it is to view Lee's stark depictions of racism and its consequences. But perhaps passive racism (Lind, 1996) offers the most insight into these spectators' cultural subjectivities and subsequent interpretations of *Do the Right Thing*: in this construct, people assume that the "struggle for equal rights does not matter," and the "continued existence of racist practices" is irrelevant because such practices do not intrude on their lives (p. 72). Indeed, many of the non-African-American spectators' statements indicate their lack of identification with the film, precisely because racism is not a part of their everyday experiences, and consequently, can be ignored. While these forms of racism are subtle, they are nonetheless "more insidious forms" than overt racism (Dovidio, p. A60) because subtle racists "justify their behavior on grounds other than race," and consequently "underestimate the continuing impact of race," dismissing "racism as a motive for their own behavior," and ultimately believing that "Blacks or members of other minority groups see prejudice where it doesn't really exist" (Dovidio, p. A60). Unfortunately, racism in all of its forms may be a "consequence of speaking about and understanding the world in Black and White terms" (McPhail, 1994, preface), resulting in a society in which racial prejudice towards Blacks by non-Blacks is "the subtext, often unspoken or slyly encrypted, in thousands of acts, big and little, every day" (Teepen, 1997, p. 6A).

Conclusion

Do the Right Thing presents spectators with "shockingly outspoken" images of racism in America (Klawans, 1989, p. 99) and recasts cinematic representations of race relations from a White to a Black perspective. For the spectators, such a radical reversal of the cinematic norm is provocative and seen as either threatening or affirming, depending on their own life experiences and resulting cultural subjectivities. Regardless of their demographic or cultural backgrounds, the non-African Americans tend to find Lee's film threatening, but for the African-American spectators, Spike Lee and his controversial film may represent an affirming recognition of the marginalized status inherent in their everyday lives that is too seldom reflected in the film industry, and that, in turn, non-African Americans may find unsettling. Perhaps Lee is right when he suggests that Blacks in America grow up with a different "mind set" from Whites (cited in Svetkey, 1997, p. 21) that allows them to identify with his depiction of racism in *Do the Right Thing* precisely because their film experiences are linked by their personal encounters with racism: "I think all of Black America threw that can," Lee says. "Black America is tired of having their brothers and sisters murdered by police for no other reason than being Black" (cited in Kunen, p. 67).

Acknowledgements

Originally published in *The Howard Journal of Communications, 9* (1998), 205-228. Reprinted by permission of the author and *The Howard Journal of Communications.*

Endnotes

1. I collected the self-report essays from the New York City area students between 1992 and 1994, and from the students in the West between 1994 and 1996.

2. The breakdown of race and gender of the student spectators is: 10 African Americans (5 women and 5 men), 7 Hispanic (5 women and 2 men), and 48 White (31 women and 17 men). Thirty of the students attend the university located in the rural Western college town, and 18 of these women and 8 of the men are members of the conservative religion. Until 1978, African-American men

were banned from holding priesthood positions within this church.

3. An additional benefit to using self-report essays is the increased participation and openness of the students. For instance, before I began collecting data for this study, I would ask my students to express their reactions to controversial films such as *Do The Right Thing* during our class discussions. Although some students were eager to voice their opinions, more were hesitant to have their peers hear and possibly criticize their reactions; for example, many students attending the New York City area university expressed their concern about being perceived as racist by the Black students during our classes discussions, while the student members of the conservative religion are taught to avoid any conversations that might be perceived by others as confrontational. When I gave my students the opportunity to express their experiences of the film confidentially, their levels of disclosure and expression increased significantly.

4. Judith Mayne (1993) discusses the potential problems of researchers projecting their own ideals onto their interpretations of spectators' responses to media texts. For example, she argues that Janice Radway's (1984) analysis of women readers devoted to romance books reflects her personal projection of "American, middle-class, academic feminism" in her analysis of responses from her "ideal" readers (p. 84). While such a concern is important to acknowledge, Mayne is not suggesting that analyses of spectator responses are not valid, but that researchers need to recognize this potential bias. Although it is never possible to separate ourselves and our personal value systems fully from our research, I make every effort to bracket my own presuppositions to try to alleviate these types of potential projections. Further, I do not discuss the film with my students until after they have completed their essays; we view the film at the beginning of the term, before any discussions or readings related to media representations of race are presented. Finally, I assure my students that there are no right or wrong answers for this assignment, as I simply want to hear their reactions to the movie.

5. The results I report are not meant to imply that all non-African Americans or all African Americans will respond to *Do the Right Thing* similarly to the spectators participating in my case study.

6. In order to identify the statements abstracted from the essays of the spectators, as well as to distinguish between the responses of women and men and their respective races, essays are labeled with numbers as follows:

1-5   African-American women (New York City area university)

6-16   White women (New York City area university)

17-36   White women (rural Western university; 19-36 are members of the conservative religion)

37-41   Hispanic women (37 attends the Western university)

101-105 African-American men (New York City area university)

106-112 White men (New York City area university)

113-122 White men (Western university; 115-122 are members of the conservative religion)

123-124 Hispanic men (123 attends the Western university)

7. Ten spectators are Italian-American (11-15, 109-113).

8. Lind (1996) found similar results: White viewers interpreted the news account of housing discrimination against Blacks from a discourse of race, in contrast to the discourse of racism exhibited in the interpretations of the Black viewers.

Name: _____

Date: _____

1. Explain the concept of relevancy discussed in this chapter. How does this concept help you understand your personal interpretations of film and television narratives? Can you think of a time when your reactions to a film conflicted with those of your friends? How can you use the concept of relevancy to explain different interpretations of the same film?

2. What is Christine Gledhill referring to when she argues that media narratives can have a "double-sidedness" quality? What is the relationship between the "double-sidedness" of media narratives and the role of relevancy in individual interpretations of media narratives?

3. Spike Lee has suggested that the only way to make a movie that accurately depicts African Americans and their experiences is to have a Black filmmaker in charge. Do you agree or disagree with Lee's assessment? Why?

4. The vast majority of Hollywood film directors and screenwriters are White men. How do you think the roles of Whites and Blacks in *Do The Right Thing* might have been different if it had been written and directed by White filmmakers?

5. Suppose *Do The Right Thing* actually *had been* produced and directed by White men, but the film is exactly the same as Spike Lee's version. Do you think the charges that the film was racist would have been as strident? Do you think racism toward Blacks played a role in the negative reactions to Lee's movie?

6. Media scholars have suggested that the most popular and well-received African-American actors are those who seem the most non-threatening to White audiences (e.g., Bill Cosby). Consider this statement in light of both the critics' and students' responses to *Do The Right Thing* cited in this chapter. Do you think White audiences generally felt the Black characters were threatening or non-threatening in Lee's movie? Do the reactions of the non-African-American students described by Cooper support or contradict this idea?

Name: _____

Date: _____

1. After critically viewing Spike Lee's film—*Do The Right Thing*—write a short reaction paper (2-3 pp.) describing your interpretation of the movie. After you've finished writing, re-read your paper, considering the role of relevancy in your personal reactions to the film. Then, write a few additional paragraphs in which you discuss your insights.

2. Conduct informal interviews with a few students who are of a race different from your own. Ask them how they feel about the way their race is depicted in entertainment media. Your goal is to increase your understanding about how interpretations by other races may differ from your own. After completing your interview, write a short reaction paper (2-3 pp.) describing the responses you collected. What insights did you gain from the interviews? Can you use the concept of relevancy to help understand the students' responses? In other words, how are individual interpretations of media related to our own experiences?

3. Team project: For this exercise, you and your team members will compare (A) media images of people of color produced by mainstream, predominately White, male, heterosexual Hollywood, to (B) how filmmakers who are people of color depict their own races. The goal is to determine how media representations of people of color in America change when people of color are in charge of their own media images. For example, if you want to examine how interracial relationships are depicted in dramatic films, you could compare the 1960s film, *Guess Who's Coming to Dinner* to Spike Lee's 1990 movie, *Jungle Fever*. Another option would be to compare Spike Lee's *Malcolm X* to other films related to the Civil Rights era, but limited to those produced by non-African-American filmmakers. How is race depicted differently in the two movies? Prepare a class presentation based on your findings.

REFERENCES

American cinema: Right or wrong? (1989, July 15). *The Economist, 310-313*, 88-89.

Ansen, D. (1989, July 3). Searing, nervy, and very honest. [Review of the film *Do the right thing*]. *Newsweek, 114*, 65-66.

Bobo, J. (1988). *The color purple*: Black women as cultural readers. In E. D. Pribram (Ed.), *Female spectators: Looking at film and television* (pp. 90-109). New York: Verso.

Chrisman, R. (1990). What is the right thing: Notes on the deconstruction of Black ideology. *The Black Scholar, 21*(2), 51, 54-57.

Cohen, J. R. (1991a). The "relevance" of cultural identity in audiences' interpretations of mass media. *Critical Studies in Mass Communication, 8*, 442-454.

Cohen, J. R. (1991b). Intersecting and competing discourses in Harvey Fierstein's *Tidy Endings*. *Quarterly Journal of Speech, 77*, 196-207.

Corliss, R. (1989, July 3). Hot time in Bed-Stuy tonight. [Review of the film *Do the right thing*]. *Time, 134*, 62.

Crouch, S. (1989, June 20). Do the race thing. *The Village Voice*, pp. 73-74, 76.

Crow, B. K. (1981). Talking about films: A phenomenological study of film signification. In, S. Deetz (Ed.), *Phenomenology in rhetoric and communication* (pp. 5-16). Washington, D. C.: Center for Advanced Research in Phenomenology and University Press of America.

Dates, J., & Pease, E. C. (1994). Warping the world—Media's mangled images of race. *Media Studies Journal, 8*(3), 89-96.

Denby, D. (1989, June 26). He's gotta have it. [Review of the film *Do the right thing*]. *New York, 22*, 53-54.

Diawara, M. (1988). Black spectatorship: Problems of identification and resistance. *Screen, 29*, 66-76.

Diawara, M. (1990). Black British cinema: Spectatorship and identify formation in *territories*. *Public Culture, 3*(1), 33-47.

Dovidio, J. (1997, July 25). 'Aversive' racism and the need for affirmative action. *The Chronicle of Higher Education*, p. A60.

Ellsworth, E. (1986). Illicit pleasures: Feminist spectators and *personal best*. *Wide Angle, 8*(2), 45-56.

Enda, J. (1997, July 12). Clinton's difficult mission is to annihilate stereotypes. *The Salt Lake Tribune*, p. A5.

Entman, R. M. (1990). Modern racism and the images of Blacks in local television news. *Critical Studies in Mass Communication, 7*, 332-345.

Farhi, P. (1997). A television trend: Audiences in black and white. In S. Biagi & M. Kern-Foxworth (Eds.), *Facing difference: Race, gender, and mass media* (pp. 202-205). Thousand Oaks, CA: Pine Forge Press.

Fiske, J. (1988). *Critical response*: Meaningful moments. *Critical Studies in Mass Communication, 5*, 246-251.

Fiske, J. (1992). British cultural studies and television. In R. C. Allen (Ed.), *Channels of discourse, reassembled* (2nd. ed.) (pp. 284-326). Chapel Hill, NC: University of North Carolina Press.

Gledhill, C. (1988). Pleasurable negotiations. In E. D. Pribram (Ed.), *Female spectators: Looking at film and television* (pp. 64-89). New York: Verso

Glicksman, M. (1989, July-August). Spike Lee's Bed-Stuy BBQ. *Film Comment, 25*, 12-16, 18.

Griggers, C. (1993). *Thelma and louise* and the cultural generation of the new butch-femme. In J. Collins, H. Radner, & A. P. Collins (Eds.), *Film theory goes to the movies* (pp. 129-141). New York: Routledge.

Hall, S. (1980). Encoding/decoding. In S. Hall, D. Hobson, A. Loew, & P. Willis (Eds.), *Culture, media, language: Working papers in cultural studies, 1972-1979* (pp. 128-138). London: Hutchinson.

Handelman, D. (1989, July 13-27). Insight to riot. *Rolling Stone, 557,* 104, 107-109, 174.

Henry, W. A. III (with Blackman, A., Johnson, J., Epperson, S. E., & Monroe, S.). (1994, February 28). Pride and prejudice. *Time, 143,* 21-27.

Klawans, S. (1989, July 17). Films: *Do the right thing* [Review of the film *Do the right thing*]. *The Nation, 249,* 98-100.

Klein, J. (1989, June 26). The city politic/Spiked? *New York, 22,* 14-15.

Kroll, J. (1989, July 3). How hot is too hot? [Review of the film *Do the right thing*]. *Newsweek, 114,* 64-65.

Kunen, J. S. (1989, July 10). Spike Lee inflames the critics with a film he swears is *The right thing* [Review of the film *Do the right thing*]. *People Weekly, 32,* 67-68.

Jhally, S., & Lewis, J. (1992*). Enlightened racism: The Cosby Show, audiences, and the myth of the American dream.* Boulder CO: Westview Press.

Jones, J. (1990). In Sal's country. *Cineaste, 17*(4), 34-35.

Lacayo, R. (with Benson, J., Graff, J. L. , Hornblower, M., Rivera, E., & Witkowski, T). (1997, September 1). Good cop, Bad cop. *Time, 150,* 26-30.

Lee, S. (Producer & Director). (1989a). *Do the right thing* [Film]. (Videotape available from Universal City Studios, Universal City, CA).

Lee, S. (1989b, July 17). Spike Lee replies: "Say it ain't so, Joe.' [Letter to the editor]. *New York, 22,* 6.

Lee, S. (1989c). *Do the right thing: A Spike Lee joint.* New York: Simon & Schuster.

Lind, R. A. (1996). Diverse interpretations: The "relevance" of race in the construction of meaning in, and the evaluation of, a television news story. *The Howard Journal of Communications, 7,* 53-74.

Lull, J. (1987). Critical response: Audience texts and contexts. *Critical Studies in Mass Communication, 4,* 318-322.

Mayne, J. (1993). *Cinema and spectatorship.* New York: Routledge.

McPhail, M. L. (1994). *The rhetoric of racism.* Lanham, MD: University Press of America.

Morley, D. (1980). *The "Nationwide" audience: Structure and decoding.* London: British Film Institute.

Morley, D. (1985). Cultural transformations: The politics of resistance. In M. Gurevitch & M. R. Levy (Eds.), *Mass communication review yearbook: Vol. 5,* (pp. 237-250). Beverly Hills, CA: Sage.

Morley, D. (1986). *Family television: Cultural power and domestic leisure.* London: Comedia.

Nelson, J. L. (1986, November). The linguistic turn in television research. Paper presented to the annual convention of the Speech Communication Association, Chicago, IL.

Nelson, J. L. (1987). *Critical response:* On media and existence. *Critical Studies in Mass Communication, 4,* 311-318.

Pease, E. C. (1995, October 15). O. J. trial puts perception to the test. *The Logan Herald Journal,* p. 10.

Pertman, A. (1994, October 16). The race angle in the Simpson case; issue can sway juries, consultants and studies say. *The Boston Globe,* p. 2.

Peterson, E. E. (1987). Media consumption and girls who want to have fun. *Critical Studies in Mass Communication, 4,* 37-50.

Radway, J. (1984). *Reading the romance: Women, patriarchy, and popular literature.* Chapel Hill, NC: University of North Carolina Press.

Sanoff, P. (1989, Feb. 6). Do the controversial thing. [Review of the film *Do the right thing*]. *U.S. News and World Reports, 106,* 51.

Stadler, H. A. (1990). Film as experience: Phenomenological concepts in cinema and television studies. *Quarterly Review of Film & Video, 12*(3), 37-50.

Staiger, J. (1992). *Interpreting films: Studies in the historical reception of American cinema.* Princeton, NJ: Princeton University Press.

Studlar, G. (1990). Reconciling feminism and phenomenology: Notes on problems and possibilities, texts and contexts. *Quarterly Review of Film & Video, 12*(3), 69-78.

Svetkey, B. (1997, March 7). The race question. *Entertainment Weekly, 369,* 20-21.

Teepen, T. (1997, August 19). Black-White issue still central in dialogue. *The Dayton Daily News,* p. 6A.

Thomas, S. (1981). Learning what people learn from the media: Some problems with interviewing techniques. *Mass Comm Review, 8*(2), 2-10.

Travers, P. (1989, June 29). The right stuff. *Rolling Stone, 555,* 27, 29.

van Dijk, T. A. (1993). *Elite discourse and racism.* Newbury Park, CA: Sage.

Walker, A. (1996). *The same river twice: Honoring the difficult.* New York: Scribner.

Wall, J. (1989, August 16-23). *Do the right thing*: A jarring look at racism. *The Christian Century, 106,* 739-740.

White, J. E., (1995, June 26). Uncle Tom justice. *Time, 144,* 36.

Zucker, J. (Executive Producer). (1995, October 11). *Today.* New York: NBC.

CHAPTER 11

Reading in Black and White: Girls, Race and the Mediated Feminine Ideal

Lisa Duke and Michelle Sisson

This research is part of a longitudinal study that addresses the seldom explored phenomenon of racial differences in interpretations of mediated ideals, in this case, femininity and beauty. In an initial inquiry by Duke and Kreshel (1998), ten White, middle-class, female participants, ages 12 and 13, were interviewed for their interpretations of *'Teen, Seventeen, YM,* and *Sassy* (which is no longer being published). These girls' readings centered on images of beauty: specifically, the "perfect" feminine body. Girls seemed ill-equipped to critically analyze magazines' images of the feminine physique, even when they recognized that these images did not accurately reflect the girls they knew. One of the most pressing questions left unanswered by that study is the impetus for this one: How might race influence girls' readings of teen magazines and the magazines' portrayals of the feminine ideal? The most popular teen magazines are arguably culturally specific in their execution of major themes, yet enjoy a substantial African-American audience.

Our approach to this research is informed by reader response theory, which offers cognitive and affective insight on how girls might interpret fashion/beauty texts and advertising. According to Beach (1993), Rosenblatt (1938, 1978), and others like Fish (1980) and Bloome (1988),

the reader brings her/his past and social context to the "ordered symbols of text...[and] crystallizes out from the stuff of memory, thought, and feeling a new order, a new experience" (Rosenblatt, 1978, p. 12). Fish introduced to the literature the concept of the "interpretive community"—a group of readers who, through some common life circumstance such as race, share assumptions about the nature and purpose of the text and develop strategies for constructing meaning in interaction with the work.

To address the question of how race mitigates girls' interpretations of the feminine ideal, Black and White girls who read teen magazines were interviewed to determine how they used or ignored material in those texts in constructing notions of beauty. In particular, this paper addresses how material on feminine self-presentation (makeup and fashion) and body image is interpreted by girls of different races. (Participants in this study are described as African American or Black, interchangeably, or White, as these were the terms and uses preferred by participants.) The literature on African-American attitudes toward beauty, body image and self-presentation suggested that Black girls would negotiate teen magazines very differently from White girls; for example, because of stronger cultural support for heavier women, Black girls might suffer far less negative impact on body image. Because African Americans rely on a sense of community and other ties to their culture as a whole in order to negotiate life as a racial minority (Arnez, 1980; Cornelius, 1991; Graham, 1994; Hull, Bell-Scott & Smith, 1982), this research explores how Black adolescents mesh interaction with mass-mediated texts with culturally transmitted ways of knowing and feeling (see Scholes, 1989; Benton, 1983).

Fresh Eyes: Theoretical Perspectives on the Power of the Audience.

How is it that readers become involved with the texts that they read? How does this individual connection become collective communication with other readers? Ruddell and Unrau (1984) have conceptualized reading as a "meaning-construction process" that enables the audience to create other worlds. It is the nature of making meaning through engagement with a text that is the central concern of reader-oriented theorists and practitioners who have revolutionized ideas about reading and how the interaction between reader and text is meaningful.

Prior to the advent of reader response theory and practice, meaning was assumed to reside in the text itself, to be extracted by the reader. The works of Louise Rosenblatt (1938, 1978) provided much of the framework shifting meaning-making emphasis from the text to the reader. Building on the ideas that Rosenblatt pioneered, Beach (1993) has offered a typology of approaches for discussing the triad of reader, text and reading experience. Beach categorizes the interactions as textual, social, cultural and psychological. Textual theorists focus on the reader's use of literary conventions in making meaning out of a text; experientialists like Coles (1989) and Booth (1988) emphasize an interaction that is closer to Rosenblatt's concept of experience being "lived through" a text.

Cultural theorists accentuate the reader's attitude as a determinant in the reading process and how the interaction is driven by ways of knowing that are culturally transmitted to the reader (Scholes, 1989; Benton, 1983). Similarly,

Fish (1980) and Bloome (1985) privilege the social context as most influential in meaning-making. As this research will show, it is the transmission of cultural "ways of knowing" that is the source of what Fiske has described as: "The intransigence of the people in the face of this system, their innumerable tactical evasions and resistances, their stubborn clinging to their sense of difference, their refusal of the position of the compliant subject in bourgeois ideology that is so insistently thrust upon them" (cited in Bobo, 1995, p. 5).

Individual Readers, Polysemic Texts, Shared Interpretations

Hall has described texts as "polysemic," or subject to multiple interpretations. Thus, the audience may choose to "decode" words and images in ways that have the most relevance for them (Hall 1979). However, Condit (1989) has noted that even though a text may be polysemic, that does not neutralize its ideological potential; readers are limited by their culture and experience to a fairly circumscribed range of interpretations for familiar symbols and images. Condit's position is that it is more accurate to call such texts polyvalent, in that the audience may differently value even the most consistently interpreted messages. However, others have noted that polyvalence is no more variable than polysemy. Walkerdine (1990) suggests that offering a wider array of images with which girls might identify is problematic, because such a solution does not take into consideration culturally proscribed valence, "how we come to want what we want":

It assumes that when the little girl sees the veil of distortion lifted from her eyes, she too will want to engage in those activities from which she has been precluded by virtue of her gender.... Content...is not just grafted onto a...waiting subject, who can be so easily changed. Rather, the positions and relations created in the text both relate to existing social and psychic struggles and provide a fantasy vehicle which inserts the reader into the text (p. 89).

Recent inquiries into girls' media interpretations have illustrated how girls' socialization occurs amidst powerful and sometimes contradictory influences, such as peers, family, culture and media (Durham, 1999). Meaning is not given but negotiated, in a process that alternately privileges and repudiates each of these influences. In media studies, the notion of an active audience (active interpreters rather than passive accepters of messages) found its first expression in the uses-and-gratifications approach to studying audiences (Blumer & Katz, 1974).

The uses-and-gratification approach to media research is frequently suggested as the most appropriate for study of adolescents and the media (Arnett, Larson & Offer, 1995) and is compatible with reader response theory in that both perspectives posit an active audience that interprets and uses media texts purposefully, creating meaning that is culturally and personally relevant. Arnett et al. (1995) have suggested that active models of development, in which "...children and adolescents actively select the environments that influence their development," mesh well with uses-and-gratifications perspective because both position adolescents as "self-socializing" (pp. 513-514). That is, adolescents actively choose those media influences to which they expose themselves and to which they potentially respond.

The uses-and-gratifications approach assumes that "individuals are able to articulate their own needs or motives for media use and communication behavior" (Rubin, 1986, p. 286). For example, African-American girls choose to read mainstream teen magazines, which have traditionally disregarded Blacks, because these texts gratify needs that may not be readily apparent to others. Therefore, this research explores the ways girls explain and use mediated material that includes or excludes girls based on their similarity to the texts' images and the congruity of the text with girls' cultural reality.

In addition to Hall's positions, reader response and the uses-and-gratifications approach also allow for Clarke's (1990) concept of "passive dissent" (pp. 28-44), a variation of the negotiated position, in describing female reception of gendered messages. In Clarke's view, while some percentage of an audience segment may express textual interpretations at odds with those of the dominant society, this is not necessarily indicative of political resistance. Clarke further argues that opposition to the dominant stance need not be overt, and that unspoken opposition is not the same as acceptance. Thus, in order to more fully understand the positions of girls in relation to fashion/beauty texts like teen magazines, it is important to ascertain which parts of the magazines they regularly attend to, which they routinely ignore and the meaning they make of their choices.

Arnett, Larson, and Offer (1995) have explicated five ways adolescents use the media: for entertainment, identity formation, high sensation, coping and youth culture identification. Although these scholars are clear in outlining how the model is appropriate to the study of Western children at different developmental stages of self-identity, they do not suggest how race—as it mitigates socialization—is addressed by their model.

For example, Comstock and Paik (1978) have posited that media help teens formulate scripts for guiding their behavior in unfamiliar situations. This scripting function of teen magazines was evident in Duke and Kreshel (1998), where early adolescent girls used teen magazines to provide them with insights on how to interact with boys in romantic situations they might encounter in the future. However, this work focused almost exclusively on the responses of White adolescent girls.

The degree to which teens are affected by media is largely determined by the relevance of the message (Cohen, 1991) and whether the behavior or belief advocated is useful and socially appropriate (i.e., in line with local norms and approved or discouraged by society at large). Thus, instead of positing an all-powerful text that prohibits interpretive leeway, it is important to consider factors—such as race—that moderate the audience's negotiation of meaning.

Does the kind of feminine beauty celebrated in teen magazines resonate with all girls, or is it a concept with specific appeal for girls of the dominant culture? When Walkerdine (1990) asks how "we come to want what we want," it is important to first examine who "we" are.

Who is Reading?

Of the 14 million girls between the ages of 12 and 19 in the United States, it is estimated that over half read *Seventeen*, the best-selling teen magazine. Although the majority of readers of the three largest teen magazines, *Seventeen*, *'Teen*, and *YM*, are White, the magazines have a significant audience among girls of color: *Seventeen* reaches 44 percent of "ethnic females twelve to nineteen" (defined as African American, "other" race, or from a Spanish-speaking household); *'Teen* and *YM* each reach 34 percent of these same girls. African-American girls ages 12 to 19 make up the single largest non-White group of readers—they comprise, on average, about 12 percent of the readership for each of the three major teen titles [all from Mediamark Research Incorporated (MRI)/Teenmark, 1997]. The 1997 MRI TwelvePlus notes that although only 12 percent of people over the age of 12 identify themselves as Black, 16 percent of *Seventeen*'s readers do—meaning that the magazine draws a greater percentage of African-American readers than are represented in the population. The median age of readers of teen magazines is 15 to 16; the median household income is between $39 thousand and $43 thousand annually (MRI/Teenmark, 1997).

The content of *Seventeen*, *'Teen* and *YM* is formulaic and relatively consistent from one magazine to the next. *'Teen* is targeted to a younger group, and *YM* is seen as depicting more diversity in its models, but girls in this study generally find the content of the magazines to be very similar. This is consistent with Evans (Evans, Rutberg, Sather and Turner, 1991), who found that the topic of fashion dominated the three most popular teen magazines, followed by beauty and entertainment. These themes have remained important across time: 60 percent of the magazines' copy was devoted to "beauty, fashion, cooking, and decorating" in each of the years 1961, 1972 and 1985 (Pierce, 1990, p. 491). The most prevalent identity-related theme of articles, interpersonal relationships (male/female dating and peer relations), was also consistent within and between magazines.

Models depicted in *Seventeen*, *Sassy* and *YM* have been found to be fairly homogeneous. One study found that 65 percent were White females, and depictions of White males outnumbered non-White females by more than three to one (Evans et al., 1991).

Other Magazine Studies

Although teen magazines represent only one type of socializing influence in the lives of girls, these publications communicate in concert, offering adolescent and young-adult females a monthly reiteration of the same interrelated values, images and ideals. Because girls experience significant physical and developmental change in adolescence, media like teen magazines serve as guidebooks on acceptable appearance, gender roles and relationship formation in adolescence, replacing parents and augmenting or surpassing peers as primary information sources (Roberts, 1993).

Media have been implicated in establishing atypical standards of appearance as the social norm (Myers & Biocca, 1992; Silverstein, Perdue, Peterson & Kelly, 1986) and encouraging girls' preoccupation with their looks (Richins, 1991; Martin & Kennedy, 1993). Researchers attempting to make the link between media exposure and negative effects on women and girls, that is, trying to identify the effects of models on adolescents' assessments of their physical attractiveness, frequently use the theories of *social learning* or *social comparison* to ground their work. Social learning theorizes that behaviors are modeled by significant others and then imitated if deemed appropriate. Social comparison theory focuses on the human drive to evaluate opinions and abilities by considering similar others. Although some researchers have found evidence that such processes occur with negative consequences to female self-perceptions or self-esteem (Cash, Cash & Butters, 1983; Stice & Shaw, 1994), others have reported mixed results (Martin & Kennedy, 1993; Richins, 1991; Thornton & Moore, 1993).

While social learning and comparison explain the possible mechanisms by which fashion/beauty media such as teen magazines may affect some women and girls, to date, most studies have focused on largely White groups of women (see, for example, Valentine, 1994; Martin & Gentry, 1997a; Martin & Gentry, 1997b). Because teen magazines primarily picture White models (Evans et al., 1991), it has been unclear how relevant and influential these images might be to girls of color.

In an effort to address the cultural and class differences they locate as key to individuals' varied responses to media messages, British cultural-studies scholars have used a framework devised by Hall (1979) for explaining audience reception of messages. Audience members read or "decode" a text from one of three positions: *dominant hegemonic, negotiated* or *oppositional*.

In the dominant hegemonic view, audience interpretation is predetermined by the text's producer. This characterization of the text as ideologically charged and powerful was at the foundation of the work of one of the most active British cultural-studies researchers, Angela McRobbie. In a textual analysis of what was then the best-selling British teen magazine for girls, *Jackie!*, McRobbie (1978) focused on exposing the "monolithic" mass-mediated hegemony she said conditioned girls' willing embrace of ideals that relegated them to social and economic subordination. She argued that "codes of femininity" were incorporated into the text to "shape the consent of the readers to a set of particular values"; among these were codes of romance, personal and domestic life, and fashion and beauty. These codes were the essential elements of scripts the magazine provided for girls to use in their everyday lives. All girls were presumed to have identical interests and equal needs and desires for such scripts. The false norms created by such limited scripts were presumed to have a devastating effect on girls, encouraging competition for boys and isolation from other girls.

In a content analysis of American teen magazines, Evans, Rutberg, Sather, and Turner (1991) reached a similar conclusion: "Articles and advertisements mutually reinforced an underlying value that the road to happiness is attracting males for a successful heterosexual life by way of physical beautification" (p. 110). In contrast, Frazer (1987) has disputed the dominant hegemonic view that posits transformation of *ideology* to *meanings/'culture'/representation* to *beliefs/attitudes/opinions* to *behavior*. Based on her analysis of girls' group discussions of teen magazines,

Frazer rejected the passive reader implied by studies such as McRobbie's and instead argued that girls interacted with the text and with each other to create meanings. These meanings shifted and were modified according to the contexts in which the meanings were elicited.

In a more recent study of girls' interpretations of teen magazines, Currie (1996) proposed to bridge work that posits a helpless audience held in the thrall of an all-powerful, ideologically charged medium and work premised on an audience equally formidable in its determined use of media for its own pleasures. She has claimed that teen magazines are neither script nor ideological monolith, but they are imbued with ideology nonetheless. A self-perpetuating ideology of femininity seamlessly meshes with the reader's own commonsense understandings, for example, "the ideological appeals of romantic love and motherhood were so strong that they overrode the criterion of logic" (p. 470). The logic borne of personal experience did not prevail when girls were asked to evaluate "images of adult femininity," leaving the magazine to project, unchecked, the accepted social mythology. The pleasures girls derived from the magazines were "ideologically charged representations of 'what it means to be a woman.'" (p. 474).

Similarly, Finders (1996) has argued that the scripts found in teen magazines will continue to affect girls until the texts' embedded messages are made visible and are no longer taken for granted. Finders portrayed participants as "vulnerable readers" who used "borrowed authority" from the magazines to denigrate non-readers. She urged teachers to counter the authority of the text by "inviting students to ponder over the implications of advertising ...toward more fully understanding how economics enable and constrain texts" (p. 87).

As her research focus moved from text to audience, McRobbie (1994) herself called into question the dominant hegemonic perspective that grounded her initial analyses of teen magazines. She found, as Johnson (1986) has argued, that it should not be assumed that the "text-as-produced" is identical to the "text-as-read." McRobbie (1994) has subsequently claimed that femininity, as modern girls are redefining it, has revolutionary potential, an assertion that is consistent with Hall's negotiated and oppositional positions.

In the negotiated position, the text producer's intended meaning is understood by the audience, but is not necessarily accepted. In an oppositional reading, the audience commandeers a text's intended meaning and turns it inside out, intentionally redefining meaning against the grain. Cultural studies scholars see oppositional or "resistant" readings as a way in which subcultures, or groups of people marginalized in society, assert themselves against social disempowerment.

Durham (1999a) has noted: "There is a paucity of studies wherein girls' spoken voices are heard…but what there is provides little evidence that any girls are able to engage in what Hall classified as oppositional readings of media messages" (p. 220). In her study of girls' interpretations of mediated standards of femininity and sexuality, Durham (1999b) found that resistance "was not obviously manifested" in the groups she observed, primarily Latinas and Anglo/European girls. This study expands our understanding of how girls interpret media images by adding the long-absent voices of African-American girls to the literature.

Gender and Adolescence as Mitigated by Race and Class

Researchers have documented that adolescent girls experience more stress and self-image disturbance than do boys (Brown & Gilligan, 1992; Harter, 1986). In an American Association of University Women study (1992), only 29 percent of high school girls (race unspecified) said they were happy with themselves, compared to nearly half of boys. Girls, who are more likely to judge themselves based on their physical attractiveness (Franzoi, 1995), suffer declining self-esteem and estimations of their attractiveness in adolescence (Harter, 1986). Adolescence is the time when girls learn that the right look and being "nice" are vital to acceptance by others (Brown & Gilligan, 1992).

Teen magazines are thought to contribute to the socialization of girls into traditional, appearance-based standards of femininity, and to ac-

centuate girls' plunge in self-confidence by inviting self-comparison to textual images of feminine "perfection." The implication has been that this pressure is keenly felt by all girls; however, the literature described in the next section suggests that African-American girls may be less susceptible to teen magazines' versions of femininity than are their White counterparts.

Adolescence, like gender, is a social construct, and the experience of this period of life is highly variable according to girls' different cultural backgrounds and stage of identity development (Schlegal & Barry, 1991). To understand how and why girls read, it is important to understand the socially situated positions from which they read. Because of researchers' focus on White youth, the unique adolescent experience of African-American girls has seldom been addressed (Smith, 1982). In fact, race has profound implications for studies of what it means to be an American female; it is one of the most important indicators of girls' self-image.

Prendergast, Zdep, and Sepulveda (1974) found that Black girls rated themselves consistently higher than White girls did on several dimensions of self-esteem (e.g., being good looking, being athletically adept). These results have been supported by later studies, which have found that African-American girls rate their overall attractiveness much higher than White girls (e.g., Parker, Nichter, Nichter & Vuckovic, 1995). In extensive interviews with African-American girls, Leeds (1994) suggested that girls' and women's magazines might be less important to them in defining and reinforcing beauty standards than were "…the appearance of favorite video stars, what they had heard their older brothers say, the opinions of peers and lectures from their mothers" (p. 149).

Black women may hold ideas about the ideal body type quite different from those of their White counterparts, regardless of their economic backgrounds. For example, Parker, Nichter, Nichter, and Vuckovic (1995) found that Black girls and women are more satisfied with their bodies, and suffer from far fewer eating disorders, than White girls, despite the fact that Black girls begin to outweigh White girls in adolescence (Rucker & Cash, 1992). Black girls have indicated their belief in a heavier body shape as ideal (Flynn & Fitzgibbon, 1996; Rucker & Cash, 1992), and heavier women are viewed as powerful and healthy by African Americans (Flynn & Fitzgibbon, 1996; Millman, 1980). Additionally, Black girls indicated that their beauty is based in "attitude and style," whereas White girls in the same study believed their attractiveness was judged in large part by how thin they were (Parker et al., 1995). These findings are consistent in investigations of working-class and middle-class Black youth.

Middle-class adolescence, typically described as occurring between the ages of 12 and the early 20s, ends much sooner for a large number of lower-income Black females—at about age 18—because economic factors necessitate greater family responsibility at a younger age (Nightingale & Wolverton, 1993). However, middle-class girls of both races are said to enjoy a similar, extended period of adolescence, relatively free of the family and economic responsibilities borne by girls in earlier times or by contemporaries in less fortunate circumstances.

Research Questions

The questions to be addressed by this research are:

1. Why do these African-American and White girls read teen magazines? How well do teen magazines satisfy these girls' desire/need to read them? What parts of the magazine are most/least gratifying to its readers?

2. How do girls read teen magazines? Are girls in this study critical readers of fashion/beauty texts? How does race influence the way these middle-class girls interpret teen magazines' images and text? Are there similarities among readings based on race or age?

Methods and Procedures

As previously noted, this paper is part of a larger, longitudinal study that traces the magazine interpretations of girls as they age from early to late adolescence. The data are drawn from in-depth interviews with three groups of middle-class girls who are regular readers of teen magazines (six or more times a year); participants were selected via a snowball method, where each participant suggested additional girls to be interviewed. The first group is comprised of ten White girls who were interviewed, first, when they were 12 to 14 years old, and, again, when they were 16 to 18. The second and third groups include 16 African-American girls—eight in early adolescence, ages 12 to 14, and eight who are 17 and 18.

Prior to the interviews, girls were provided with funds to purchase the teen magazine of their choice. All participants were interviewed individually, in their homes, at the homes of their best friends or, in one case, at the mother's place of business. The names of the girls and some distinguishing details have been changed in order to protect participants' anonymity.

In interpretive, qualitative approaches such as the one used in this study, the researcher serves as the instrument of data collection and analysis (Lincoln & Guba, 1985). As a White woman researching, in part, African-American youth, it was important to the design of the study to have built-in checks on the first author's interpretations. First, girls verified my interpretations post-interview, that is, through member checks (Lincoln & Guba, 1985). Two female African-American university students heard about this work and volunteered as research assistants. As an additional check on the validity of the cross-race interviews, one of these assistants conducted a focus group with Black participants to see how differently girls might express themselves with a same-race moderator.

Although these interpretations have been corroborated by the participants, certain aspects of the analysis, such as the precise language of themes and ways of linking certain data, result from the first author's socially situated frames of reference. Therefore, this analysis is but one in what should be a wide array; other researchers working with similar subjects would no doubt enrich the description begun here.

White Participants

The first group of White participants consists of three girls who live in a small coastal city in the Southeast. The first author was introduced to them by one of the mothers, with whom she attended graduate school. These girls have known each other for most of their lives. Throughout their early teens, they attended the same private Christian school.

The second group of White girls lives in the first author's subdivision, a suburban "bedroom community" outside a major Southern city. These girls described themselves as a trio of best friends; two were sisters. They do not claim any particular religious affiliations, and were generally less interested in school and adult approval than any other group interviewed.

The third group of White girls is Jewish and lives in the suburbs of a major Northern metropolitan city. In their early teens, they attended public schools with a predominately middle-class to upper-middle class Jewish student population. Duke was introduced to the group by a young male relative, who described these girls as popular.

BLACK PARTICIPANTS

The first African-American girl recruited lives in Duke's neighborhood; this girl introduced the first author to one of her friends. Two sisters were recruited while buying teen magazines at the corner drugstore; the eldest introduced Duke to two of her friends. Another girl attended a summer journalism camp where Duke was an instructor. Other girls were referred through an African-American colleague; those girls put us in touch with other friends.

The African-American participants live in and around a major Southern metropolitan area. Ten live in the suburbs, six live within the city limits. The girls in the suburbs attend schools that are largely White; the girls in the city proper attend schools with a majority African-American population. All girls were interviewed in their homes, with one exception; that girl's mother requested the interview take place at the mother's place of work, a school library.

In general, the Black mothers were far more interested than White mothers in the nature of this study and the part their daughters would play in its development. It was not unusual for Black mothers to conduct a "mini-interview" with me regarding the goal of the study before their daughters were interviewed.

INTERVIEW FORMAT

After agreeing to participate in this study, girls were provided with money to purchase the teen magazine of their choice, which they were asked to read before their scheduled interviews. Half the White girls bought *Seventeen*; the other half chose *YM*. The younger Black girls chose to purchase *Seventeen* (four girls), *'Teen* (three girls), and *YM* (one girl). Six of the older Black girls chose *Seventeen*; the remaining two bought *YM*.

The teen magazine of a girl's choice was used as a stimulus device during the interview, a technique called auto-driving (McCracken, 1988). Auto-driving requires that participants be provided with photographs, music, text or video as prompts for their interpretations. Through the use of this technique, girls were able to provide more vivid interpretations of the text, and often used the magazine to strengthen descriptions of their reading experiences.

Interviews began with a grand tour question, "Tell me, and show me, how you read this magazine" (Crabtree & Miller, 1992). This method allowed the participant to talk at length, with the magazine serving as a prompt. Although an interview guide was used in initial exchanges with participants, the conversation flowed naturally and the guide was used only to ensure all important issues were covered.

As a check on the cross-race interviews with Black girls, several of these girls participated in a focus group led by an African-American moderator, a 21-year-old female college student. Six of eight girls in the older African-American group agreed to participate, five of those six actually attended. Girls were provided with dinner in return for their participation in the focus group.

Questions from individual interviews were rephrased and asked again for verification. We also used the focus group as an opportunity for feedback on results from a partial, preliminary analysis, and to clarify points girls made during their individual interviews.

ANALYSIS

After transcribing tapes of participant interviews, Lincoln and Guba's (1985) method of categorizing data was used to establish emergent themes and organizing constructs. Transcripts were examined for instances of language, descriptions of content, particular uses of text and units of information to be grouped into categories (e.g., identity formation, self-expression through artifice). Using a variation of Lincoln and Guba's (1985) representation of constant comparison, units were examined individually and sorted into sets that were subsequently labeled with the abstract functions that unified them. Next, function categories were examined to see if they contained substantially more units from girls of one racial group. All data were categorized unless judged to be unrelated to the topic or so atypical as to not be thematically viable. Analysis was complete when categories were saturated with compelling data instances, emergent patterns and regularities were identified, and additional analysis would not contribute significantly to the findings (Lincoln & Guba, 1985).

Findings

IMAGES OF THE FEMININE IDEAL

INTERVIEWER: What do you think the magazine says about girls?

FAITH, 14, BLACK: It says that they try to be perfect and stuff.

INTERVIEWER: What do you think about that?

FAITH: I think that you ain't got to be perfect for nobody. You ain't got to try to prove yourself to nobody.

All the girls in this study, regardless of race, described the mediated ideal in similar terms. To the girl, participants described the magazine ideal as "thin," or "skinny," or even "scrawny." The ideal's dress and makeup were seen as extremely fashionable and elaborate. In the sense that the typical magazine model represents a media-endorsed standard of beauty, girls are well aware that the standard is White—as was made explicit by participants' frequent references to long blonde hair and blue eyes.

Participants in this study believed themselves virtually impervious to ill effects from mediated images of ideal beauty, yet Black and White girls claimed they saw the influence of these images on other White girls their age. While most White girls were satisfied with their overall looks, they were less satisfied with their body shape and weight. In response to specific images in the magazines, they frequently discounted the appearance of the models as atypical or unachievable.

That girls realize attaining the mediated ideal is difficult if not impossible does not mean that the image has no power over them. Whether media scholars believe fashion and beauty magazine images have an effect on girls' self-images, girls themselves do. Black and White girls spoke of the power of the image to "put a picture in your head," and in the heads of boys, about how highly desirable girls should look. Nearly all the girls found some aspect of the models' appearance they admired or wished to emulate. Likewise, nearly all girls said they had friends who negatively compared themselves to the images in the texts.

Whereas White girls had an endless stream of fairly uniform White models to confront, Black girls usually had only one or two well-known Black models to assess:

NICOLE, 17, BLACK: I was looking at an old, OLD *Seventeen*… — it was like a '95 or '96 — Alicia Silverstone was on the cover. And there wasn't a Black NOTHIN' in there. It was even like all blonde-haired, blue-eyed models.

MODERATOR: Has it changed?

(All the voices that follow are girls age 17, Black)

VOICE #1: Tyra Banks was on the cover a month ago.

VOICE #2: I got that one.

VOICE #3: There's more dark hair now—

SHAWN: But then again, when I think about it, Tyra is the only Black model they ever use. And she's like, in between, you know what I'm saying? When they pick a Black model, it's always just Tyra.

Black girls do not particularly admire or seek to emulate models; instead, they pointed to the more infrequent images of African-American performers or athletes, or people with power, as the ones on which they build their fantasies. Kira, 17, said of all the people in her magazine, she would choose to be the editor, "because he probably makes a lot of money. But other than that, no one."

Nicole noted, "White people perceive beautiful in a different way than we do." For African-American girls, beauty was as much a question of character as appearance. When asked to identify their favorite thing about themselves, White girls were apt to name two things: something physical and something in their character. Black girls consistently identified their favorite thing about themselves as something in their character or personality—seldom mentioning a physical characteristic. White girls' descriptions of what makes a girl beautiful focused almost exclusively on looks; African American girls' descriptions usually contained references to personality and attitude:

> INTERVIEWER: What do you think makes a girl beautiful?
>
> KIM, 13, BLACK: Her personality.
>
> INTERVIEWER: Why don't you describe a beautiful girl you know?
>
> KIM: Nice and has her own beliefs and listens to other people but doesn't necessarily always do what they say.

Shawn says a woman's personality is what makes her beautiful. When asked for an example, she names actress Angela Bassett, because "I think she has a beautiful face and everything, and she has to be a lovely person to be around.... She just has this outgoing attitude and it...just catches everybody.... You can just see it from a mile away."

THE THIN, WHITE BODY TRAP

In 1994, the early adolescent White girls whom Duke and Kreshel (1998) studied looked at teen magazine models' bodies as how they should have been but were not—with some degree of anxiety. This was particularly the case when girls assessed the bodies of models, which for the most part reinforced the rigorous, largely

unattainable standards girls set for themselves and others. They looked forward to a day when their more mature bodies might approximate those of the older models, but they envisioned this as a natural course of events or a necessity, more the fulfillment of a social requirement than a deeply held personal desire.

Black girls saw more to dislike than like in most images of the teen magazine ideal, which often exemplified characteristics Black girls—and Black males—did not find attractive. The models' bodies were seen as unhealthily thin:

> ANDI, 17, BLACK: What White guys find attractive is so different from Black guys.... My hips being big, they like that. Big behind. That's great. Big chest. That's great, too.... I'd rather just be what I am, eat what I like to eat and...be acceptable. That's why I don't look at [models], 'cause that's not what I want to look like.... If my grandmother saw me looking skinny like that, she'd freak out.

For African-American girls, no cultural imperative demands a certain body size, although most girls agreed a buxom shape was appealing; therefore, they viewed magazine models and read or ignored the text on exercise and diet with virtually no anxiety. Festinger's (1954) theory of social comparison indicates that people seek out similar others against which to evaluate themselves; Black girls said they seldom saw Black models in their magazines and dismissed most of the ones they did see as either very dark and exotic or very light:

> NICOLE, 17, BLACK: I'm sorry, they don't look like... Black girls to me. They don't even have what I consider to be a Black-girl body at all. ...Their hair's in little ringlets. ...And it's just not realistic.
>
> INTERVIEWER: Is that the kind of woman they feature in the magazine?
>
> NICOLE: Nine times out of ten, it's... that "borderline Black woman," is what I call it. It's like she could probably pass for White if she tried.

Whereas young adolescent White girls were transfixed by the images of the models' bodies, African-American girls assess themselves and the bodies they see represented in the magazines with different eyes. They see "sick looking" bodies where White girls see perfect ones. Black girls see average women where White girls see heavy women. For example, Sylvie estimates her ideal size as size 12 or 14. She thinks the models in the magazines wear a size 10. This is in contrast to the size 4 or 6 White girls were striving for and estimated as the size of magazine models. Black girls were generally dismissive of the models and model figures they saw in teen magazines; they espoused a philosophy of self-acceptance and embraced a full range of body shapes as acceptable:

> SHELLY, 17, BLACK: I don't have the mindset like I got to be perfect. Because how the Black environment is, there isn't one specific way a Black girl has to be, so you fit in everywhere…. In the White environment, they have a more specific way of how you are supposed to look and dress.

Many Black girls mentioned the roles their mothers, grandmothers and boyfriends play in reinforcing a confident body image. It is worth considering how Black girls will negotiate the tension between mediated and cultural ideals, as more African-American and other minority models take center stage in the pages of fashion and beauty magazines.

THE GREAT DIVIDE:
CONTRASTING VIEWS OF COSMETICS

> CARA, 17, WHITE: I love make-up. I'll go and think, okay, I'm just buying mascara…. [Then] I'll find myself saying, "Isn't this lipstick pretty?" I think, okay, it's only $10 more. So I'll go ahead and get that, too.

Duke and Kreshel (1998) found that adolescent White girls had an ambivalent attitude toward cosmetics and the ubiquitous makeup ads and features in teen magazines. Almost all the girls wore makeup, but none of them wanted to appear to be wearing it. At this young age, makeup was viewed by girls as a necessity—in their age of acne, makeup was a tool for returning to normal appearance, rather than an agent of change or improvement. Magazines capital-

ized on this necessity by constantly helping girls identify their flaws, and offering advice on how to fix them.

White girls' attitudes toward makeup did not change significantly with age. Four years later, the same girls spoke in detail and at great length about makeup and its place in their lives, even if they did not wear much makeup on a daily basis. White girls often spoke of not looking like themselves or looking "awful" without makeup:

> INTERVIEWER: You didn't think you looked awful before [age 13] — what changed?

> RITA, 16, WHITE: When I started putting on makeup, it's like when I took it off, then I wouldn't look like myself.

> INTERVIEWER: You only look like yourself when you have the makeup on?

> RITA: I look like myself, but I just think it's like a better image of myself when I have makeup on. …I feel insecure going somewhere without makeup.

At 13, White girls wore makeup to make their skin look normal. At 17, makeup has a different normalizing function. For the girls most heavily invested in makeup as a daily ritual, cosmetics were a way of blending into a group of similarly made-up girls. Girls learn how to talk about makeup from the text in teen magazines; the words girls use to describe cosmetics and the attributes they look for in the makeup they buy seem to be drawn directly from magazine advertisements and articles.

In contrast with the uneasy alliance White girls had with cosmetics, Black girls usually described makeup as unnecessary and largely foreign to their experience of maturing into women:

> NICOLE, 17, BLACK: I wasn't allowed to wear makeup when I was younger…. My friend, who is White, is like, "Yeah, my mom let me play around with makeup when I was six years old." She could wear lipstick out and that sort of thing. Or she'd buy those little makeup kits…I didn't get those. It was like, "You don't need makeup." My mom doesn't even like to see me in lipstick now.

Only 2 of the 16 Black girls interviewed expressed any interest in makeup. The self-confidence most of the Black girls felt about their appearance was striking in their comments on makeup. Seventeen-year-old Davida's comments were typical: "There's nothing wrong with my face to put on makeup for."

Most Black girls echoed Kira's comments about the makeup tips and cosmetic advertising in teen magazines, "They don't have anything to do with me." In general, African-American girls believed the makeup information in the magazines was uninteresting because they wore cosmetics only rarely. The colors were frequently seen as incompatible with their skin tones. Their socially significant others, such as peers, parents and boys, did not encourage cosmetic use, and girls said they saw little change in their appearance when they did wear makeup:

> SYLVIE, 17, BLACK: To make a Black woman beautiful, since we [are] already the color we are, we really don't need all that makeup and stuff; just keep herself clean and have a nice attitude.

> INTERVIEWER: Do you think you'll wear makeup when you get older, or not?

> SYLVIE: I don't know, because I think I'm beautiful.

The cosmetic experience seemed frivolous to most of the African-American girls in this study, but they understood precisely how the beauty tips in teen magazines apply to White girls—as prescriptive for acceptance and success. Nicole observed White girls reapplying their makeup in class: "Like, because they have to. I don't have time to worry about that." She believes that Black girls in general judge themselves and others on characteristics other than appearance because they have been judged on appearance—the color of their skin—all their lives:

> NICOLE, 17, BLACK: White girls...have that kind of belief that, "If I'm pretty and ...if I'm real cutesy to my boss, I can get things." And it's like, yeah, you might be able to...But it doesn't work that way for most Black people.

READING OVER RACE

Why, then, do African-American girls purchase these magazines? The reasons differ for younger and older girls. Younger African-American girls did not seem to recognize that much of the content was oriented to White girls. For example, Chris, 14, was mystified by makeup tips that would make sense only on White skin. Early adolescent girls of both races sought out teen magazines for learning about boys and heterosexual romantic relationships, accessing information on sex and their bodies and learning about social issues such as teenage pregnancy, HIV, binge drinking and eating disorders.

Articles claiming real boys as authors were particularly riveting to younger girls of both races, because they seldom had close relationships with real boys to confirm or deny the perspectives presented by the magazines. Older Black girls believed the magazines presented a flawed picture of boys—the images did not jibe with their realities. However, they were still interested in articles and features intended to give girls greater insights on their own personalities and the nature and future of their heterosexual relationships. Older black girls showed greater interest in images and material that was judged "real" than content that was staged, contrived or imaginary: features like "School Zone" and issue-oriented stories incorporating anecdotal stories from real girls' experiences were particularly well liked. They enjoyed articles and features that promised them greater self-knowledge, understanding of the vagaries of life and a subsequent sense of increased control of the future; quizzes, features detailing girls' embarrassing moments and horoscopes were favorites.

> NICOLE, 17, BLACK (from focus group): Some stuff is universal. But then there's the makeup and stuff you can't relate to, and it's like, you know, we live in a White world. ...I try not to think about stuff like that, but basically, yeah, it is.

Summary

Analysis of the data showed that most African-American girls in this study were uninterested in striving for or achieving the ideal feminine physique, as the magazines portray it. Similarly, there was little interest in makeup and grooming advice that was seen as inappropriate for Black girls, due either to formulations intended for White girls or African-American girls' belief that cosmetics were superfluous to being attractive. African-American girls tended to evaluate themselves and others on character and personality rather than appearance. Subsequently, they showed more interest in articles on singers, athletes, actors and real girls than in pictures of models.

Most White girls maintained their interest in cosmetics from early adolescence and contended that some kind of makeup was necessary for girls to look their best. They admired the physiques of models and agreed that the amount of self-denial and hard work necessary to achieve such a body was admirable but difficult to emulate. White girls' evaluative statements about themselves and others generally centered on appearance; personality was something a girl depended on if she was unattractive.

African-American girls see teen magazines as having limited utility as a source of information on beauty and product information. The magazines provided a one-way mirror, through which African-American girls could see White girls and all the trappings of White beauty culture, but the White producers and consumers of the beauty culture seemed unable to look through to see Black girls. African-American girls simply read around the images and information they perceived as excluding them and focused on what they saw as the truly generic content, such as health information and fashion:

> INTERVIEWER: Do you think they use enough Black girls in the magazine?
>
> KIM, 13, BLACK: It doesn't make a difference to me.
>
> INTERVIEWER: Would you like to see more girls like you in the magazine?
>
> KIM: I don't care. I just like the clothes.

White girls seemed unaware of the bias in their magazines until they were asked to consider the material in light of racial representation. Although older White girls recognized relatively few models of color in teen magazines, they argued that somehow this was less important than that the text was appropriate for all girls. Many White girls make emphatic statements that the visual inequity between girls of color and White girls was not an indication of the magazines' prejudice. Rather, the current dearth of these images was attributed to demands of the market ("Black girls don't read these magazines") and oversight ("There are usually a lot more picture of Black girls—this is not a good issue"). White girls had no conception of how the text might change to reflect more closely the needs and concerns of Black girls. Due in part to their exposure to White-oriented teen magazines, African-American girls were explicit and opinionated about White girls' orientation to a beauty standard that Black girls did not share.

White girls, who are more culturally aligned with the material in the major teen magazines, consistently invest more authority in the magazines' counsel and images of beauty, regardless of age. In early adolescence, White girls regarded the well developed bodies of the magazine models as promises of bodies to come as they matured. The text served as a crystal ball, illustrating for girls the ideal they might one day approximate, and a map, showing the way to satisfaction, beauty, and ultimately the opposite sex, via cosmetics, diet and fashion. However, even the interpretations of these girls must be read in context; a compliant or resistant stance toward the magazines stayed relatively consistent from ages 13 to 17.

Girls of both races looked for confirmation of ideas, attitudes and behaviors about which they were less than sure. The portraits of real teens featured in *Seventeen*'s "School Zone" feature were especially powerful in this regard— "School Zone" depicted actual teens of style, and no contrived fashion layout could match the power of the real in enticing girls to entertain new possibilities for self-presentation.

Discussion

Although media critics speak of the negative influence that mediated ideals of beauty have on girls, the underlying assumption of such a statement is that girls view media as their looking glass, in which idealized versions of themselves are reflected. While this may be true in many ways for girls who see images in teen magazines congruent with their Anglo/European physical characteristics and White cultural ideals, the girls of color interpret these images differently. Their resistant interpretations of White-oriented material in fashion and beauty magazines make sense in light of research that has shown that African-American girls have higher levels of self-esteem and more positive body images than White girls.

By choosing to read teen magazines produced for a primarily White audience, it could be said the Black girls in this study are making a choice equivalent to those of the minority children in Clark and Clark's (1947) doll study—choosing White dolls over Black ones. Clark and Clark's study, and subsequent, similar studies, have been said to demonstrate minority children's negative identification with their race. However, the observations of Baldwin, Brown, and Hopkins (1995) clarify the questionable assumptions that have allowed a Black self-hatred theory to proliferate in spite of conflicting findings; such studies "…propose that Black people, especially children, acquire their self-conception from their interaction with the Euro-American community rather than from the African American community" (p. 49). The authors conclude that the Eurocentric paradigm that orients most research of people from different ethnic and cultural backgrounds must be challenged, and that research involving African Americans must consider their Afrocentric cultural orientation.

Prior to conducting this research, we, too, thought one of the outcomes might be that, because African-American girls are largely excluded from the dominant discourse on feminine beauty, those who read teen fashion and beauty magazines would have a more negative self-image than White girls who read the same material. However, quite the opposite was true—African-American girls recognized that the magazines were unable to guide them to ways of looking and behaving that are valued in their families and cultural communities. Instead of translating their relative exclusion from the major teen magazines into negative self-assessments, Black girls generally viewed the magazines as biased and largely irrelevant to their ideas about beauty, though enjoyable for other reasons. However, it does appear that older African-American girls' interpretations were more culturally aligned with those of the African-American community writ large—the culture derives its power not only from the values and ideas communicated to girls, but also from girls' experience in the culture. With age, girls grow in their experience of their culture and solidify their racial identity.

However, when African-American girls were asked if they would prefer a teen magazine just for Black girls, most said no. The magazines produced just for Black teens were perceived as poorly produced or lacking in editorial content; additionally, these magazines are not always easily attainable. For girls who want a high quality, well produced fashion magazine targeted to their age group, 'Teen, Seventeen and YM are frequently the only choices available on magazine racks.

Girls' differing cultural legacies cannot be overlooked in any analysis of how they interact with fashion and beauty texts. Andi, a 17-year-old Black girl, observed that White girls have had to learn the lessons of femininity embedded in teen magazines if they were to succeed in attracting a successful, White man. Although fashion and beauty texts like teen magazines may lose much of their relevance as White women become more financially self-reliant, the texts consistently demonstrate for girls that the goal of achieving a pleasing appearance should be paramount in their lives. White girls struggled to dismiss this textual imperative as frivolous, but did so inconsistently and with difficulty—material that they said was worthy of their attention, and material that they actually attended to and read, were frequently at odds.

African-American girls said they are more discerning, critical readers of texts such as teen magazines because of how they were raised.

African-American girls observed that their White classmates' unhealthy focus on looks was encouraged not only by the magazines but by White mothers as well, who steered their daughters into behaviors like makeup play from an early age. African-American girls often expressed sympathy for White girls, whom they saw as unwitting victims in a quixotic beauty quest of their own making. Black girls saw this emphasis on unrealistic beauty standards being reinforced by White male classmates, who some Black girls felt were as influenced by mediated ideals as White females.

African-American girls in this study frequently referred to cross-generational negotiations of femaleness in their families. How grandmothers and mothers felt about their bodies and self-presentation was far more important to Black girls than White girls. For African-American girls, mothers and grandmothers were frequently cited as purveyors of beauty norms—if they did not need makeup, why should their (grand)daughters? Alternatively, White girls seldom mentioned mothers as influential in their feelings about their bodies or appearance, other than in instances where girls spoke of first wearing makeup borrowed from their mothers.

One African-American participant argued that the experience of being a racial minority made Black girls less apt to buy into a value system that placed a premium on a standardized way of looking. They understood what it was to be judged as lesser based on color, and resisted assessing and disparaging others on media-reinforced, White standards of beauty. Black girls' views of what constituted beauty was simply less restrictive—they understood and appreciated White standards of beauty as well as Black. For example, whereas White girls were striving for a narrowly defined body size and shape, Black girls saw unattractiveness only at the far reaches of either side of the weight continuum; however, they were far more likely to describe a girl as too thin than too heavy. Their more realistic, inclusive view of the female physical norm was reinforced by elder female family members, who were said to view heavier girls as healthier, and by African-American males, who prize "thick" or amply filled-out girls as sexually appealing and desirable.

Limitations and Implications for Future Research

In the interest of limiting my study to a manageable size, we have focused our research on White and African-American, middle-class girls—their combined number make up the vast majority of teen magazine readers. However, as the percentage of other people of color in this country continues to grow, so grows the likelihood that their readership will make up an increasing percentage of the audience for this type of publication. Durham (1999G) found evidence for interpretive congruity between the Anglo/White girls and Latinas she studied, a very different outcome from the one presented in this study. How might the interpretations of first- and second-generation Asian girls differ from one another, and from the girls in the aforementioned research?

Although it is believed that most of the girls who read the magazines regularly come from families with moderate discretionary income, there may be a large number of girls from less affluent families who also read them. Teen magazines have a huge pass-along readership, and are available for girls to read in schools, in public libraries and at points of purchase. How do girls use these texts when they are financially excluded from the mediated ideal?

Roberts (1993) has suggested that the polysemic nature of many media texts should be positively exploited; teachers, parents and other adults with influence in girls' lives can help guide girls to more constructive interpretations of media. However, observations made in this study are similar to those of Currie (1996), who noted that at a time in girls' lives when parents have generally diminished influence anyway, adolescents tend to read teen magazines in isolation. Therefore, we contend that it is at the level of production that interested adults can most effectively assert their influence—demanding a more complete range of feminine images, attitudes and behaviors to fill the pages of girls' magazines and minds.

Walkerdine (1990) has claimed that such a view misses the point, because it does not consider how the mediated beauty montage is maintained by consent, for example, how girls come to want to see images of female perfection. However, this inquiry has demonstrated that American teen magazines are lagging behind girls' desires to see new, more inclusive images of femininity. *Seventeen*'s "School Zone," a feature that highlighted real girls with a wide range of styles and cultural backgrounds, was far more interesting to most girls than were the routine models in more stylized spreads. However, "School Zone" is comprised of only a small number of pages in one publication; the remainder of the images in this and other magazines are consistently idealized and, in the view of this study's participants, less inclusive of minority girls than they should be. In this regard, McRobbie's (1994) observation that British girls are pushing their magazines to portray girls and women more positively and realistically may foreshadow a similar process in updating American teen publications.

Media critics contend that as long as the vast majority of producers and consumers of media are White, the authentic experiences and images of other cultures will have difficulty coming to light (Gitlin, 1983). To date, the most prevalent images of African-American women and girls in mainstream teen magazines closely approximate White standards of attractiveness. On that basis, they are easily dismissed by most African-American girls in this study, who feel no need to compare themselves to women who they say are "borderline Black."

However, the producers of mainstream teen magazines and other marketers are becoming increasingly sensitive to the needs of people of color, for one simple reason: the U.S. Census estimates that by year 2010, 39 percent of the teen population will be made up of African Americans, Hispanics, Asians, and other non-Anglo/ Whites. Once Black girls' perspective on the mediated beauty culture has been changed from that of outsider to insider, will African-American girls lose some of the critical distance that has allowed them to sustain relatively high levels of body confidence and self-esteem? Alternatively, would the celebration of broader, more

diverse standards of beauty ease White girls' relatively negative physical self-assessments? The range of beauty embraced by the Black community could serve as a dynamic model for how the dominant culture can progress in redefining femininity for the good of all women. But the result of more and different media representations of feminine beauty will result in a narrowing of the interpretive gap that now separates White and African-American girls— for better and worse. If images of real girls rather than models ever become the mode, it may be more difficult for all girls to resist comparing themselves to magazine images.

Younger White girls tended to defer comparing themselves to the models they saw in 1994 teen magazines, contending that the models were older and more developed. As they grew older, most of these girls continued to distance themselves from the professional models, whom they knew to be atypical. White girls were more successful in resisting notions of beauty related to makeup and fashion than body shape, which in a sense represented a physiological reality rather than a trend. As one White girl noted, "Some girls…must look like that, or else they wouldn't be in the magazine." It was easier for African-American girls to opt out of self-evaluation, given that they seldom saw their racial equivalents represented in teen magazines.

It is imperative that future research determines whether images of girls who are not professional models, selected because they are presumably more typical and representative, invite more image-comparison among readers. An important complement to such a study would be to track how such portrayals of real girls may change (e.g., become more made-up) as they become more prevalent in the text.

African-American participants cited the Black family and culture as most influential in Black girls' relatively positive assessments of their appearance and self-worth. It is vital to consider how African-American cultural values, which have thus far served Black girls well, could be co-opted by beauty media that feed on feminine insecurity. Future studies should monitor how the authority of the Black family and community as arbiters of African-American beauty is affected by the inclusion of more minority models and real girls of color in mainstream teen magazines.

Our research goal is to increase awareness of how one subset of the media, the teen magazine, is used by girls in defining who they are and what it means to be a woman in American society. As a result of their greater awareness, women and girls can be more effective in redefining the gender system that exerts such profound effects on our values, behavior and destinies. It is our hope that through the words of girls, we can learn more about our own becomings, and initiate more positive influence on women yet to be.

NICOLE, 17, BLACK (from focus group): There is the TV answer, 'Be yourself, find out who you are.' But I think part of it is, you gotta figure out what's important to you, what's going to get you where you need to be. Once you figure that out, you know where to draw the line between what the media tells you and where you really need to be.

Name: _____

Date: _____

1. Discuss your view on how idealized images affect adolescents. How do you think race, gender and age might influence how an audience member negotiates these images?

2. Describe how you think of ways in which mediated images have influenced your perception of yourself.

3. Do you believe that, as more images of African Americans are included in mainstream beauty magazines, it will become more difficult for African-American girls to continue to define their own beauty ideals? Why or why not?

4. Do the media have an obligation to provide the public with images that are more representative? Realistic? Why do you think non-representative, unrealistic images continue to proliferate?

Name: _____

Date: _____

1. Evaluate the content of leading women's fashion/beauty magazines against the content of teen magazines for girls. How are themes that are introduced in teen magazines developed in the publications for women? What can you infer about their intended audiences from the content of the magazines?

2. Teen magazines have been criticized for promoting images that are racially biased and/or psychologically damaging to girls. In a paragraph or two, address the following: Do you believe these magazines should change, and if so, how could such change begin? What is your vision for a new and improved fashion/beauty magazine for teen girls? Are such magazines inherently "bad" for girls?

REFERENCES

American Association of University Women Educational Foundation (1992). How schools short-change girls. Washington DC: American Association of University Women.

Arnett, J.J., Larson, R., and Offer, D. (1995). Beyond effects: Adolescents as active media users. *Journal of Youth and Adolescence, 24*(5), 511-533.

Arnez, N. (1980). Black poetry: A necessary ingredient for survival and liberation. *Black Studies, 11*(1), 3-22.

Baldwin, J.A., Brown, R.B., and Hopkins, R. (1995). The black self-hatred paradigm revisited: An Africentric analysis. In Kenneth P. Monteiro (Ed.), *Ethnicity and psychology: African-, Asian-, Latino-, and Native-American psychologies.* Dubuque: Kendall/Hunt Publishing Company.

Beach, R. (1993). *A Teacher's introduction to reader-response theories.* Urbana, IL: National Council of Teachers of English.

Benton, M. (1983). Secondary worlds. *Journal of Research and Development, 16*(3), 68-75.

Bloome, D. (1985). Reading as a social process. *Language Arts, 62*(4), 134-142.

Blumer, J. G. and Katz, E. (1974). *The uses of mass communication.* Newbury Park, CA: Sage.

Bobo, J. (1995). *Black women as cultural readers.* New York, NY: Columbia University Press.

Booth, W. (1988). *The company we keep: An ethics of fiction.* Berkeley, CA: University of California.

Brown, L.M. and Gilligan, C.R. (1992). *Meeting at the crossroads: Women's psychology and girls' development.* Cambridge: Harvard University Press.

Cash, T.F., Cash, D.W., and Butters, J.W. (1983). Mirror, mirror, on the wall...: Contrast effects and self evaluations of physical attractiveness. *Personality and Social Psychology Bulletin, 9*, 351-358.

Clarke, J. (1990). Pessimism versus populism: The problematic politics of popular culture. In R. Butsch (Ed.), *For fun and profit: The transformation of leisure into consumption* (pp. 28-44). Philadelphia: Temple University Press.

Cohen, J. (1991). The "relevance" of cultural identity in audiences' interpretations of mass media. *Critical Studies in Mass Communication, 8*, 442-454.

Comstock, G., and Paik, H. (1978*). Television and the American child.* San Diego: Academic Press.

Coles, R. (1989). *The call of stories.* Boston, MA: Houghton Mifflin.

Condit, C. M. (1989). The rhetorical limits of polysemy. *Critical Studies in Mass Communication,* June, 103-122.

Cornelius, J. (1991). *When I can read my title clear: Literacy, slaves, and religion in antebellum south.* Columbia, SC: University of South Carolina Press.

Crabtree, B.F., and Miller, W.L. (1992). *Doing qualitative research.* Newbury Park: Sage Publications.

Currie, D.H. (1996). Decoding femininity: Advertisements and their teenage readers. *Gender and Society, 11*(4), 453-478.

Durham, M. G. (1999a). Articulating adolescent girls' resistance to patriarchal discourse in popular media. *Women's Studies in Communication, 22*(2), p. 220.

Durham, M.G. (1999b). Girls, media, and the negotiation of sexuality: A study of race, class and gender in adolescent peer groups. *Journalism and Mass Communication Quarterly, 76*(2), 193-216.

Duke, L.L., and Kreshel, P. (1998). Negotiating femininity: Girls in early adolescence read teen magazines. *Journal of Communication Inquiry 22*(1), 48-71.

Evans, E.D., Rutberg, J., Sather, C., and Turner, C. (1991). Content analysis of contemporary teen magazines for adolescent females. *Youth and Society, 23*(1), 99-120.

Finders, M.J. (1996). Queens and teen zines: Early adolescent females reading their way toward adulthood. *Anthropology and Education Quarterly 27*(1), 71-89.

Fish, S. (1980). *Is there a text in this class?* Cambridge, MA: Harvard University.

Fiske, J. (1988). Critical response: Meaningful moments. *Critical Studies in Mass Communication, 5*(3), 246-250.

Fiske, J. (1989). *Reading the popular.* Boston: Unwin Hyman.

Flynn, K., and Fitzgibbon, M. (1996). Body image ideals of low-income African American mothers and their preadolescent daughters. *Journal of Youth and Adolescence, 25*(5), 615-630.

Franzoi, S. L. (1995). The body-as-object versus the body-as-process: Gender differences and gender considerations. *Sex Roles, 33*(5/6), 417-437.

Frazer, E. (1987). Teenage girls reading *Jackie! Media, culture and society. 9*(4), 407-425.

Garner, D. M., Garfinkel, P. E., Schwartz, D., and Thompson, M. (1980). Cultural expectations of thinness in women. *Psychological Reports, 47*, 483-491.

Gitlin, T. (1983). *Inside prime time.* New York: Pantheon.

Graham, S. (Spring, 1994). Motivation in African Americans. *Review of Educational Research, 64*(1), 55-117.

Hall, S. (1979). Encoding/decoding. In S. Hall, D. Hobson, A. Lowe, and P. Willis (Eds.), *Culture, media and language: Working papers in cultural studies, 1972-1979* (pp. 128-138). London: Hutchinson.

Harter, S. (1986). Processes underlying the construction, maintenance, and enhancement of the self-concept in children. In J. Suls and A.G. Greenwald (Eds.), *Psychological Perspectives on the Self, 3* (pp. 137-181). Hillsdale, NJ: Lawrence Erlbaum Associates.

Hull, G., Bell-Scott, P., and Smith, B. (Eds.). (1982). *All the women are white, all the blacks are men, but some of us are brave.* Westberry, CT: Feminist Press.

Johnson, R. (1986). What is cultural studies anyway? *Social Text*, 16, Winter.

Leeds, M. (1994). Young African American women and the language of beauty. In K.I. Callaghan (Ed.), *Ideals of feminine beauty: Philosophical, social and cultural dimensions.* Westport, CT: Greenwood Press.

Lincoln, Y.S., and Guba, E.G. (1985). *Naturalistic inquiry.* Newbury Park: Sage.

Martin, M.C., & Kennedy, P.F. (1993). Advertising and social comparison: Consequences for female pre-adolescents and adolescents. *Psychology and Marketing, 10*, 513-530.

Martin, M.C., & Gentry, J.W. (1997). The role of esteem-relevance and perceived control in determining the effects of physically attractive models in advertising on female and male adolescents. *Psychology and Marketing, 10*, 513-530.

McCracken, E. (1993). *Decoding women's magazines: From Mademoiselle to Ms.* London: Macmillan.

McCracken, G.D. (1988). *The long interview.* Newbury Park, CA: Sage.

McRobbie, A. (1978a). *Jackie!: An ideology of adolescent femininity.* Birmingham: The Centre for Contemporary Cultural Studies.

McRobbie, A. (1978b). Working-class girls and the culture of femininity. In Women's Studies Group (Eds.), *Women take issue* (pp. 96-108). London: Hutchinson.

McRobbie, A. (1984). Dance and social fantasy. In A. McRobbie and M. Nava (Eds.), *Gender and generation* (pp. 130-161). London: MacMillan.

McRobbie, A. (1991). *Feminism and youth culture: From "Jackie!" to "Just Seventeen."* Boston: Unwin Hyman.

McRobbie, A. (1994). *Postmodernism and popular culture.* London: Routledge

Millman, M. (1980). *Such a pretty face.* New York: W.W. Norton.

Parker, S., Nichter, M., Nichter, M., and Vuckovic, N. (1995). Body image and weight concerns among African American and White adolescent females: Differences that make a difference. *Human Organization, 54*(2), 103-114.

Parnell, K., Sargent, R., Thompson, S. H., Duhe, S. F., Valois, R. F., & Kemper, R. C. (1996). Black and white adolescent females' perceptions of ideal body size. *Journal of School Health, 66(3)*, 112-117.

Peirce, K. (1990). A feminist theoretical perspective on the socialization of teenage girls through *Seventeen*. *Sex Roles 23(9/10)*, 491-500.

Peirce, K. (1993). Socialization of teenage girls through teen-magazine fiction: The making of a new woman or old lady? *Sex Roles 29(1/2)*, 59-69.

Richins, M. L. (1991). Social comparison and the idealized images of advertising. *Journal of Consumer Research, 18* (June), 71-83.

Roberts, D. F. (1993). Adolescents and the mass media: From Leave It to Beaver to Beverly Hills 90210. In R. Takanishi (Ed.), *Adolescence in the 1990s: Risk and opportunity* (pp. 171-186). New York: Teachers College Press.

Rosenblatt, L. (1938). *Literature as exploration*. New York, NY: Appleton, Century, and Crofts.

Rosenblatt. L. (1978). *The reader the text and the poem*. Carbondale, IL: Southern Illinois University.

Ruddell, R. and Unrau, N. (1994). Reading as a meaning-making construction process: The reader, the text, and the teacher. In R. Ruddell, M. Ruddell, & H. Singer (Eds.), *Theoretical models and processes of reading*. Newark: NJ: International Reading Association.

Schlegal, A. and Herbert III, B. (1991). *Adolescence: An anthropological inquiry*. New York: Free Press.

Scholes, R. (1989). *Protocols of reading*. New Haven, CT: Yale University.

Smith, E. J. (1982). The black female adolescent: A review of the educational, career and psychological literature. *Psychology of Women Quarterly, 6(3)*, 261-288.

Stice, E., & Shaw, H. E. (1994). Adverse effects of the media portrayed thin-ideal on women and linkages to bulimic symptomatology. *Journal of Social and Clinical Psychology, 13(3)*, 288-308.

Walkerdine, V. (1990). *Schoolgirl fictions*. London, NY: Verso.

ABOUT THE EDITORS AND CONTRIBUTORS

Co-Editors

Guy T. Meiss received his Ph.D. in mass communication from the University of Wisconsin-Madison and is Professor Emeritus and former Chair of Journalism at Central Michigan University. His research interests include gatekeeping in the mass media, the development of critical thinking skills and interactive communication technologies. He is a former management consultant with Hay & Associates (Philadelphia) and a doctoral fellow and consultant at the East-West Communications Institute (Honolulu, Hawaii).

Alice A. Tait is the mother of Joseph Conrad Smith, II, the grandmother of Leiah, Joseph III, Brigham and Robert. She received her Ph.D. in mass communication theory from Bowling Green State University and is Professor of Journalism at Central Michigan University. Her research interests include the effects of mass media on society and individuals, specifically on African Americans, Native Americans, Hispanics, Asians, women and people with disabilities. She has published numerous articles on the Detroit television series *Profiles in Black*. Her work has also appeared in the *Michigan Academician, Western Journal of Black Studies, News Computing Journal, Journal of Mediated Communication, Feedback,* and the *Handbook on Mass Media in the United States*.

Contributors

Richard L. Allen received his Ph.D. from the University of Wisconsin-Madison and is Professor Emeritus in the Department of Communication Studies at the University of Michigan. He studies symbolic representations of socially identified groups, with an emphasis on continental and diasporic Africans. More recently, he has been researching the concept of propaganda and its contemporary manifestations.

Susan Angulo completed an undergraduate degree and a Master of Arts in foreign language education at Florida State University, and later completed an Ed.D. at Nova University in higher education administration. She began her professional career with the Florida Migrant Child Compensatory Education Program, developing ESL programs for migrant elementary school children in Ft. Myers, Florida. Subsequently she accepted a full-time position at Florida International University as coordinator of a Title VII bilingual education grant. Currently she is Assistant Vice President for Academic Affairs at St. Thomas University in Miami, Florida. For the past 7 years Dr. Angulo has served the Miami community as Co-Director of The Miami Latin Film Festival.

Judith Bachay received her Ph.D. in counselor education from Barry University in 1994. Her dissertation research focused on counselor inventions that would enhance ethnic identity in Haitian adolescents. Post-doctoral research and scholarly writing have focused on the intersection of race, gender, culture and the media. She has worked as a National Consultant for the Peace Education Foundation since the group's inception in 1980. Dr. Bachay has researched and published extensively in the field of conflict mediation and resolution, and is a founding member of the Center for Loss and Healing, as well as Associate Professor within the Social Science and Counseling department at St.

Thomas University. Dr. Bachay is a member of the corporate training team, Diversity Trainers, Inc. She is a core member of the Women Waging Peace global network at the John F. Kennedy School of Government, Harvard University.

Rev. Edward A. Blackwell, Jr., has 25 years of higher education administration experience. He is the Director of Campus Ministry at St. Thomas University, Miami, Florida. He serves as a member of the Archdiocese of Miami Worship Commission, President of the Campus and Community Alliance for North Dade, Member of the North Dade Regional Chamber of Commerce Board of Directors and Project Director for the Building Civic Leadership and Pride grant. He holds degrees in sociology (B.A. Bloomsburg University), theology (M.A. from Mt. St. Mary's College and Seminary) and educational administration (Ed. D. from Florida International University). In addition to his campus ministry duties, he is Associate Professor in the Department of Education.

Rebeca Brasfield is an elementary school teacher in New York City. She received her Bachelor's degree in psychology from the University of Illinois, Champaign-Urbana. Ms. Brasfield has written a weekly column for the *UIC Today* and has worked as an assistant editor for *Black Thought*. Her research interests include feminist theory, gender studies, critical race theory, educational policy studies and queer theory.

Tamika J. A. Carter is a doctoral candidate in the Department of Communication Studies, University of Michigan. She researches issues of race and gender in the media. She studies the effects of media images of race on the self-identity of individuals belonging to stigmatized groups, and how the media aggravates or alleviates racial tension in communities.

Brenda Cooper is Associate Professor in the Department of Journalism and Communication at Utah State University, where she also served as Director of the Women & Gender Studies Program. Cooper's research and teaching are guided by a strong feminist stance and commitment to promoting diversity. Her research focuses on issues of media representations of diversity, including spectators' conflicting interpretations of film narratives, analyses of film translations of women's stories and strategies of resistance articulated through the challenging lens of the female gaze. Cooper's most recent research investigates the strategies through which film and television narratives may work to disrupt the strict boundaries and biases of heteronormativity.

Prabu David is Associate Professor in the School of Journalism and Communication at Ohio State University. His research focuses on media effects, information seeking and human-computer interaction. He received a doctorate in mass communication research from the School of Journalism and Mass Communication at the University of North Carolina at Chapel Hill.

Fernando Delgado is Associate Vice Provost for Academic Programs and Graduate Studies at Arizona State University West, where he is also Associate Professor in the Department of Communication Studies. His research focuses on cultural and ethnic identities and their intersection with popular culture, particularly sports, film and television, and music. He is a member of several editorial boards, and his research has been published in a variety of outlets, including *Communication Theory*, *Text & Performance Quarterly* and the *Journal of Sport and Social Issues*. He teaches a variety of courses in rhetoric and cultural studies.

Lisa Duke, Ph.D. A former advertising copywriter, Dr. Duke teaches creative courses and a graduate course in qualitative research in the Advertising Department at the University of Florida. Her research interests include advertising creativity, gender studies, pedagogy, racial identity and social learning. Her work has been published in *Journalism and Mass Communication Quarterly, Psychology* *and Marketing, Journal of Advertising Education, Journal of Communication Inquiry* and *The Annals of the American Academy of Political and Social Science.*

Gary Feinberg is Professor of Sociology and Chairperson of the Department of Social Sciences and Counseling at St. Thomas University, Miami, Florida. He holds a Ph.D. in sociology from the Union Institute, and has done doctoral and post-doctoral work in sociology at New York University and the University of Oxford. He has published numerous articles and book chapters on international and comparative criminal justice, including works on Britain, Vietnam, China, Tibet, Russia and the Baltic States. He is currently investigating the impact of New Labour's appropriation of managerial objectives relative to Britain's justice system. His contribution to the present chapter centers on the materials related to stereotyping, its functions, dysfunctions and consequences.

Melissa A. Johnson is Associate Professor in the Department of Communication at North Carolina State University. Her research focuses on content, uses and effects of U.S. ethnic media and international news flow between Latin America and the United States. She holds a doctorate in mass communication research from the School of Journlism and Mass Communication at the University of North Carolina at Chapel Hill.

Dawn Huey Ohlsson graduated from North Carolina State University with a bachelor of arts in communication, specializing in public relations. She is director of marketing for one of the largest media market research firms in the United States, and travels throughout the U.S. moderating specialized focus groups.

Byron Renz received his Ph.D. from Wayne State University. He has been Associate Professor or Independent Scholar at Wayne State University, Central Michigan University, the University of Northern Iowa, Northern Kentucky University, Northern Arizona University and Northern Michigan University. He has taught a wide range of practical and theoretical courses in mass communication, journalism and public relations, and has been active in curriculum development and program administration. He has also worked as a radio news writer and anchor and on-air program host in major markets, such as New York, Chicago and Detroit. He served as a Fulbright professor in mass communication, journalism and public relations at the University of Latvia and Rigas Stradina University from 1998 to 2000, and as a Fulbright professor in communication and journalism at Belarusian State University, Minsk, Belarus, from 2003 to 2004. His research interests focus on the interrelationship of mass media and society. He is author of *Art and Technique of Audio Production* and has published articles in the *International Journal of the Sociology of Language, Yearbook of German American Studies, Communication Education, Feedback* and the *Michigan Speech Association Journal.*

Diana I. Rios is Associate Professor in the Department of Communication Sciences and the Puerto Rican and Latino Studies Research Institute (PRLS), at the University of Connecticut. She is Associate Director of PRLS. Her teaching and research addresses ethnicity, race and gender in mass communication and cross-cultural processes, as well as mass communication theory and effects. Much of her writings, based on survey and field work, have focused on Latino audiences and how women use media. Her recent research centers on Latino and African-American representation in news and entertainment.

Beatriz Gonzalez Robinson is Associate Professor in the Department of Social Sciences and Counseling and the Director of Planning and Evaluation at St. Thomas University. She is a licensed psychotherapist, and is certified in school counseling, administration and English education. Her research includes work in leadership, gender and culture issues, particularly as they relate to the fields of mass media, public policy, education and counseling. Her work has been presented for the American Psychological Association, the White House Initiative on Educational Excellence for Hispanic

Americans and Columbia University's Annual Winter Roundtable on Cross-Cultural Psychology and Education.

Gloria P. Ruiz is Associate Professor in the Communication Arts, English and Humanities Department at St. Thomas University in Miami, Florida. She was a Title VII Fellow at Stanford University, a Walter Kaitz Fellow and a Faculty Fellow with the National Association of Television Program Executives; she served as State Chairperson for the National Association of African American, Hispanic/Latino Studies and Affiliates. Her research interests address multicultural and diversity issues as they relate to communications, and she has published several articles on this topic. Recent publications include "Crossing the Cultural Divide: Cultural Adaptation and AIDS Prevention Among Cuban American Women." Her professional work involves developing multicultural training and educational programs for media organizations as well as educational institutions.

Michelle Sisson, Ed.D. is Associate Professor of Middle, Secondary and Adult Education at Armstrong Atlantic State University. She has published in the *National Association of Secondary School Principals Bulletin*, and presented for the International Conference on *The Future of the Book* in Cairns, Australia, the American Association of Adult and Continuing Education, and the International Reading Association. Her research interests include adult-learning theories, cross-racial interviewing and reader response in adult literacy.

INDEX